NIGHT TERROR

She lay completely still. In fear, but quiet. She glanced up at the intruder who stood over her with one knee on the bed. He aggressively placed a sharp blade on the left side of her throat. It was a ten-inch knife with a seven-inch blade, almost three inches wide. The sharp edge grazed against her cheek. Shelly stifled a scream. She had no idea what to do.

The man added to the tension when he leaned into her face, his breath smelling of liquor and cigarettes.

"Do you have any sharp kitchen knives?" he inquired. Shelly looked up at him with pleading eyes. She did not want to answer. "Sharp enough to cut your throat with?"

Shelly closed her eyes and began to cry. She did not want to die here. Not like this. "I don't know," she replied.

"Don't worry, mine is."

A Message from the Author

My wife, Lisa Mitchell, died unexpectedly on April 28, 2002. She was 1,200 miles away visiting her parents, while I was halfway through with this book.

For the next eight months I could not think of anything but my grief. The last thing I wanted to do was to write a book about rape and murder. But I remembered how she listened to me read the manuscript while she cooked pasta in our cozy West Hollywood apartment. How she made helpful suggestions when I went astray. How she desperately wanted me to tell this story.

Lisa wanted me to tell it because she had also been a rape victim. Lisa, always stoic by nature, maintained an untarnished demeanor her whole life. She chose not to discuss it. That began to change in the last couple of years. She started to express an interest in speaking out about what happened to her. She hoped I would become a successful writer so she could help others.

One of Lisa's two rapists was freed in early 2002. He supposedly "found God" and was living a "righteous" life. She worried that this man could become another Rex Krebs, freed from prison for a vicious crime, only to be paroled and allowed to walk the streets. She wanted this book to be published to alert the public to the absurdity of paroling rapists.

On the morning of April 28, I completed the section on recidivism among rapists as well as the underreporting of rapes by victims. Lisa never got to read those passages.

At 8:00 P.M. I got the call from my Mom. Lisa had died in her childhood home from sudden arrhythmic death syndrome. She was only thirty-eight years old. She never got to help other rape victims.

Maybe now she can.

DEAD AND BURIED

COREY MITCHELL

PINNACLE BOOKS
Kensington Publishing Corp.
http://www.kensingtonbooks.com

PINNACLE BOOKS are published by

Kensington Publishing Corp.
850 Third Avenue
New York, NY 10022

All Kensington Titles, Imprints and Distributed Lines are available at special quantity discounts for bulk purchases for sales promotions, premiums, fund-raising, educational or institutional use. Special book excerpts or customized printings can also be created to fit specific needs. For details, write or phone the office of the Kensington special sales manager: Kensington Publishing Corp., 850 Third Avenue, New York, NY 10022, attn: Special Sales Department, Phone: 1-800-221-2647.

Pinnacle and the P logo Reg. U.S. Pat. & TM Off.

First Printing: October 2003

10 9

Printed in the United States of America

PART I

RACHEL

ONE

November 12, 1998
San Luis Obispo, California
Midnight

Rachel Lindsay Newhouse stumbled outside of the brightly lit restaurant onto the dark, chilly streets of San Luis Obispo. She was intoxicated and upset. She had a fight with her roommate Andrea West, and she was ready to go home. The only problem was she did not have her car. The girls rode together in Andrea's car and Rachel was not about to ask her best friend for a ride. Not after their argument.

Rachel gathered her wits about her and stepped onto Nipomo Street, where the restaurant Tortilla Flats, or "the Flats," as the locals liked to call it, is located. The Flats is a trendy Mexican-food restaurant that serves passable California Mexican cuisine, but whose main priorities are their top-shelf margaritas. That was the reason why Rachel was there in the first place. She was out celebrating with the Beta Theta Pi fraternity on this Thursday night and was ready to partake of the Sauza-tequila-and-lime concoctions with no hassles. At twenty years of age, however, Rachel Newhouse was not old enough to drink legally in the state of California.

Neither was Andrea West, her roommate. It was because of that that Rachel found herself standing outside the restaurant and shivering instead of inside throwing back another margarita with some cute guys from her college, Cal Poly.

Andrea, who was also only twenty, could not get into the bar side of the Flats. Both girls had employed the old "smudged stamp" routine to attempt to get inside. Some drinking establishments will mark the top of their customers' hands with a black felt-tip marker or a black stamp, which is a signal to the doorman that they have already been inside and can reenter without hassle. Minors who want to circumvent the whole identification process at the door merely get someone who has legally gained entrance into the bar to offer up their stamp. The minor licks the top of his or her hand and rubs it against the marked customer, thus creating a reasonable facsimile of the stamp.

At least that was the game plan.

Rachel Newhouse's smudged stamp worked with no problem. She immediately bolted in and began to enjoy the festive atmosphere. Unfortunately for Andrea, the doorman stopped her and informed her that she would not be allowed in the bar side. She could only enter the restaurant side. Andrea stood by herself for the next hour, until she finally saw Rachel leave the bar side and head toward the rest room. Andrea met her at the door and began to complain. Soon the girls started to argue. Suddenly Rachel tore out of the restaurant, leaving Andrea behind. Once outside, Rachel waited shortly, hoping her friend would follow her. When Andrea did not appear, she took off.

As Rachel headed east on Nipomo Street, she began to shiver in the brisk Central California coastal air. Downtown San Luis Obispo is located only seventeen miles from the Pacific Ocean and decorated with such gorgeous beaches as Shell Beach, Pismo Beach, and Avila Beach. The usually picture-perfect sunny enclaves are harbingers for fog and cold weather in the wintertime and make for a chilly environment all around. Dressed only in black jeans and a dark blue silk shirt, Rachel was very cold. She was also nearly two miles away from her comfortable white wooden house located on the dead-end Gerda Street.

Rachel took a left onto Higuera Street and walked another half mile. At this time of night, it was not crowded. Had she walked out an hour earlier, she would have encountered several stragglers from the weekly farmers' market. The market is a gathering of hundreds of revelers who enjoy shopping for fruits and vegetables, reading informative brochures from political-minded organizations and several nonprofits groups, eating barbecue ribs and brisket sandwiches from an outdoor smoker, catching a live puppet show, and dancing to the strains of a new musical group every week. The internationally known gathering takes over this area of downtown for the evening and keeps it well populated. By the time Rachel left the Flats, the market had already dispersed. The streets were almost empty.

Rachel passed the Downtown Centre, the local minimall. She eventually came to Osos Street, where she took a right and headed east. Rachel walked along the sidewalk past several well-kept Victorian-style homes and past a few apartment complexes. She headed toward familiar territory—the Jennifer Street Bridge, an intriguing structure that had only gone up earlier that year. Its intentional rust-colored exterior loomed over the local train tracks like some kind of manic erector set, but it served a useful purpose—especially for Rachel. The bridge crossed over the railroad tracks in front of the restored Amtrak station and allowed pedestrians and bicyclists to cross over into the Jennifer Street neighborhood.

Rachel's neighborhood.

Rachel had no reason to be scared as she walked home. She was almost to the halfway point to her three-bedroom house nestled in the southeastern section of the neighborhood. There was only one semilarge task for Rachel.

Crossing the Jennifer Street Bridge.

The Jennifer Street Bridge is an ominous structure, even in the daylight, with its hulking, rusted exterior and a maze of stairs, handicap ramps, and railings. Not to mention the poor lighting. When you climb the fifty-eight stairs to reach the height of a three-story building, you are thrust out onto the crossover that is encased with a firm crisscross wire system in every direction—on both sides and overhead. The encasing allows one to see the underlit train station, which is located approximately fifty yards to the northwest. The bridge itself, however, maintains a slight hovering glow due to the sporadic lights festooned along the lower portion of the railing.

Rachel turned off Osos Street and onto Jennifer Street, a cul-de-sac of sorts that provides access for automobiles to park in the train station waiting area. It also provides space for patrons of several popular hangouts, including Café Roma and a corner convenience store. It was a heavily populated area.

She felt safe.

Rachel grasped the rust-colored handrail and thought about heading up the stairs. Instead, she walked a little farther and shuffled up the winding handicapped-access ramp. The shadows played tricks on her eyes as they cast a shimmering maroon shadow through the rails. The combination of shadows and an inebriated mental state caused Rachel to move at a slow, deliberate pace.

Rachel's actions had drawn the attention of a man in the parking lot facing the bridge. He had been sitting in his 1993 blue Ford Ranger pickup truck. He could comfortably hide underneath the shadows inside his huge vehicle. The man watched as the young woman staggered toward the bridge. He assessed the situation laid out before him and decided to take action. He grabbed something from the front seat of the truck and headed up the stairs. He hustled up the poorly lit concrete-and-metal staircase before she arrived at the bridge. She had no idea what waited for her up top. Besides, her focus was on one task and nothing else.

Getting home.

Instead of waiting for her at the top of the staircase, he stepped onto the crosswalk portion of the bridge. He liked the darkness of his perch. The wire seemed to remind him of something, but he could not quite conjure up its importance.

He stealthily glided one-quarter of the way up the bridge and turned around. The girl was only now about to reach the head of the staircase. He looked down at the item he grabbed from the front seat of his truck and chuckled under his breath. He then pulled it over his head.

He peered through the eyes of a skull mask left over from a recent Halloween party. It was the perfect addition to an increasingly frightening scenario. As he looked through the eyeholes, he saw the beautiful girl. She was petite, but large-breasted. She had gorgeous shoulder-length blond hair. She was breathing heavily.

And she did not even notice him.

Maybe she just acts like I don't exist.

Just like the others.

The excitement began to course through his body. He was aroused and angered. He knew what he had to do.

Rachel Newhouse was on the bridge and she knew she was almost home. She tried to ignore the other person. She just wanted to get home. Once she made it to the other side of the Jennifer Street Bridge, she would spot something special—a street sign for Rachel Street. It always brought a smile to her face when she saw it.

As soon as that glimmer of hope popped into her mind, she finally glanced at the other person on the bridge. Something seemed odd about the man. At 5'7", he   to be near her height. He was much broader, however, and his face seemed unusual. She could not really make out why he looked so strange, due to the poor lighting. To make matters worse, the man wasn't walking across the bridge. He had stopped and was actually facing her. Rachel tried to blow it off and keep on toward her final destination. She walked within three feet of the man when she looked up into the face of horror.

All she saw was a huge skull. At the same time she heard a loud *thwack!* as something hard smashed up against her temple.

Rachel Newhouse would never see Rachel Street again.

TWO

At 8:30 A.M., Friday the 13th, Cal Poly student Theresa Audino crossed the Jennifer Street Bridge to retrieve her car, which she parked downtown. She and her boyfriend had spent the previous evening at the farmers' market, where she purchased her weekly supply of vegetables. She decided to walk home and left her car downtown. She crossed the Jennifer Street Bridge at 11:30 P.M. on Thursday night. She did not notice anything unusual.

This morning, however, she definitely saw something that scared her.

A pool of blood, at least a foot across, lay conspicuously near the staircase at the top of the bridge. The blood still seemed thick and fresh. It was still wet.

Audino noticed several drops of blood, about the size of her thumb, on the stairs. She decided to see how far they stretched. As she slowly descended the fifty-eight steps, she noted that the blood drops went all the way to the bottom stair. She followed the blood to the right of the stairs, onto the sidewalk, and then left to the train station parking lot. Suddenly, the drops disappeared. They stopped right at a tree planter located next to the first parking spot.

Audino contacted the police. They informed her that they had already heard about the blood.

San Luis Obispo police officer Christopher Staley, who worked the day shift from 7:00 A.M. to 7:00 P.M., reported to the Jennifer Street Bridge. He noticed the large pool of blood on the top of the stairs. He proceeded to obtain a blood swab in case it might be helpful in the future. Later that morning, he did something inexplicable. He asked the city cleaning crew to wash the blood off the bridge.

They did.

"Have you heard from Rachel today?" asked Kirk Williams, an assistant manager of the SLO Brewing Company, where Rachel worked as a hostess. He was speaking to one of Rachel's three roommates, Nichole Tylenda.

It was 6:00 P.M.

"She was supposed to come in to work this afternoon," Williams continued.

"I actually haven't heard from her all day. Apparently, she didn't show up for her class and she didn't come home today. It's not like her to not call," Tylenda said worriedly.

Rachel usually let someone know what she was up to. The attractive Cal Poly nutrition major made sure her circle of friends knew what she was doing almost every day. These included Andrea, her other roommates, her coworkers, and her family. SLO Brewing coworker and occasional date Adam Olson told Williams, "It's unlike her to disappear like this. There's no way for her to vanish without telling anybody where she was going."

Nevertheless, no one could find Rachel Newhouse.

By Saturday, November 14, a full-scale search was on. Rachel's friends created hundreds of missing-person posters, with Rachel's pertinent information listed, and posted them all over downtown. The San Luis Obispo police were also on the trail of the missing college student. They were led by Captain Bart Topham, who secured a search-and-rescue team made up of anywhere from twenty-five to sixty searchers. Several tracking dogs assisted and a California Highway Patrol helicopter tracked the team's progress from the sky.

Captain Topham had all the people on the search-and-rescue team follow Rachel's potential route home from Tortilla Flats to the Jennifer Street neighborhood. They also searched several creeks in the area that lined the peaceful neighborhoods.

San Luis Obispo was up in arms over the prospect of a missing college girl.

Rachel Newhouse was the prototypical California college girl. She was an attractive, full-figured, 5'6", 120-pound blonde who was athletic, academically blessed, hardworking, and honest to boot. Her grandmother Patricia Newhouse described her as a "conscientious, hardworking girl" with "lots of friends." Her grandmother also stressed that her kin was not really a "party person—she's more into taking care of business and getting things done."

Rachel was getting things done at Cal Polytechnic Institute. She was a junior-year nutrition major, with a strong B average. She was used to getting things done. Just as she did at Irvine High School in Orange County, where she maintained a straight-A average and also excelled at sports, including soccer and cross-country track. She was a student body officer and member of the California Scholarship Federation. She was also very popular and good at making friends and keeping them.

One friend that Rachel kept was Andrea West. They were both freshmen at Irvine High School, where they met in 1992. They became fast friends and maintained their close bond over the years. Andrea described Rachel as "the perfect friend. She's always there when she's needed. She's a happy and cheery person. She cares."

Rachel Newhouse also cared about doing the right thing. Her aunt Patricia Turner described Rachel as a bit too hard on herself. Andrea furthered the idea of Rachel as a hardworking, conscientious person. She informed the police that in addition to her studies, Rachel also baby-sat and worked at SLO Brewing.

Rachel Newhouse kept busy and stayed out of trouble.

By Monday, November 16, 1998, Andrea West had not heard from her friend. Neither had her boss Kirk Williams. Nor had Captain Topham. No one in town knew where she was located. Word began to spread around the Cal Poly campus about her disappearance. By Wednesday, the mood of the town and the campus shifted in a dark direction. Samina Khan, Rachel's lab mate, headed for the Women's Center on campus. Her mission: to buy pepper spray. She was afraid and looking for a way to defend herself.

"I was thinking about getting some last year, but I didn't feel unsafe," she said forlornly as she clutched her new purchase.

Parents of several Cal Poly students began to contact Captain Topham. They also had one thing on their minds: protecting their children.

Why was there so much panic in a seemingly routine missing college student case? After all, it was no big deal for a young college student to take off a few days from school and not call friends. Extended trips to Tijuana or Las Vegas were not out of the ordinary. Why were the parents and, indeed, many of the students concerned?

It was not the first time a female Cal Poly student had gone missing in recent years.

THREE

On May 25, 1996, the beginning of the Memorial Day weekend, many students were packing their bags and getting ready to return to their hometowns. The semester had ended and, for some, it was time for one last celebration. Kristin "Roxy" Smart, a 6'1" statuesque blond freshman from Stockton, California, was ready to join the fun.

Kristin was the progeny of intelligent parents. She was born at 2:00 A.M. in Augsburg, Germany, on February 20, 1977, to two teachers, Stan and Denise Smart. When her family relocated to the United States, her father became a high school principal in Stockton. She also had a brother and sister, Matt and Lindsey. All three of the Smart children loved swimming. Kristin excelled at the sport in high school. She also had a strong love for the state of Hawaii and the Pacific Ocean. Her love for aquatics led her to choose Cal Poly for college because of the school's close proximity to the ocean.

Kristin had successfully made it through her first year in college, where she majored in speech communications. She looked forward to returning home for the summer, but first she wanted to party. After all, she deserved it.

Kristin started her end-of-the-year celebration at an off-campus party thrown by fellow student Ryan Fell. The party took place on Crandall Way, less than a quarter mile from Kristin's dorm. According to police reports, Kristin arrived at the party sober.

Two hours later, she was not.

At approximately 2:00 A.M. Kristin Smart lay in the next-door neighbor's yard passed out. Cheryl Anderson, who knew Kristin but was not close friends with her, and another Cal Poly student, Tim Davis, spotted her. After they roused Kristin out of her inebriated state and got the lanky, tall blonde to her feet, they began to walk her back to her dorm. About a quarter mile later, another student, Paul Flores, popped up alongside them. He informed Anderson and Davis that he met Kristin at the party earlier that night.

Flores offered to walk Kristin back to her dorm.

Kristin, Paul, Cheryl, and Tim walked northwest on Via Carta, from the raucous party, onto the main campus drive known as Perimeter, which is a three-quarter circular road that connects all of the main arteries on campus. Davis was the first to break off and go to his dorm. It was only a short trip to Muir Hall, Kristin's dorm, so Anderson assumed everything was fine. Even though Kristin stumbled and could barely stand up straight, Anderson decided to let Flores walk her home the rest of the way. After all, it was only another one hundred yards or so. Anderson parted ways and headed off to her own dorm. Flores assured Anderson that he would get Kristin home safely.

No one has heard from or seen Kristin Smart since.

The next morning, witnesses saw Paul Flores with a black eye. He did not have it the night before at the party, according to several witnesses who attended.

No one reported Kristin as missing until May 28, 1996. The Cal Poly campus police supposedly took their sweet time in looking further into her disappearance. They eventually contacted her father, Stan Smart, who was now the principal at Vintage High School in Napa, California. Mr. Smart assumed that Kristin had done something wrong at school. He was frustrated to learn that no one had seen her for almost three days.

The Cal Poly police treated Kristin's case as a simple missing-person case. They told her parents that it was not unusual for a student to run away and not tell their family. The Smarts, however, did not buy that theory. They knew Kristin would tell them anything if she was upset, depressed, or in some kind of trouble. As the days ticked off the calendar, however, their fear increased substantially.

The campus police conducted interviews with several students from the party—at least the students that remained on campus. They also spoke with Paul Flores and mentioned the black eye to him. Flores claimed that he got it during a basketball game. At a second interview he recanted his story and claimed that he received the black eye while fixing his car. For some reason, the campus officers did not bother to ask him why he lied about the basketball game.

Later, Flores would tell his close friends that he had lied twice. He claimed he did not get the black eye while fixing his car. In fact, he had no clue as to how he got the shiner. He laughed as he told his friends that he was embarrassed that he did not know how it got there, so he had to make up something.

One month after the disappearance of Kristin Smart, the case switched hands from the Cal Poly campus police to the San Luis Obispo Police Department and the San Luis Obispo County Sheriff's Department. Former San Luis Obispo sheriff Edward Williams immediately pegged Flores as the main suspect in her disappearance and began a full-scale investigation into the young man.

Unfortunately, for the police, Flores hired an attorney and refused to speak to anyone about Kristin Smart. Despite Flores's antagonistic stance, Sheriff Williams was able to conduct a search of Flores's dorm room. The only problem was that Flores had moved out over two months earlier and had thoroughly cleaned his room up in the process. Despite the cleaning, the sheriff's three cadaver-sniffing dogs made a direct beeline for Flores's dorm room. The dogs were having a field day in Flores's old room. They bounced up and down all over the young man's mattress, which was property of the school; therefore, it remained in the room. Unfortunately, no specific physical evidence was located.

Soon thereafter, Paul Flores dropped out of college.

His headaches were only beginning.

The Smarts began a relentless campaign to get Paul Flores to speak. They believed that he was the key to the whereabouts of their daughter. They did everything in their power to get him to come forward and, if not confess, at least tell them what he knew about Kristin's final moments. Their pressure campaign consisted of sending out photo collages of Kristin to Flores's parents, grandparents, and other relatives. The collages showed their daughter enjoying the sun, laying out at the beach, or enjoying the water with her friends. They were images of a typical gorgeous California girl, and they believed Paul Flores had a hand in her potential demise. Friends of the Smart family would also send postcards to members of Flores's family asking them why their son would not speak with authorities. The Smarts wanted to make sure that the Flores family knew their son was the main suspect.

The Smarts indicated that the envelopes always came back to them—open. They at least knew that the Flores family was getting the message.

The Smarts, frustrated by Paul Flores's refusal to speak, decided to pay him a visit. They traveled to a Central California gas station, where he worked. Their intentions were honorable; they just wanted him to help them find their daughter. According to sources, however, Flores hid in the back of the gas station and refused to speak to the bereaved family.

The Smarts made sure Paul Flores knew someone had their eye on him at all times. Private investigators volunteered their services to the family to track Flores down wherever he relocated. He eventually ended up in Southern California.

In Irvine.

Where Rachel Newhouse grew up.

The private investigators were able to find out where

Flores sought employment. Anytime a potential employer encountered Paul Flores, they also received a packet of newspaper clippings from the Smarts that detailed Flores's potential involvement in her disappearance. If they could not get the packet to the companies before they hired him, they usually received it soon thereafter. Most times, the result was the same: Paul Flores was not hired, or if he already had the job, he was asked for an explanation. Usually, they asked him to leave. He lost jobs at a video store, a fast-food hamburger restaurant, and Outback Steakhouse.

Frustrated, Paul Flores tried to join the U.S. Navy. The Smarts were right behind him with their packet of information. The navy refused to accept the wayward youth.

Later in 1996, the Smart family sued Paul Flores in civil court. Once again, the purpose was to force him to talk. Flores, however, remained silent by invoking his Fifth Amendment right against self-incrimination, and the family eventually dropped the lawsuit.

The entire incident not only left the Smarts devastated, but the Flores family was shattered as well. According to sources, Flores's parents could no longer handle the strain of their son as a suspect in an abduction, or even murder case. Ruben and Susan Flores eventually divorced because of their son's situation, among other problems they experienced.

Curiously, despite the hardship the Smarts have caused him, Paul Flores has never sued the family. He has also never asked for a restraining order against them.

When they realized they could not corral Paul Flores, the Smarts turned to the local police. Their frustration with the authorities, however, was apparent from the beginning. They did not understand why it took the campus police a month before they requested the services of the San Luis Obispo County Sheriff's Department. They were outraged when the sheriff's department took forever to search Flores's room, long after he vacated the premises. They were also upset that the sheriff failed to test any of Flores's items from the room for DNA evidence. This could have included the mattress and any hairs, scabs, skin flakes, and other potential DNA evidence left in the room.

The Smarts decided to turn to higher authorities: the Federal Bureau of Investigation, as well as Janet Reno, the United States Attorney General. They wanted someone on their daughter's case.

They needed to find her.

The Smarts took charge of the search for their daughter by running a full-court press on the media. They were able to get Kristin's name and face out to millions of viewers by making numerous appearances on shows such as *20/20*, *Sally*, *Inside Edition*, and *America's Most Wanted*. They even visited a psychic for a show on the Sci-Fi Channel called *Sightings*.

The Smarts feared that the case would simply languish, so they contacted a family friend, California State Senator Mike Thompson, St. Helena, Democrat, who was eager to lend a hand. Senator Thompson immediately drafted legislation that would require campus police departments and local law officials to draw up written agreements as to who would handle homicides and other violent crimes in their overlapping jurisdictions. The bill would act as a response to the monthlong lag time between Kristin's disappearance and the time the sheriff's department officially got involved in her search. Willie Guerrero, a spokesman for Senator Thompson, stated that the law creates a "minimum threshold" between law enforcement agencies and how they should handle the investigations of violent crimes on California's college campuses.

Governor Pete Wilson signed House Assembly Bill (SB) 1729 on August 11, 1998. It is better known as the Kristin Smart Campus Safety Act.

FOUR

With Kristin Smart's disappearance fresh in their minds, the police wasted no time in attempting to find Rachel Newhouse. Indeed, it seemed as if the entire 43,000-person community of San Luis Obispo was on alert.

Members of the community welcomed Rachel's family, including her father, Phillip, her mother, Montel, her brother Travis, twenty-two, her sister, Ashley, nineteen, and her uncle Peter Morreale, a defense attorney from Riverside, California. Morreale acted as spokesperson and expressed the family's gratitude to the warm people of San Luis Obispo who took them in, fed them, and attempted to comfort the Newhouse clan as the investigation was under way. Morreale informed the press, "Phil and Montel are very appreciative. They don't feel like strangers up there."

It was an easy time to feel uncomfortable as the search for Rachel continued. On Wednesday, November 18, another shock occurred in the community. A local resident, Richard Wall, was shot and killed less than one mile away from Cal Poly. The seemingly safe bastion of San Luis Obispo seemed to be under arrest.

Fear and panic soon began to take over.

Cal Poly senior Malia McKee expressed that "no way will I walk home at night." McKee vividly recalled Kristin Smart's disappearance and how "it really scared us, but it wore off."

Architecture major Julie Bebeikin talked about her late nights on campus. She said that some nights she would not leave until 2:00 A.M. and that "I feel like I'm in a complete ghost town." She even carried an X-ACTO knife for protection.

Sharon Perkins, coordinator of the Cal Poly "Take Back the Night" program, an annual campus gathering to foster awareness about violence against women, spoke of Rachel's disappearance as a wake-up call. She matter-of-factly informed the local press, "I think a lot of people have the opinion that Cal Poly is really safe." In her mind women must be on their guard at all times and that "this is a reality check that in San Luis Obispo it can happen here."

By Thursday Captain Topham could tell that a crime had occurred in his sleepy little burg. He began to feel the pressure of the Newhouse case. The previous day, he called off the cadaver-dog search teams. Furthermore, review of several local businesses' surveillance videotapes showed no sign of Rachel and hundreds of interviews led nowhere.

Captain Topham knew that each day they did not locate Rachel Newhouse, the more difficult it would be to find her. He also began to hint that this was probably a case of violent crime, mainly due to the blood found on the bridge. There was no match made yet between the blood drops found on the Jennifer Street Bridge and Rachel Newhouse. Captain Topham, however, could not deny the inevitable conclusion: the blood probably was hers.

Despite his initial reluctance to turn the reins over, Captain Topham decided to appeal to a higher authority. He contacted the Sacramento office of the Federal Bureau of Investigation and requested assistance. He believed the FBI was better equipped and had a stronger workforce to locate Rachel Newhouse. He made the call. He could only hope that it would help to find the missing twenty-year-old from Irvine.

The Newhouse family also got involved in the search for their daughter. They printed up thousands of flyers at the downtown Kinko's and distributed them throughout the town and the surrounding county. They also posted flyers in the

San Joaquin Valley and in Southern California, in hopes of spreading the word.

Morreale stated that the Newhouse clan was extremely pleased with the efforts of Captain Topham and the sheriff's department in the search for their daughter. He was perturbed, however, by a statement made by San Luis Obispo police chief Jim Gardiner about Rachel's drinking. The Newhouses believed that Gardiner insinuated that Rachel got what she deserved. She was only a minor who was partying and drinking when she should not have been. Morreale was quick to stress that Rachel did not have a drinking problem of any kind.

Even Captain Topham talked about common sense among the town's residents when they ventured out at night. He insisted that the residents of San Luis Obispo had no reason to be afraid. Topham calmly reassured his constituents when he said, "We have no indication this incident fits a pattern." He was quick to add that Rachel Newhouse's disappearance should not "change our perception that this is a pretty safe community."

FIVE

The police were doing everything in their power to alleviate the town's fears. Others chipped in to help search for Rachel Newhouse as well. Rachel's family offered $10,000 for information leading to the recovery of their daughter. Fellow Orange County resident and Anaheim Angels centerfielder Jim Edmonds and his agent, Dwight Manley, each kicked in $25,000 for the search for Rachel. Edmonds, a father of two girls, felt Rachel's story hit close to home.

"I know what it's like to be out there and be on your own and have to rely on people you don't know," Edmonds stated to the *Orange County News*. "This is a situation where everybody needs to get out there and help the cause and try to bring her home."

Manley added his reason for helping: "We all need to realize that Rachel Newhouse could be our child, niece, friend, and hope this effort will help the police in Rachel's safe recovery."

Part of that recovery effort by police was to search the Cold Canyon Landfill, south of San Luis Obispo, on Friday, November 20. Captain Topham described the check of the nearby Edna Valley garbage dump as a routine measure in a missing-person case and not the result of any specific lead. He informed the media that no clues had been located concerning Rachel's case.

The media had also received numerous bogus contacts.

Dave Colby, news director for local NBC affiliate KSBY-TV, claimed to have received twenty-five to thirty phone calls a day about various dead bodies in the neighborhood.

"Every time one of us goes to lunch," Colby related, "we've heard conversations that a body has been found."

The rumor mill, needless to say, became a source of irritation for Captain Topham.

"If people really want to help, quit gossiping," he angrily snapped.

Meanwhile, the FBI began to set up equipment—their main purpose in the case was to devise a computer tracking system to organize all of the various interviews and searches that had already been conducted and "to manage the huge volume of information that has been developed."

Some members of the media attempted to arrange a meeting between the Newhouses and the Smarts. Tabloid television program *Hard Copy* wanted to get the families together for a special program, but the Newhouses did not want to take part. They kept to themselves and wanted no part of the press attention. Peter Morreale stressed, "The Smarts' grief is a private matter, and so is ours." He also claimed it was impossible for the Newhouses to talk to anyone because they could not even speak among themselves without crying.

The Newhouse family believed there was nothing left for them to do in San Luis Obispo. They headed back to Irvine on Thursday. Morreale again emphasized that the family was pleased with the police's handling of the case; however, some believe there was some underlying frustration on the part of the family. That lay with Police Chief Jim Gardiner, who again stressed the importance of eliminating underage drinking among coeds. Gardiner stated that he did not blame Rachel Newhouse or Kristin Smart for their disappearances, but he believed alcohol might have played a part. He spoke of how alcohol can impair an individual's decision making, can numb a person's brain, and toss common sense out of one's mental window.

"I've seen too many situations where alcohol destroys lives," Gardiner stated. He also believed that neither Rachel nor Kristin would be missing if they were sober.

Other people wanted to help. Heritage Oaks Bank set up a Rachel Newhouse Help Fund. A young girl even broke open her piggy bank and brought $6 in coins to the bank to do her part. One fraternity charged money for parking at football games and donated the proceeds to the fund. Another fraternity threw an alcohol-free barbecue bash, which attracted over two hundred students and raised $1,200 before local police shut it down at 9:00 P.M. Also, a former police reserve officer, Frank Dufault, and his Internet partner Randy Falcke donated the monthly proceeds from their Smart Date Web site to the Rachel Newhouse search fund. Dufault and former pilot Jerry Noble created the Smart Date Web site in 1996 after the disappearance of Kristin Smart. Their concept, which won the London-based Crime Social Innovations award, provided a service wherein females could register their personal information and give detailed descriptions as to whom they were dating and where they would be going with their date. Noble, who used to file preflight plans before every takeoff, described the site as a way for a woman to file a "predate plan." The service cost its users $12 a month and the entrepreneurs offered to donate their entire profits for the month of December.

Despite the efforts of the police, volunteers, and concerned citizens, there still was no sign of Rachel Newhouse. The police were further disappointed when the initial test results of the blood found on the Jennifer Street Bridge came back inconclusive. They would have to wait another three weeks before the DNA test results came back.

Rachel's friends at Cal Poly were frustrated as well. Several of her friends from Irvine who attended Cal Poly or Cuesta College, the local junior college, gathered at a house on Luneta Drive in Rachel's neighborhood for Thanksgiving. Rachel used to park her car at this house every day when she stopped by to talk with her friends. She was not with them on this day of remembrance. Instead, her friends reminisced about Rachel while they ate a potluck turkey lunch. Most of the time they cried.

Other Cal Poly students who did not know Rachel personally felt her presence in their own homes when they returned for Thanksgiving. School officials from Cal Poly sent home a letter to every student's parents about her disappearance. The school believed they had a right to know what was happening at their child's campus. Juan Gonzalez, vice president of student affairs, hoped the letter, combined with the now more than $60,000 reward, would stimulate discussion between the students and their parents.

One former student who did not receive one of those letters was Paul Flores. The prime suspect in the Kristin Smart case was once again a target in many people's eyes. The San Luis Obispo Police Department released an official statement, however, that Flores was *not* a suspect in the Rachel Newhouse disappearance: "We wish to announce that Paul Flores, who has been the subject of much attention during the investigation into the disappearance of Kristin Smart, has been eliminated in the disappearance of Rachel Newhouse."

No one gave an official explanation as to why the police ruled Flores out. Sheriff's Department sergeant Sean Donahue sternly stated, as far as Flores's involvement in the Smart case, "Nobody is ruled out. We haven't ruled him out yet."

On Sunday, November 29, the investigators received a disturbing call from Ventura County. Apparently, a group of avid bird-watchers had been traipsing about in an area known as Hungry Valley, when they made a gruesome discovery.

A young woman's dead body.

SIX

Captain Bart Topham breathed a sigh of relief when he got more information on the body found in Hungry Valley. It turned out to be an eighteen-year-old runaway from Simi Valley named Melinda Marie Brown. Captain Topham cranked up the Rachel Newhouse search team anew and ignored the persistent rumors that swirled around his head like a devilish Santa Ana wind spinning out of control.

Captain Topham and the FBI continued to interview as many San Luis Obispo residents as possible. They spoke with the night manager of Tortilla Flats who estimated that there were probably fifty people in the restaurant on the night of Rachel's disappearance. He explained to the police that minors, patrons under the age of twenty-one, were allowed into the restaurant on the dance floor side, while those over twenty-one, able to drink alcohol, were allowed on the bar side of the Flats.

The police also viewed more surveillance videotape from Sandy's Deli and Liquor, located next door to the Flats. As was par for the course, they could not see anything on the tapes. Randy Pound, manager of Spike's Place, a bar near the Flats that Rachel frequented, told reporters that when interviewed, he claimed that Rachel did not come in on November 12.

Police continued to search the neighborhoods, creeks, and back alleys of San Luis Obispo. They also reinterviewed several of Rachel's friends and school acquaintances, but still with no luck.

The Newhouses' hopes began to diminish with each passing day. They desperately wanted to know the results of the blood test. Officers used sample blood from other family members to attempt to make a determination if the Jennifer Street blood was hers. Police took hair from one of Rachel's hairbrushes. Still, they would have to wait. Rachel's aunt Stephanie Morreale had a horrible feeling in her gut. Her instincts were that the blood would belong to her niece and that someone had snatched her out of thin air like a nimble magician with evil intentions.

"Rachel was the kind of girl who called home four or five times a week," she stated with concern. Her niece was not the type to go missing for four weeks without a single word as to her whereabouts.

On Tuesday, December 15, the investigation received some positive news. Governor Pete Wilson kicked in an additional $50,000 in reward money for information that may lead to the discovery of Rachel Newhouse.

In a press release the governor implored, "Rachel is a good student, a loving daughter and a caring friend to many. She has a bright and promising future, and I pray that she is returned safely to her family and friends."

The additional contribution by the governor upped the reward total to more than $110,000. Surprisingly, Chief Gardiner made the request for the additional money.

"Anything we can do to increase the incentive to come forward will help," he added.

On Wednesday Chief Gardiner held a press conference with Jim Edmonds and Peter Morreale. They discussed the reward money, but their real purpose was to keep Rachel's case in the public eye. They did not want people to become disinterested and not attempt to help locate Rachel Newhouse. Several news outlets and one special guest attended the press conference. A television crew from the hit series *America's Most Wanted* was there. They were planning a special that would air that Saturday. They wanted to spread the story of Rachel Newhouse to a national audience. The crew was also anxiously awaiting the test results of the blood found on the Jennifer Street Bridge.

News on the blood finally came through on Wednesday, December 16. Captain Topham, however, did not release the information to the public until Friday. The captain informed the press corps that the Department of Justice laboratory in Fresno, California, did not give a specific indication as to whom the blood belonged. They did state, however, that the blood might belong to Rachel Newhouse. The odds that it was hers were quite astronomical—8 million to 1.

It had to be Rachel's blood.

Captain Topham acknowledged that the results probably meant that Rachel was almost home on November 12, just blocks away. He reiterated also that it did not mean she was dead. He stated that there was not enough blood at the scene to indicate that she may have bled to death on or near the bridge. He stated that more evidence was located at the scene and it belonged to Rachel. He did not mention any other information that may have indicated an attacker was present on the bridge with Rachel.

Nevertheless, everyone in the room knew: someone had violently attacked Rachel Newhouse less than half a mile away from her quaint, quiet San Luis Obispo home.

Their sanctuary was no more.

PART II

AUNDRIA

SEVEN

March 11, 1999
Branch Street, San Luis Obispo, California
2:00 A.M.

Aundria Lynn Crawford was ready to call it a night. The twenty-year-old Cuesta College student had made it through another hectic day of school and she was pooped. She had worked hard ever since she moved to San Luis Obispo to attend the respected junior college. Aundria had been an excellent student and ballerina, until she turned sixteen. That year she discovered that she walked on her feet incorrectly and would have to rework her bones to correct the problem. The pain on her point toe, the one she tiptoed on, was unbearable. It forced her to quit her first true passion. As a result Aundria missed the one thing that helped her stay focused and disciplined. Subsequently, with her diminished enthusiasm came diminished grades. Her senior year at Clovis High School proved to be a killer. Academically she performed poorly. Her lack of a solid grade report prevented her from attending her dream college—Cal Polytechnic Institute. Therefore, she settled into the next best thing—she enrolled in junior college.

Aundria spent her first year of college at Fresno City College, where she drastically improved her grades. She then transferred in her sophomore year to Cuesta College, another junior college, in San Luis Obispo. She intended to do everything in her power to transfer to Cal Poly. Cuesta College had one of the highest transfer rates in the state, so she knew if she stayed focused, her chances were excellent.

This evening, however, she was worn out and ready for bed. She kissed her cat, Riley, good night and stripped out of her clothes. She usually slept in her panties and a well-worn T-shirt, in her cozy upstairs loft bedroom. The brown duplex reminded her of a ski lodge in Colorado. Aundria retired to her bedroom and read a little before turning off the lamp on her nightstand.

She was not aware of the man standing outside.

Or that he wore something over his face.

The man had pulled a pair of panty hose over his mug and crept toward Aundria's duplex. It was the fourth time he had been there, spying on the lithe, dirty-blond-haired college student. The half a fifth of Jack Daniel's that he had drunk earlier in the evening seemed to release his inhibitions. Before when he had spied on her, he did not have the courage to approach her.

Aundria had turned out the lights in her bedroom. It was time to go to sleep.

Now was his chance.

The man strode directly toward the front door of the duplex. It was locked. He went around back. He checked the large windows, but they were locked. He went back to the front. He looked around, wondering what to do, when he spotted her bathroom window. It was a tiny window, but he was determined to get inside. Much to his surprise and glee, it was unlocked. He quietly removed the screen and began to crawl through the window. It was an amazingly tiny window. Too tiny for his hefty frame, but he was determined. There was a reason he wanted inside so badly and he was going to get in, no matter what happened to him. He continued to squeeze through the window; however, he hurt himself in the process. Despite the pain he successfully made his way into Aundria Crawford's duplex.

"Meeeoooowwwwww!"

The loud screeching noise that emanated from the bathroom temporarily paralyzed the man. He had no idea what caused the shrill sound.

It was Riley.

Aundria awoke from her slumber. She decided to go check on her cat. Riley had felt sick, due to a recent surgery.

The intruder stood quietly, but anxious, in her bathroom. The encounter with the damned cat had increased his heart rate substantially, and he seriously contemplated getting the hell out of there. Just as he was ready to turn around and sneak back out, the bathroom door opened.

A sleepy-eyed Aundria Crawford looked at the man standing in her bathroom. They both froze in their tracks for a split second and then the intruder reared his arm back and punched her solidly in the mouth, splitting her lip and slamming her up against the bathroom wall. He then advanced on her and continued the forceful melee. He punched her, at least three or four more times in the face, until he knocked her unconscious.

The man stopped for a moment and looked down at the attractive girl lying at his feet in the cramped bathroom. He then pulled out a rope from his back pocket, which he purposefully brought just for this occasion, and knelt down on the floor and grabbed Aundria's limp body. Immediately he wrapped the rope around her wrists and secured them behind her back. He also tied her feet together and wrenched them up her backside until they reached her bound wrists. He then looped the rope around her feet and her wrists so she was in a hog-tied position. He then looped the rope around her neck. He checked the rope to make sure it was secure. She was not going anywhere.

He also made sure she could not make a noise, so he grabbed a roll of silver duct tape, which he also brought for the occasion, and unfurled it across her mouth.

Still not feeling entirely confident, he bolted up Aundria's staircase and into her bedroom. While there, he grabbed one of her pillowcases and quickly returned to the bathroom. He grabbed Aundria's still-unconscious body and draped the pillowcase over her head. He did not want her to see him in case she woke up.

Aundria was unconscious, hog-tied, gagged, and blindfolded. But she was still alive.

The intruder returned to her bedroom and grabbed another pillowcase. He began to survey the room and realized that he wanted to take some of this girl's items with him. Using the pillowcase as a carrying bag, he stuffed random items inside. He took some of Aundria's country and classic rock CDs, videotapes, and even a VCR. He also grabbed some of her clothes.

The intruder rushed outside to Branch Street and located his blue Ford Ranger pickup in front of her house. It was nestled under several large oak trees, which served as a natural canopy over the quiet neighborhood street. The darkness created by the trees provided a cover, so no one would see him. He tossed the pillowcase full of stolen items into the car and returned to Aundria's brown duplex.

When he returned, he panicked.

She was conscious!

She was valiantly struggling against her numerous restraints, but the exertion only frightened her more and slowed her down. The man did not punch her again. Instead, he grabbed her in a bundle, tossed the 5'6", 120-pound girl over his shoulder, and headed out onto Branch Street. He placed her in the back of the truck cab behind the seats and quietly shut the passenger door. Instead of getting into the truck and driving off, the man returned to the duplex.

He scurried to the bathroom and grabbed a towel. He used it to wipe off Aundria's blood from the floor. There were only small spots, but several dispersed throughout the house. When he finished, he turned off the lights and headed out. As he was about to exit the back door, something shiny caught his eye.

Aundria's keys.

He raced over to the dining-room table, where they lay. He grasped them in his large hand. There was something unusual attached to the keys.

A tiny black eight ball key chain. He looked at the key chain with a certain sense of bemusement.

It brought back memories. Just as quickly, he was gone.

EIGHT

March 12, 1999
Clovis, California
12:15 A.M.

"This is Gail Eberhart. I need to report that my daughter is missing."

A San Luis Obispo Police Department dispatcher took the call. The woman caller did not sound too stressed, but concerned. The dispatcher calmly asked the woman for her daughter's name.

"Aundria Crawford," the woman replied. "She lives on Branch Street in San Luis Obispo, near the Greyhound bus station."

"When was the last time you spoke with your daughter, Mrs. . . ?"

"Eberhart. I spoke with her this past Tuesday. But I paged her last night and I haven't heard from her since. She always returns my beeps."

The dispatcher could tell Eberhart was getting slightly more frantic as the conversation continued. He wanted to calm this situation down before the woman became too upset.

"Ma'am, I am going to send someone over there right away," he assured her. "We will check it out for you right now."

The dispatcher did not want to waste a second in tracking down the young woman. It had been four months since the disappearance of Rachel Newhouse. The last thing the police force of San Luis Obispo wanted was for word to spread that another local college girl had gone missing. He hoped he could nip this problem in the bud before it blew up into an all-out frenzy. Besides, he assumed, she probably just took off for an early weekend and decided not to call her mother. The mom is probably just overprotective and panicky.

The dispatcher put a call out to beat patrol officer Jon Paulding, who whisked over to the small brown duplex, less than a half mile from the Jennifer Street Bridge. Officer Paulding pulled up in front of the apartment and noticed a white Ford Mustang in the driveway. He jotted down the plate numbers and made a mental note to check them out later. Officer Paulding walked up to the front door on the right-hand side of the duplex and knocked. No one answered the door. The officer, not too concerned, wrote a note to Aundria and informed her that she should call her mother. He left it on her Mustang.

Meanwhile, back in Clovis, Gail Eberhart began to get scared. She continued calling for several more hours and still could not get a hold of Aundria. Finally, at 5:15 A.M., she called the San Luis Obispo Police Department again. The dispatcher directed her call directly to Officer Paulding.

The police officer returned to Aundria's duplex. This time he attempted to gain entry into Aundria's home. Once he realized he could not enter through any of the doors, he asked for Eberhart's permission to break in. She agreed without hesitation. He did not need to, however, as the dispatcher had already contacted the landlord, who would arrive soon with the keys.

Officer Paulding checked Aundria's car again. He clasped the door handle, and to his surprise, it was unlocked. He looked in and noticed a brown leather purse, which belonged to Aundria, lying on the floorboard. He searched the purse for a set of house keys but found nothing. At the same time the landlord arrived.

Officer Paulding called for assistance and a second officer arrived at the Branch Street residence. The landlord unlocked the front door and both officers began to search the duplex. Officer Paulding checked upstairs in Aundria's loft. He looked up at a countertop and spotted her pager.

Nothing looked unusual to the officers.

Officer Paulding contacted Gail Eberhart to inform her that nothing looked suspicious. She asked him if they should go ahead and file a missing-person report. The officer agreed and took the pertinent information.

NINE

Aundria Crawford did not know Rachel Newhouse. They did not go to the same college, even though they lived in the same town. They did not hang out with the same crowd, even though they were the same age. They did not live similar childhoods, even though they would both end up in the central coastal town of San Luis Obispo.

Many people knew Aundria Crawford as Aundria Eberhart. She was born on July 10, 1978, in Pasco, Washington, to Jim and Gail Eberhart. Her parents were hardworking middle-class Americans. Her mom worked in retail for the local Sears department store and her dad worked as an electrician. Despite a love for their only daughter, Mom and Dad did not share a love for one another. They divorced when Aundria was only six months old. After the divorce Gail packed up the car and relocated with Aundria to her grandparents' home in Fresno, California. Don and Jody Crawford gladly took them in and nurtured their precocious granddaughter.

Aundria enjoyed growing up with her grandparents. They were warm and loving and did everything possible to assure that she had a normal childhood. She loved to play outside and inspect the creatures that wandered the yards in their neighborhood. Her grandfather recalled her deep love for animals: "When she was a child, she would get mad at me for crushing snails."

Aundria also developed a fondness for ballet. She danced

in *The Nutcracker* and *Alice in Wonderland* and impressed everyone with her ability.

After Aundria's foot problem forced her out of ballet, she turned her attention to horses. Her father owned some horses and she always loved to ride them when she visited him. Even though she already knew how to ride, she took additional lessons. She got so good that she began to compete in barrel racing. She even won several awards.

As Aundria got older, she branched out beyond stereotypical female obsessions. Despite a definite feminine exterior, Aundria accepted her masculine side. She especially loved working on cars. She was not just some weekend warrior wanna-be either. She knew her way around the inside of an engine block and even learned how to change an alternator. She met some boys who were also into cars and racing and she started to attend various car races around Fresno Valley and Bakersfield.

Aundria attended Bullard High School in Fresno and made several friends. She also began to slip while she was there. Some of her friends ran in some interesting circles and were not the best of influences. She allowed too many distractions to take away from her schoolwork and soon fell behind. She was not into drugs or alcohol; she just liked to hang out. Her grandfather Don Crawford stressed the point that "she did not do drugs and she didn't drink. She was just a good girl."

Gail and Aundria relocated to Clovis, California, in 1996, her senior year. By then, Aundria was prepared not to graduate with her classmates. Her grades had fallen so far that she had to attend a special home-study program known as ReStart to help get her back on track. Embarrassed by her lack of discipline, she took her studies seriously this time. Her ReStart instructor, Joy Cravens, met with Aundria once a week and went over her assignments to make sure she showed signs of improvement. Cravens explained that Aundria was studious, considerate, and quiet, but had a tendency to show up late for their meetings. Cravens also stated that Aundria did not leave much of an impression on her because the teacher mainly remembered the bad students.

Aundria's efforts paid off. She upped her grade point average and walked in her senior high school graduation ceremony with all of her classmates.

She was extremely proud of her redemption and was determined to continue the cycle.

Aundria's first collegiate adventure took place at nearby Fresno City College. After a year of doing well there, she was ready and eager to be on her own. With financial help from her grandparents, she packed up her 1988 white Ford Mustang and headed out to Central California. San Luis Obispo was her destination. Her ultimate goal was to attend Cal Polytechnic Institute, but first she would have to earn her way in one more time. Aundria's high school and junior college grades were not quite good enough for Cal Poly's standards, so she had to register at another junior college and work her way up. Aundria was used to obstacles and looked forward to the challenge. She enrolled at Cuesta College, located on Highway 1, less than five miles from Cal Poly. On the surface Cuesta College appeared to be the rougher of the two colleges—a smaller campus, with older, more run-down buildings, and more students standing around smoking and flashing multiple piercings and tattoos. In many ways it is the polar opposite of Cal Poly, which exudes a more polished exterior. Its student body is populated by the Hollywood stereotype of the surfer dude jock types and beautiful blond California girls.

Underneath the rough outer shell of Cuesta College lies a launchpad for better and brighter things. Cuesta has one of the highest transfer rates for its students in the state. Many students attend the junior college to get their grades back up so they can attend colleges such as UCLA, USC, and Cal Poly. Aundria was fully aware of Cuesta's exceptional transfer rate. She planned to take full advantage of the opportunity.

Aundria began in general studies but switched to interior designing. She exhibited a knack for how to make a room look good—if it involved furniture positioning, drapery hanging, or color schemes, it coursed through her bloodstream. Her favorite class during the spring 1999 semester was interior-space planning. She learned about the effects and value of proper lighting, use of space, and the power of walls.

Margaret Collier, dean of the school's design department, spoke highly of Aundria. "She loved school," the dean praised. "Her teachers thought she was doing great."

Aundria made a positive impression on her coworkers as well. Since money was always tight, Aundria usually stayed employed to keep up with the bills for school and her duplex. Aundria turned her love of cars into a job working for the local Kragen Auto Parts in San Luis Obispo. Her auto knowledge, positive demeanor, and ability to communicate with total strangers proved to be a winning combination at the huge automotive repair superstore. Her coworker Robert Santos, who was also a classmate of hers from Cuesta College, sang her praises. He spoke highly of her intelligence, wit, and confidence.

"She wasn't afraid to speak her mind and tell you how she felt," Santos recalled. "I think she was going to do good in life. I think if there was something she wanted, she would go get it."

Santos was surprised when Aundria quit her job at Kragen after five months to go work for veterinarian James Waldsmith at the Equine Center in town. Her family, however, was not. They knew how much Aundria loved animals. For her, it was the dream scenario: this beautiful California girl, who loved the ocean and animals, working in a vet's office and living in gorgeous San Luis Obispo.

What more could she ask for?

Unfortunately, the veterinarian's assistant position did not work out for Aundria. Dr. Waldsmith let her go after only one month of employment. Aundria had shown up late to work far too many times in her short stay at the company. Dr. Waldsmith found her congenial yet unreliable.

"She was a nice gal," the doctor recalled. "The typical Cal Poly kid [she was a Cuesta College student] that shows up at our door."

Aundria would not let this setback throw her off course. She set out to get back her job at Kragen. Her former manager, Gil Luera, spoke with her just before she disappeared. Luera stated that Aundria had "just come back to reapply here when all this came down." Luera also stated he was looking forward to giving her old job back to her.

He never got the chance.

TEN

Captain Bart Topham knew he only had one chance to keep the citizens of San Luis Obispo calm. After the third college coed disappearance in nearly three years, he needed to put a lid on this case immediately, before he had vigilante groups forming and citizens packing up their trucks and moving out. He called a press conference on March 15 to let everyone know that the police were on top of this latest missing-person case.

Captain Topham wanted to make one point explicitly clear: "There is no evidence of a connection between this missing-person case and any other at this time," referring, of course, to the Kristin Smart 1996 disappearance and the Rachel Newhouse disappearance just four months earlier. The last thing the captain wanted was for the people of San Luis Obispo to be afraid to walk out in the streets at night for fear of a serial killer.

The townsfolk did not believe Topham and they were scared.

"It's too weird for this to happen three times," stated nineteen-year-old Cuesta College student Jodi Simonson. "It makes me nervous."

Some of the students tried to move on with their lives. Mandy Daniels, a twenty-year-old Cuesta College student, stated, "I take good precautions, but I also try not to let it alter my life."

Ralph Wessel, a resident of the nearby town of Cayucos,

did not believe Topham for one second. "I think it's the same person," he stated with supreme confidence. "I know the police don't think there's a connection, but it's probably a serial killer after the same type of student."

Adrielle Ray, another Cuesta College student, also had little faith in the captain's assurances. "I wouldn't be surprised if it takes a number of these before police realize a pattern, like four or five."

Some of the residents were tired of the terror. Some expressed a strong desire to move out of their little oasis because of the crimes. Erica Ruiz seriously contemplated packing up her stuff and moving out. "It scared me because it's so close to home," she recalled. "This definitely is encouraging me to move. I'm thinking about it even more."

Her husband, Benjie, weighed in on the latest disappearance: "I've been here twenty-two years and never seen anything like this. Tourism could drop because of this, and there might be a drop of students who come to Cal Poly."

Captain Topham knew it was going to be rough. He could sense that the people of his community were changing. The humble little area, hidden off the 101 Freeway, engulfed in the grassy, mountainous protective arms of the Nine Sisters volcanoes, was no longer a safe haven.

"I think things are changing, and we've just been incredibly lucky for a long time," observed Topham.

Now he hoped he could be lucky in tracking down another missing college student. He hoped he was lucky, not for his sake or even the sake of his town, but because of concern for one person—Aundria Crawford.

The prospects for finding her were not positive. Despite extensive searches for four months, the authorities in San Luis Obispo had never located Rachel Newhouse. Her uncle Peter Morreale had reached a point of resignation upon the news of Aundria's disappearance. He was no longer optimistic that the police would find Rachel: "After four months it doesn't look real good that she's alive."

The spring of 1999 had gotten off to a rotten start, even before Aundria's mysterious disappearance. On February 16 a mother, Carole Sund, her daughter, Juli, and foreign exchange student Silvina Pelosso disappeared from the Cedar Lodge in El Portal, California, near the basin of the Yosemite National Park. The three women were celebrating Juli's participation in the American Spirit Association cheerleading competition and had decided to take a side trip to the famed park of natural wonders before returning to their home in Eureka, California. The last time anyone saw the three women, they had just eaten at the Cedar Lodge Restaurant at 7:35 P.M. No one had seen or heard from them since.

Carole's husband, Jens Sund, and her parents, Francis and Carol Carrington, relocated to El Portal in an attempt to locate their daughter, granddaughter, and charge. They scoured high and low in the mountains and valleys outside and inside the park. They checked gullies in case Carole's red Pontiac Grand Prix rental car may have plunged over the side. They checked old mines. The kidnappers may have tossed their bodies into deep chasms off the roads of the mountainous area. They interviewed several former convicts who populated the outskirts of the park in secluded trailer homes, but they found nothing.

The combination of Rachel Newhouse's disappearance and the three missing women from Yosemite had everyone on edge in Central California. Emotions were even tauter in San Luis Obispo after Aundria Crawford's disappearance. Captain Topham organized two neighborhood searches on Friday, March 12, and a more thorough search the following day. By Monday, March 15, the police called the searches off. Captain Topham had to concede that Aundria Crawford had more likely than not been abducted. The break-in at her apartment, the blood on the floor, the missing items, and the Mustang in the driveway all pointed to her disappearance as a kidnapping.

Police Chief Jim Gardiner informed the media that the

Aundria Crawford investigation would include possible kidnapping and maybe murder.

"We're hoping that's not the case," he cautiously intoned.

Captain Topham continued his stubborn refusal to acknowledge that the Crawford and Newhouse disappearances had any correlation. More and more people were getting tired of his stance, but he insisted that the cases were too disparate.

"The specifics of all three [including the Smart case] are all different," Topham stressed. He spoke of how both Kristin and Rachel disappeared after they drank alcohol. He mentioned it appeared as if Aundria had been abducted from her residence. Furthermore, he pointed out that Aundria did not drink.

"She doesn't drink. She's not a partyer."

Emotions increased after that statement.

Instead of focusing on Captain Topham's backhanded slam of his niece, Peter Morreale spoke of the striking similarities between Rachel and Aundria.

"It's remarkable that she was the same size and build as Rachel." Morreale was convinced that a serial killer had gotten both Rachel and Aundria. Both girls were college students in San Luis Obispo. Both were intelligent and outgoing people. Both were 5'6" tall. Both girls weighed exactly 120 pounds. Both girls had blond hair. The similarities were too obvious to ignore.

Morreale also expressed his concern for Aundria Crawford's family and hoped they could still stand after the shock and dismay that go hand in glove with news of a loved one's disappearance. "Obviously, her family is going through living hell. We can relate to that."

Another family expressed dismay over the disappearance of Aundria Crawford. Denise Smart, mother of Kristin Smart, who disappeared almost three years earlier, stated, "I'm sure everyone there is shocked. It's hard to believe this happened in one small city, but it could have happened anywhere."

PART III

DISCOVERY

ELEVEN

March 16, 1999
Pismo Beach Athletic Club, Pismo Beach, California
Morning

David Zaragoza jumped on his favorite Lifecycle exercise machine as he did every weekday. He picked up the *San Luis Obispo Tribune* and scanned the cover of the front section. Staring back at him was the winsome face of the missing Cuesta College student, Aundria Crawford. As Zaragoza pumped away on the Lifecycle, he read the story of how Captain Topham suspected a break-in at her apartment, only ten blocks from downtown San Luis Obispo. Topham also mentioned that he believed Aundria might have been abducted. While Zaragoza's sweat beaded into his eyes, one person's face popped into his head. Bizarre stories swirled around in his brain. Something bothered him, but he could not pinpoint it.

Twenty minutes later, gleaming with sweat, Zaragoza dismounted from the exercise machine. He grabbed a towel, wiped his forehead, and took a swig from his water bottle. The routine did not relax him as it usually did. Instead, he was irritable. The Aundria Crawford story nagged at him incessantly and left him unfocused.

He took another swig from his water bottle. Suddenly he realized what was bothering him. He grabbed his gear and newspaper and bolted out the door.

* * *

David Zaragoza was a parole officer in San Luis Obispo County. The thirty-seven-year-old family man grew up in Northern California. His father ran a farm, where Zaragoza worked as a kid, but David had bigger dreams for himself. He attended Cal Poly in the early 1980s. He kept his interests in the family line, but he wanted to run a plethora of farms. He was eager to achieve this goal when he signed up for courses and received his degree in agricultural business. Upon graduation Zaragoza found the job market to be almost nonexistent, so he applied for a job in the California penal system. He assumed he might find a job in the field of corrections.

Zaragoza began his run with the California penal system in January 1989. He started out as a state prison guard for three years before he received a promotion to correctional counselor at California Men's Colony East in San Luis Obispo.

By April 1992 he advanced yet again to the position of parole agent, but he went back to being a prison counselor from November 1992 to November 1993. He then returned to his parole position in San Luis Obispo.

By 1999 David Zaragoza was a seasoned parole officer and his specialty was sex offenders. And there were plenty of them in his region.

San Luis Obispo, despite its beauty and small-town mentality, is located in a potentially volatile portion of the state of California. It is located within 140 miles of eleven security prisons. One of the most notorious facilities in the country, the California Men's Colony (CMC), is located within one mile of Cuesta College and five miles from Cal Poly. CMC has housed numerous high-profile criminals within its walls, including the serial-killing duo of Lawrence Bittaker and Roy Norris, who met there in the late 1970s and, upon their release, terrorized Southern California by kidnapping, torturing, and murdering teenage girls.

Some of the other ten prisons include the California State prison—Corcoran. It is home to notorious 1960s cult figure Charles Manson, the leader of the Manson Family, which killed at least seven Los Angelinos in 1969 including eight-and-a-half-month pregnant B-movie actress Sharon Tate; Robert Kennedy's assassin Sirhan B. Sirhan; and Juan Corona, a migrant farm worker who killed and buried twenty-five people in Yuba City, California.

The other prisons nearby include the Valley State Prison for Women in Chowchilla, the Central California Women's Facility, the Substance Abuse Treatment Facility and State Prison located in Corcoran, the North Kern State Prison, the Wasco State Prison, the California Correctional Institution in Tehachapi, the Correctional Training Facility of Soledad, the Salinas Valley State Prison, the Pleasant Valley State Prison, and Avenal State Prison.

In addition to the multitude of correctional facilities, San Luis Obispo County also houses one of the state of California's largest mental hospitals for criminals, Atascadero State Hospital. Before he went to prison, the aforementioned serial killer Roy Norris spent five years there after he raped and assaulted two women in San Diego. Atascadero doctors declared him "no further harm to others." Three months later, he raped a young woman from Redondo Beach. Norris ended up in CMC, where he met Lawrence Bittaker.

One of the misnomers of California is that it is a mecca for violent crime, especially rape. While it is true that the total numbers of rapes are high, the percentage of violent, forcible rapes of individuals is one of the better percentages in the United States. According to the U.S. Crime Index Rates, in the year 2000, there were 90,186 reported forcible rapes in the country. Of that total, 9,785 occurred in the state of California. That same year the state's population reached almost 34 million; therefore, the rate of occurrence of a forcible rape in California in 2000 was 28.9 out of every 100,000 people. This placed California as the thirty-first best state in the

Union. The nationwide average recorded that year stood at 32 per 100,000 people.

Despite these surprising numbers, the individuals who committed these crimes are some of the most notorious in our country.

David Zaragoza's parole beat included some of these notorious criminal sex offenders. At the time of Aundria Crawford's disappearance, his roster consisted of more than one hundred of California's most reviled offenders.

As he chewed over the Crawford information, one parolee's name sprang to mind: Rex Krebs.

Krebs, a prison parolee, lived deep in the woods of Davis Canyon, near Avila Beach, just south of San Luis Obispo. Zaragoza had been assigned the Krebs case back in 1997 after he was released from Soledad State Prison. Krebs had been incarcerated for rape charges in two cases that occurred ten years earlier in nearby Arroyo Grande and Oceano. Zaragoza remembered that the Krebs attacks involved break-ins of women's residences. There was a ring of familiarity to his modus operandi.

Zaragoza decided to pay Krebs a visit.

TWELVE

March 17, 1999
Davis Canyon Road, Davis Canyon, California
Noon

David Zaragoza skipped his usual workout regimen at the gym. Instead, he hopped into his Jeep Cherokee and hurriedly made his way to Davis Canyon. The beautiful canyon area is home to lush vegetation and beautiful, sprawling mountains covered in towering green trees. Inside the canyon are numerous fruit and vegetable farms and vineyards. Mixed among the vast farming areas are beautiful multimillion-dollar homes that belong to the wealthy vintners. Among the gorgeous mansions sit several weathered houses and old trailer homes festooned with television satellite dishes.

From the south, one enters Davis Canyon via See Canyon Road, a well-paved road with a few twists and turns, but nothing too treacherous. Rex Krebs lived in this general area. To get to his house, Zaragoza had to drive a mile-and-a-half on See Canyon Road before he made a left onto Davis Canyon Road. This road was the reason why Zaragoza had the Krebs case in the first place.

Krebs lived in a rental home, owned by Muriel Wright, almost two miles in from See Canyon Road. Not a far distance until you actually used Davis Canyon Road, which is rocky, narrow, and skirts alongside some precarious drops over the edge. The two-tire track pathway is barely accessible by any vehicle other than a four-wheel drive. Zaragoza's Jeep Cherokee was more than sufficient.

Zaragoza was familiar with the path to Krebs's house. He had been there several times for routine parole visits. He believed Krebs was a decent enough fellow. After all, he was only thirty-three years old and had lived a rough life, in and out of reform schools, jails, and prisons for almost half his life. Zaragoza hoped that Krebs was getting his life back on track—job, girlfriend, nice secluded home. He hoped Krebs had kept his nose clean.

Zaragoza made his way up the winding dirt road. He passed only a few homes that were located nearly a half mile apart from one another. It was not unusual for the neighbors to not see one another for six months. Most of the Davis Canyon inhabitants liked their privacy and tended not to mingle. Zaragoza sensed that was why Krebs lived here.

No one would bother him.

He looked up and saw the familiar landmark that let him know he was almost to Krebs's residence. It was the beat-up wooden A-frame house, with its broken windows and menacing exterior, just off the road. It always spooked him, out in the middle of nowhere. He drove around the corner past the A-frame. The grass seemed to grow higher on either side of his Jeep Cherokee. This signaled the end of the road for him. Within fifty yards he saw the mailbox.

He was here.

Zaragoza kept the engine running; however, he depressed the brakes. He took a deep breath, glanced up at his rearview mirror and could not see his eyes behind his dark wraparound sunglasses.

That was just how he wanted it.

Zaragoza took another deep breath and placed his foot on the gas. He entered the long dirt driveway to the right and watched as the trees scraped the sides of his Jeep Cherokee— "Texas pinstripes." The driveway was about fifty feet long and descended past a small pond to the east. Just beyond the pond was a midsize royal blue wooden barn with white trim. It seemed large enough to house a couple of midsize Cadillacs. Zaragoza reached the bottom of the driveway. As he looked to his left, he saw a two-story house. It was the same color as the barn and almost twice as large. Zaragoza shook his head in disbelief as he wondered how a former convict could live on such beautiful property. Then he remembered the nearly inaccessible road and the remoteness of the location.

It made sense.

Zaragoza aimed his Jeep toward the house, when out of nowhere a bulky figure appeared in front of him. The parole officer took a quick breath yet again and realized it was his man—Rex Krebs.

Zaragoza parked his Jeep Cherokee and sat inside. The former convict, dressed in a blue short-sleeved oxford shirt, slowly ambled up alongside the vehicle until he was standing at the window. He seemed to wince in pain. Zaragoza noticed that the stocky Krebs had been limping and wore a weight belt around his ribs.

"What happened to you?" Zaragoza inquired.

Krebs tensed up and stammered, "I, uh, I—I hurt myself on the wood."

"What do you mean by that?"

"Oh, I, uh, fell off the wall into the firewood."

Zaragoza slowly exited his automobile. He watched carefully as Krebs kept reaching for his ribs. He did not believe him. He thought about the newspaper report that stated the intruder into Aundria Crawford's duplex entered through a tiny window. Furthermore, Krebs's injuries were not consistent with someone falling onto a pile of wood. He had no cuts or abrasions on his hands or arms.

"Do you want to come on inside?" Krebs asked his parole officer. It was common for Zaragoza to enter Krebs's residence. He nodded behind his dark sunglasses and followed Krebs inside. Other than the stammering response, Zaragoza believed that Krebs appeared calm and in control. They walked to Krebs's home and entered through the back door.

Zaragoza had no idea what Krebs was really hiding.

"I need to get another urine sample from you Rex."

"Sure. C'mon in."

The two men entered Krebs's barn apartment. Zaragoza gave him a plastic cup. Krebs took care of business and gingerly returned the specimen to his parole officer.

Zaragoza knew he needed to get out of there.

Immediately.

THIRTEEN

David Zaragoza returned to his parole office in downtown San Luis Obispo. Once settled in, he contacted San Luis Obispo Police Department detective Jerome Tushbant. Zaragoza informed the detective about his suspicions concerning Krebs, including his knowledge of Krebs's criminal sexual assault history, the isolation of Krebs's home, and his questionable rib injury. Despite the information provided by Zaragoza, Tushbant did not rush to act on Krebs. Instead, he sent the information to the Department of Justice representatives in town, who came on board only three days earlier. The DOJ representatives handled all seemingly innocuous tips to be sure nothing was overlooked. Since there were more than five hundred tips in just a few days concerning the Aundria Crawford disappearance, there was plenty of information to sift through.

Karren Sandusky headed up the California Department of Justice Sexual Predator Apprehension Team, out of Fresno. She was responsible for these less-than-high-priority tips in the Aundria Crawford case. On Friday, March 19, she received information from Detective Tushbant of Rex Krebs's background and noticed a couple of sexual assaults from 1987. At approximately 1:30 P.M. she decided to give Krebs a call.

It was probably nothing, but what the hell.

Sandusky picked up her phone and dialed Krebs's work number at 84 Lumber.

He did not seem shocked to hear from her. "I'm surprised you guys didn't contact me after that first girl went missing," he stated.

Sandusky and Krebs agreed to meet at his house at 6:30 P.M.

Sandusky hung up the phone and quickly got a hold of Zaragoza. She introduced herself and let him know that a meeting had been set up with Krebs.

Sandusky also contacted Department of Justice special agent Frank Navarro. The two agents drove out to Krebs's residence in the canyon so they could "become familiar with the location."

After checking out the property, Sandusky and Navarro drove back into town to meet David Zaragoza. They arrived at his office at 3:00 P.M., made the round of introductions, and got down to business. Zaragoza had Krebs's file open on his desk and the three officials began to discuss what to do next.

Zaragoza called Parole and Community Service Division (P&CSD) parole agent Victoria Wood and P&CSD administrator Dan Hoy and spoke with them about the need for a search warrant. Sandusky called the DOJ office again for more assistance. Special Agents Vince Jura and Juan Morales helped in the search.

All five personnel headed out to the isolated barn in the woods. On the way out Sandusky contacted Krebs again at 84 Lumber. She wanted to let him know that they were on their way to his property and asked if it was OK for them to begin the search. He asked that they wait until he arrived and that he would let them search then.

Once Krebs showed up, the officers began their search. They took several items from his home, including a pair of black boots, an 84 Lumber wooden box, two metal chains, index cards with lists of women's telephone numbers on them, work-related paperwork, 84 Lumber receipts with female customers' names on them, including their phone numbers and home addresses. They also discovered CO_2 cartridges and BB pellets.

Zaragoza was relieved.

They had found what they needed to bring Krebs into custody for further questioning without violating his basic civil rights. The pellets were a violation of his parole, in that he was not allowed to carry a weapon or simulated weapon of any kind. Zaragoza asked Krebs if he owned a BB gun.

"Yeah." He solemnly nodded.

"Does it look like a revolver or semiautomatic?"

"Yeah."

"Where is it?"

"84 Lumber."

FOURTEEN

The following day, at 6:15 A.M., Zaragoza, Agent Navarro of the DOJ and one of his assistants, plus two San Luis Obispo police officers organized a stakeout across the street from 84 Lumber. Their plan was to wait for Krebs to arrive at work, arrest him, and then locate the BB gun.

Krebs pulled up in his Ford Ranger. He exited his vehicle and entered the store. Less than one minute later, the five officers got out of their cars and entered behind him. Krebs looked up, saw Zaragoza, and nodded toward him.

"Rex, turn around," Zaragoza calmly ordered. Krebs turned his back to the parole officer. Zaragoza slapped a pair of handcuffs on him.

"Where's the BB gun, Rex?"

"It's under the cash register," he stated, and nodded in the correct direction.

Zaragoza reached under the register and found the BB gun. It looked exactly like a semiautomatic pistol.

"Rex, you are under arrest for violation of your parole requirements. Specifically, possession of a firearm or simulated firearm."

Zaragoza glared at the forlorn convict to see if he had any expression.

All he saw were Rex Krebs's tears.

Zaragoza, Sandusky, and Navarro returned to Krebs's residence at 3:00 P.M. to conduct a more thorough search. While at the barn Zaragoza received a phone call from San Luis

Obispo police detective Sue Murphy, who had been at Aundria Crawford's residence the day of her abduction. Detective Murphy clued Zaragoza in to what was missing from Aundria's apartment. He mentioned several items such as CDs by George Strait and Korn, videotapes, and something unique to the missing college student: an eight ball key chain.

Detective Murphy, along with Officers Janice Mangan and Mark Brady, showed up at Krebs's home to assist in the search. The six authorities began to comb over the house in a methodical fashion. They secured numerous and varied items from the house, such as feathers in a plastic kitchen garbage bag, used duct tape rolls from Krebs's upstairs master bedroom, and two topographical maps of Davis Canyon in his bedroom closet. They found an oversize belt buckle in the top drawer of Krebs's filing cabinet, along with several crudely drawn sketches and patterns of belt buckles. Zaragoza noticed a recurring theme on the drawings and the belt buckle itself—a strange figure-eight symbol. More like the number eight if it was lying down on its side.

The infinity symbol.

The officers systematically made notes of their discoveries and continued to search. They found an audiotape labeled as "House Meeting 4-21-98," more 84 Lumber receipts with customer information on them, and a Canon camera, located on top of Krebs's refrigerator. They also found a cream-colored Victoria's Secret negligee, size 5/Small.

Special Agent Navarro made the most startling discovery of all. As he canvassed Krebs's house, he abruptly stopped in the front living room. He scanned the room slowly, not quite sure what he was looking for. He noticed mainly innocuous items such as a television, a beaten-down couch, and some nondescript étagères.

Navarro was about to exit the living room when something caught his eye. It was an old hand-carved wooden box located on top of one of Krebs's bookshelves. He walked over to the shelf and grabbed the 6" x 4" x 2" box. He turned it over in his hands and looked at both the top and bottom of it. He then placed it on the coffee table in the living room and unhooked the metal locking clasp. At first it looked like a random collection of miscellaneous items: two matchbooks from Outlaws, "A Grubbin' and Guzzlin' Establishment"; a Superstar 84 star-shaped pin; yellow glass icicles; an orange Sebadoh guitar pick.

One item, however, stood out. A small black plastic eight ball key chain holder. There was no ring attached to it that would hold keys, but it was definitely part of a key chain. He quickly closed the box and held on to it tightly.

Navarro informed Zaragoza and Sandusky of his discovery. The agents decided it was time to pack up. They marked the remaining items and gathered their findings for the day. The investigation into Rex Krebs was only now ready to begin.

On Sunday, March 21, 1999, Detective Jerome Tushbant summoned investigator Larry Hobson to the San Luis Obispo Police Department. Detective Tushbant wanted Hobson to interview Krebs to learn if he knew anything about the disappearance of Aundria Crawford.

Hobson picked Krebs up from the county jail and transferred him back over to the police department. When they arrived, Hobson led Krebs into the employee break room.

Krebs waived his constitutional rights and agreed to speak with Detective Hobson.

Hobson asked Krebs where he was on the evening of March 11, 1999. The calm Krebs stated that he was nowhere near Branch Street. He told Hobson that he was out buying flowers for his girlfriend, Roslynn Moore, and purchasing groceries.

Suddenly Krebs looked up at Hobson and began to tell him a new version of the events from that night. He remembered that he *had* been in the neighborhood, on Aundria Crawford's street even. He claimed that he had visited a friend on Branch Street, two blocks south of Aundria's residence. Krebs added that he frequented nearby Manuel's Liquor Store. He also stated that he occasionally ducked into the Gaslight Lounge, located on Broad Street at the corner of Branch Street, two blocks north of Aundria's duplex.

FIFTEEN

April 22, 1999
Davis Canyon Road, Davis Canyon, California
2:00 P.M.

For over one month the residents of San Luis Obispo were unaware that Rex Krebs was in jail. Most of the people were under the impression that the Aundria Crawford case was moving at a glacierlike pace, just like the Kristin Smart and Rachel Newhouse cases. Soon after Aundria's disappearance gun sales surged, enrollment in self-defense courses increased, and people began to walk down the quiet streets in pairs and in groups, instead of by themselves. The fear had been ratcheted up several notches in San Luis Obispo.

On this day their fears would subside—but the horrors were only beginning to unfold.

The residents of Davis Canyon and See Canyon had no idea what was going on in their secluded neck of the world. Police had scoured the area the previous two days looking for something. The neighbors had no idea what they were trying to find. Several police vehicles were ushered in and out of rugged Davis Canyon Road. One Davis Canyon resident noticed a 35' x 8' sheriff's emergency response vehicle. Police officers had to trim trees that hung across the road so the truck could pass through. A coroner's vehicle also entered this beautiful, remote section of California's Central Coast.

Muriel Wright owned her own two-story house that sat on

property she shared with her adult daughter, Debbie, at the end of Davis Canyon Road. She also owned the barn apartment behind the house. She rented it out to a quiet fellow by the name of Rex Krebs. They lived on approximately 240 acres of wooded, secluded property. The neighbors had no idea why the police were heading back to her property.

Davis Canyon resident Ed Diable spotted a police car driving down the dirt road from the direction of Wright's properties. Diable glanced into the squad car driven by Detective Larry Hobson. As difficult as it was, Diable was able to catch a glimpse of a man in the backseat. He spotted a pensive face and a bushy mustache. As he glanced up to the top of the man's head, he saw the shaved dome. There was only one person with that distinctive look who lived back in this area—Rex Krebs. Diable wondered what in the heck was going on.

He would find out soon enough.

The day before, April 21, 1999, Detective Larry Hobson had taken Rex Krebs for a ride. When the two men returned to the jail, Hobson asked Krebs if he could see him tomorrow. Krebs nonchalantly replied, "Maybe. I'll deal with it tomorrow."

On April 22, 1999, Hobson returned as promised. Soon thereafter, he and Krebs were back in his police car, this time heading for Krebs's home in Davis Canyon. On the way out to the remote location, Hobson contacted fellow investigator Bill Hanley, who drove, and Officers Keith Storton and Russ Griffith, who followed in their marked San Luis Obispo Police Department vehicle, with a camcorder.

Krebs first directed Hobson to the A-frame, which was located just under a mile-and-a-half from the See Canyon Road turnoff onto Davis Canyon Road. The A-frame, on the left side of the road, was marked by a tiny mailbox with the name WRIGHT on a wooden post. The abandoned home had a natural brown wood siding that appeared slightly weathered. The walls were a fleshy tan color. Not an A-frame house in the true sense of the word, it had more of a front facade in the shape of the letter *A*. There were, however, several broken windows on the old building—a favorite for vandals severely off the beaten path. Overgrown eucalyptus trees hid the house. At night it resembled a house ripped out of the pages of a Brothers Grimm fairy tale.

Hansel and Gretel would not stop by here for a visit.

All five men piled out of their vehicles. Krebs, in his convict-issue bright orange jumpsuit, pointed up the hillside for Hobson, who scaled up the slope. Krebs pointed at a pile, nodded his head, and looked down at his feet.

SIXTEEN

April 23, 1999
Davis Canyon Road, Davis Canyon, California
8:30 A.M.

The following morning, Agent David Kice of the FBI walked to the location where Rex Krebs pointed to as the location of Rachel Newhouse's body. It was easy to spot, thanks to the yellow crime scene tape. The burial site was located almost thirty feet high on top of a grassy hill about sixty feet from Davis Canyon Road. Agent Kice was the team leader for the body recovery. Twenty men from the San Luis Obispo Police Department, the coroner's office, and the district attorney's office supported Agent Kice.

Two of Agent Kice's support team took over the digging chores. They began to dig with a deliberate, careful pace so as not to destroy any possible evidence. After several minutes one of the men hit something that made him pause. As he inspected the dirt, he noticed a mesh wire that covered a black plastic garbage bag. He began to scrape the dirt off the area and soon revealed a much larger area of the garbage bag. He knelt down to touch the bag and recoiled. He felt human flesh.

It was Rachel Newhouse's decomposed body.

She had been missing for more than five months. Her body, caked in damp dirt, contorted at an unnatural angle. According to Agent Kice, her legs were near her torso and her feet were located right next to her head. Her feet had decomposed; however, they could make out her toenails. The men gently used paintbrushes to remove the dirt. It fell from her body rather easily.

The only thing about Rachel Newhouse that was recognizable was a silver bracelet still wrapped around her left wrist with her name etched on a small plaque.

It still shone brightly.

The exhumation of Rachel Newhouse lasted until 3:00 P.M. After that work was completed, the men turned their attention up the road. They walked down the driveway that David Zaragoza had nervously entered one month earlier. The support crew went around to the back of the house. They saw the yellow tape just twenty feet from Rex Krebs's bedroom window. There they would find the body of Aundria Crawford.

The men walked up to the garbage pile enclosed within the crime scene tape. One of the men brushed away a plastic GNC bag, a crushed aluminum Pepsi can, and a black frying pan. He then grabbed his shovel and began to penetrate the solid earth beneath his feet. He dug for several minutes when he spotted what remained of Aundria Crawford.

Aundria had been missing for more than one month. Though not as decomposed as Rachel Newhouse's body, Aundria's death scene was just as horrifying a discovery.

Special Agent Kice described Aundria as being in a "fetal position on her back, with her knees drawn up to her chest and her arms underneath her back." He noticed that Aundria was wearing some type of dark-colored knit fabric. He also noticed some type of fabric on her head. There were also what appeared to be plastic flex ties, or "flex cuffs," on her arms and legs.

Rachel Newhouse and Aundria Crawford had led lives of beauty, hope, and trust. They sought to better themselves in one of the most gorgeous locations in the entire United States. They had dreams and wishes they were on the verge of fulfilling. Instead, they ended up in shallow graves beneath piles of trash on one man's property.

Rex Krebs. A paroled sex offender.

Krebs's neighbors still had no idea what was going on. When the news spread, and it spread like a Southern California wildfire around town, they were predictably shocked. They had no idea Krebs just got out of Soledad State Prison after serving ten years of a twenty-year sentence. He had been sentenced in 1987 for sexual assault of a twenty-one-year-old woman in Oceano and attempted sexual assault of a thirty-one-year-old woman in Arroyo Grande, both towns just south of San Luis Obispo and part of San Luis Obispo County.

The California Board of Prison Terms had paroled Rex Krebs in September 1997. The board, made up of several appointees from the then-governor Pete Wilson (Republican), cited his strong work ethic and good behavior while in prison.

Upon his release, Krebs moved to the town of Atascadero on Bajada Street. Krebs's stay in the small northwestern suburb of San Luis Obispo County was short-lived. One neighbor who was not impressed with the city's newest addition was Diane Morgan. She lived next door to the woman who rented a room to the ex-convict. She did not feel comfortable in his presence.

"He was really creepy," Morgan recalled. "You could tell he just got out of prison. All buffed up, all tattooed. He would drive by and just stare us down."

Instead of just feeling uncomfortable, however, Morgan decided to do something about it. She decided to pay a visit to the San Luis Obispo County Sheriff's Office. Once there, she asked the officer at the front desk if she could look at the Megan's Law list on CD-ROM.

Megan's Law was a bill signed on May 8, 1996, by then-President Bill Clinton. "Megan" refers to Megan Kanka, a seven-year-old New Jersey rape and murder victim. Her killer, two-time convicted child molester Jesse Timmendequas, lived across the street from the Kankas. Megan's parents had no idea they lived so close to a paroled sex offender. At the time police departments could not disclose such information.

Megan's Law would change that policy.

The state of California adopted its own version of Megan's Law on September 25, 1996.

Diane Morgan used the Megan's Law CD-ROM to look up Rex Krebs. She discovered that he was a recent parolee who had spent time in prison for sexual assault with a knife.

"After we found out, whenever I saw him driving down the street, it was sickening," Morgan's friend Shelly Dye remembered with disgust. The two women, however, were not satisfied simply to know that a sexual predator was in their midst. They decided to do something about it. The women organized a campaign to get rid of their new, unsavory neighbor. Morgan wrote an anonymous letter, made numerous copies, and secretly placed them in all of their neighbors' mailboxes. The letter informed the citizens of Atascadero of their newest neighbor and the horrible crimes that he had committed.

Morgan went a step further and wrote a note just for Krebs. She let him know that she was on to him: "We know who you are. We know what you did. The whole neighborhood is watching you." She relentlessly hounded the sheriff's department.

"We kept asking them, 'What can we do to get him out of this neighborhood?' "

Despite their honest feelings about sex offenders in their county, the sheriff's department informed Morgan that paroled rapists have rights too.

By July 1998 the pressure from Morgan and Dye worked. Sue Peterson, Morgan's next-door neighbor and Krebs's landlord, contacted Debra Austin, Krebs's parole officer, who, in turn, suggested to Krebs that he pack up his bags and head elsewhere.

"Old Rex the Rapist," as he had become known in Atascadero, did just that. He decided to relocate.

Larry Wright, Rex's coworker, informed him that his

mother had an attached barn apartment for rent, deep in the Davis Canyon area, less than five miles from Avila Beach. He met with Muriel Wright and told her about his past criminal history. He also informed her that he had been framed. Wright felt sorry for Krebs and agreed to rent out the barn apartment, which was located right next to her house. She failed to mention to her neighbors that her new tenant had just been released from prison.

Nine months later, everyone knew.

On Saturday, April 24, 1999, *Fresno Bee* crime beat reporter Michael Krikorian drove more than 135 miles to the San Luis Obispo County Jail. He was determined to get more information from the suspected murderer Krebs. He had a story ready to go that he believed would get him access to Krebs. Krikorian had spoken with Krebs's mother, Connie Ridley. His plan was to let the guards know that he had a message from Ridley that she needed desperately to pass on to her son. Krikorian showed up at 7:30 A.M. for his 8:00 A.M. visit and signed in at the front desk. As he put his pen to the sign-up sheet, he noticed the name Roslynn Moore. She too signed up that same day to visit Krebs. He took a seat and waited patiently. He sat next to a thin, fair-skinned African American woman. He correctly assumed it was Roslynn. He later wrote in his article about meeting Krebs's girlfriend:

A young woman also had signed up to see him. While we waited for the 8 a.m. visit, we struck up a conversation. She said she was a friend of Krebs and was coming to say goodbye to him.

"I have some things I want to tell him," she said. "But I really don't know what I'm going to say.

"Yeah, Rex was a friend of mine. But I had no idea at all. I didn't know that Rex."

The woman was about 5-foot-3 and 110 pounds. Her black glasses, covering big brown eyes, rested halfway down her small nose. She was casually but stylishly

*dressed in baggy white linen pants and a snazzy wind-
breaker. She was of Caucasian and African-American
ancestry. Her black, curly hair bounced on her shoulders in the wild morning wind.*

*After we had chatted for a few minutes, I told her
why I was there to see Krebs. Then I noticed her stomach. She appeared to be pregnant. It hit me.*

*"Is your name Rosalind (sic)?" She brought up her
left shoulder as her head bent down to meet it. Her lips,
pressed together, formed a quick smile, then a frown, as
she nodded.*

"Yes."

*She looked sad, alone and scared. She had been
avoiding the media.*

*I put my hand on her shoulder and she collapsed into
my arms. She cried for more than a minute.*

*"I don't know what I'm going to do," Rosalind (sic)
said. "I can't believe this. I was at that house a lot.
Those girls. Oh, those poor girls. I'm going to go back
home with my mom. I have to get out of here."*

*After her 15-minute visit with Krebs, she came back
to the parking lot. "His eyes are dead," she said. "He
fooled a lot of people."*

It was Krikorian's turn to look into those eyes.

The reporter made his way into the tiny holding cell. Krebs
held court behind a glass partition, a telephone in hand.
Krikorian took his seat and Krebs nodded toward the telephone. Krikorian picked his up and got straight to the point.

"Do you have anything to say to the families of the girls
you killed?"

"God. Oh God, sorry," he replied in a raspy voice.

Krikorian realized that Roslynn was right: Krebs's eyes
looked dead.

"Are you worried about the death penalty, Rex?"

"I hope they give it to me."

Krikorian wrote that Krebs expressed more sympathy for the families and seemed disgusted with his actions.

"Two girls are dead," Krebs solemnly stated as he stared at the desk. He then lifted his head and, with his soulless eyes, looked directly at the reporter.

"If I'm not a monster, then what am I?"

PART IV

REX, OR CREATION OF A MONSTER?

SEVENTEEN

Rex Allan Krebs came into the world on a cold, blustery day of January 28, 1966. He was born in Sandpoint, Idaho, in the northern panhandle, approximately five hundred miles north of Boise, Idaho, and less than twenty miles south of the American-Canadian border. His father, twenty-year-old Allan Krebs, and his mother, nineteen-year-old Connie Krebs, had only recently married due to Connie's pregnancy. It was the first marriage and child for Allan. It was the second of each for Connie. Her first child, Lecia, was born three years earlier when Connie was sixteen.

At the time, Sandpoint, Idaho, was a tiny rural town with less than three thousand people. Shadowed by the 6,400-feet-high Schweitzer Mountain, known for its excellent snow skiing, the town was primarily a farming community. Most Sandpoint residents lived on large farms spread out across vast distances from one another.

Allan grew up on a farm on the outskirts of Sandpoint. Connie had grown up in town. Allan met Connie at Sandpoint High School.

Connie, who struggled as a parent, would often nip at the bottle. Connie seemed to struggle quite often. On January 31, 1963, at the age of sixteen, she gave birth to Lecia. The father was not Allan Krebs. By 1965, however, Connie ran into Allan again and the two began to date. Soon thereafter, Connie got pregnant for the second time. Allan decided to make her an "honest woman," so they got married in Sandpoint on

June 22, 1965. After Rex was born, Allan, Connie, Lecia, and the newest addition moved in with Connie's mother, Arleta Howell, on Walnut Street.

The Krebs family lived here for a short period before they moved in with Allan's mother, Florence Krebs. The family then moved to Allan's father Alfred Krebs's farm on Colburn Culver Road, located fifteen miles north of Sandpoint. Alfred Krebs, "Grandpa," was a quiet man, with a quick temper, who worked hard on his dairy farm.

Allan Krebs got a job with the Burlington Northern Railroad company. While Rex was still an infant, Allan uprooted the family and relocated to Lester, Washington, into a house built by the railroad company. Not the largest man, Allan held his own. He was able to do heavy lifting and always managed to stay in top physical shape. Allan would usually wind down from a hard day on the job with a bottle of liquor.

Preferably vodka.

According to Lecia, the Krebs family lived at four or five different locations during the first five years of Rex's life. The uprooting of the family was always a result of Allan's sporadic success with employment. He was not one to remain gainfully employed. Allan worked numerous jobs from the railroad to farming in such different locales as Spokane, Washington, and Thompson Falls and Plains, Montana. Despite initial feelings of prosperity whenever a new job appeared on the horizon, the result was the same: Allan would somehow find a way to screw things up. As a result the unstable Krebs clan always seemed to be packing up their belongings and hitting the road for the latest pipe dream.

After another firing the Krebs family returned to Sandpoint. They moved back in to Alfred Krebs's farm and helped Grandpa Krebs with the dairy.

The uncertainty of Allan's work situation was a major source of frustration and anxiety for Connie. Having nowhere else to turn, she directed her anger toward her husband. Their tongue-lashings often took place in the bedroom, behind thin doors through which the children could hear. Their heated discussions usually centered on her disappointment in her husband and his failure to provide properly for her and the children. Her screams usually resulted from the punches he threw in her face when he could not stand the attacks.

Lecia Dotson recalled several instances when Allan Krebs brutally assaulted Connie Krebs. She remembered "when she'd come out from their bedroom, she'd have a huge black eye or her face would be swollen or her arm would be black and blue from him grabbing her and throwing her around."

Lecia remembered how she and Rex responded to the unrest in their home. "We were usually frightened. We spent a lot of time together, you know, trying to avoid it."

It was impossible, however, to avoid.

Arleta Howell, Rex's grandmother and Connie's mother, recalled a horrifying incident outside her home after Connie and she had returned from the grocery store. Allan wanted them home by 4:00 P.M. They were thirty minutes late. As the women pulled up into the driveway, Allan blasted outside to confront them.

"He came around the car and opened the door," Howell remembered clearly. "He jerked Rex out of my arms and Rex screamed, like any baby would scream. I told him, 'You're hurting the baby!' And he said, 'Who cares?'"

Howell was ready to get out of the oncoming bad situation, but she realized it would be better to stay, just in case something might happen to her daughter and grandson. She saw her daughter and son-in-law walk toward the house on either side of the car. Allan was holding Rex in his arms. Suddenly, without warning, Allan yelled out to Connie, "Catch him," and he threw Rex over the top of the car. "Luckily, she caught him," Howell recalled.

After the baby-tossing incident, Arleta Howell became truly worried. "From then on, I was really scared for Rex and Connie both, and Lecia also, because you never really knew what he was going to do."

Especially as more children were born. Two more sisters, Tracy and Marcia, cluttered up the tiny Krebs household and made life even more difficult for Allan Krebs. Tracy, a healthy girl, was born in January 1970. Sister Marcia was born the following year in January, but to add to the difficulties in the Krebs household, Marcia developed a nasty fever when she was less than one year old. The family doctor initially diagnosed the problem as an ear infection; however, it was much worse. The undetected fever lasted for several days and caused permanent brain damage to the youngest Krebs sibling. To this day she has the mental capability of a thirteen-year-old.

As the frustrations mounted in the Krebs household, so did the violence. In April 1970 tragedy struck hard. Allan's sister was murdered in Spokane, Washington. The thirty-year-old woman had been shot in the head and her body stuffed in the trunk of a car.

Allan's brother, Art Krebs, believed the homicide was the beginning of the long, downward spiral for his brother and family. "It seems like ever since my sister got murdered, our family was cursed. It was like that was the beginning of the family plague."

After his sister's murder Allan became worse. He continued to drink heavily and he continued to beat his wife.

"Allan was very good with his hands—very good," Connie recalled.

Connie spoke of how Allan used to beat her. His favorite method of control was to slug her. He would punch her while the kids were in their rooms. They did not see the violence at first, but they always heard it. Allan also used to kick Connie.

"If you were lucky, he wouldn't kick you with his boots. I pray to God they didn't see that. I'm sure that they heard it."

One time Allan had beaten Connie up so bad that she moved all of the kids into the house across the street from her mother on Walnut Street. One night Allan decided to pay his family a visit. Connie and Marcia stayed in one room. Rex,

Lecia, and Tracy all had their own rooms. Allan angrily walked over to the house, stormed up the sidewalk, and banged on the front door. Connie, with Tracy in tow, went to the front door. She knew that it was her husband and that he was furious. According to Lecia, her mother asked Allan to leave and he refused. He somehow made his way inside and began to attack Connie. He tossed Tracy aside, grabbed Connie by the wrist, and dragged her into the bedroom. Repeatedly he pummeled the defenseless woman in the face with his fists. When she was as limp as a rag doll, he raped her. Lecia heard everything. So did Rex.

Lecia also recalled another instance when Allan caused a big scene that escalated into violence. While separated from her husband, Connie became smitten with a coworker, a young man by the name of Bob Jackson. Connie thought Bob was a strikingly handsome, sweet, fun guy.

Soon the two became a couple.

One afternoon Bob and Connie went to the Laundromat in Sandpoint to wash several loads of dirty clothes. All of the kids were there. The noneventful day would suddenly change with the appearance of Allan Krebs. The father, furious when he saw Connie with another man, decided to take it out on Bob Jackson. The angry Krebs pummeled the living tar out of the scrawny Jackson in front of the kids and the customers in the Laundromat.

Neither Connie nor Bob Jackson filed charges against Allan. "You did not mess with Allan," she explained. "You just didn't. You stayed as far away from him and gave him as little stuff as possible so he would not come after you. It just wasn't done."

Connie had enough of Allan's abusive behavior. She filed for divorce in fall 1971, was granted custody of the children, and attempted to make a life for herself and her kids with Bob Jackson. The new clan lived across the street from her mother's home.

Allan Krebs, however, was not out of her life just yet.

On the night of February 23, 1972, Allan showed up at Connie's house in a rage. He was furious because their divorce had come through earlier that day. Allan came up to the front door and knocked. Connie answered it and let her ex-husband in. She told him that Rex and Lecia were upstairs in their bedrooms, Marcia was asleep downstairs, and Tracy was sleeping in a crib in her room.

Allan made sure to visit each room and spend time with each of the kids. He then went into Connie's room and asked to borrow her Polaroid camera. He wanted to take some pictures of his children, he explained. Connie shrugged her shoulders at the suggestion and turned to reach for the camera, which was located above her daughter's crib. Allan quietly sidled up behind his wife, grabbed her shoulders, and effortlessly tossed the woman onto the bed. He punched her repeatedly in the stomach; he assumed she was pregnant again.

Then he began to choke her.

Luckily for Connie, her brother Roy "Gene" Howell and some of his friends saw what was going on. Gene recalled the scene of his sister lying underneath Allan Krebs. "Both eyes were blackened when we got there. I walked in on them and he was on top of her in the bedroom and I asked him what he thought he was doing." Gene stated that Allan got "very nervous" and then Gene's friends called for help. The Sandpoint police arrived and put an end to the abuse. Connie filed a report with the officers, but despite being bloody and bruised, she did not file charges against her former husband.

She had other plans.

Less than a week later, Connie, along with all four children and Bob Jackson, packed her car with the barest of necessities and slithered away into the cold Idaho night, away from her torturer. They were on their way to Nevada. They escaped the clutches of a demented alcoholic under the darkness of night.

Or so she thought.

EIGHTEEN

Connie Krebs, now Howell, and Bob Jackson ended up almost nine hundred miles away from Sandpoint in Carson City, the capital city of Nevada. Connie hoped it would be the beginning of a better life for her and the children. A life free of verbal and physical abuse. One where her children could thrive and become wonderful people.

Connie believed that Bob Jackson was the man who could provide her such a life.

The dream was short-lived.

Bob Jackson turned out to be as bad a nightmare as Allan Krebs had been.

Just as they had for the first five years of Rex's life, Connie and the kids frequently moved around. When they first arrived in Nevada, they stayed with a friend of Jackson's for about a week. Jackson then got a job in construction and they packed up and moved to the small town of Gardnerville. The newly formed family moved into a tiny one-room apartment above the Ritchford Bar and Motel, a popular pool hall and tavern. Bob Jackson, Connie Howell, and four frightened children were living together in one cramped room, with three double beds, directly above the bar and pool hall. Connie and Bob made several trips down to the tavern. They did not go downstairs to play pool, however. They became frequent patrons at the well-worn bar, where they imbibed whenever they could. They usually dragged the kids down into the bar while they drank their problems away. Connie and Bob became such regulars in the ratty, run-down bar that they became friends with the owners. The kids became favorites of the other regulars who frequented the establishment.

Thanks to their friendship with the Ritchford Bar's owners, Connie and Bob were able to move their family out of the tiny one-room quarters above the bar and into a larger space. A cabin opened up behind the bar and the owners gave Bob first dibs on it. The cabin had all of two bedrooms. Apparently, there was not much entertainment available in the area for kids. According to Lecia, she and Rex used to play in the irrigation ditch located behind the cabin.

Bob began to prosper at his job and was able to upgrade his adopted family's standard of living. They moved away from the cabin and into a four-plex apartment. They moved into an upstairs apartment on the upper left-hand side. Things seemed to be looking up, for they lived there for almost one full year. Quite a long time for this family.

Alas, the fun ended as another move was on the horizon. Bob and Connie took off yet again, this time to the Ranchos area in Gardnerville, where they actually bought a house.

Lecia described what it was like moving from house to house all the time and how it made her life difficult. "I always needed to know where we lived at directly so that if Mom or Bob were too drunk to get home," she recalled, "I could always make sure that I got my brothers and sisters home." Lecia did not know the addresses of her various homes, but she knew how to get home if it was ever necessary. Usually on foot, sometimes by car—with her driving.

The relationship between Connie Howell and Bob Jackson actually started on a positive note. Connie was grateful that Bob had helped her escape the clutches of Allan Krebs. Bob, however, seemed to travel the same path as Allan with his inability to remain gainfully employed. To make matters worse, he liked to imbibe the old booze. What compounded the situation was that Connie was also prone to join her new mate in drowning her sorrows. In fact, she often encouraged Bob to get drunk with her. The decreased inhibition brought on by the alcohol consumption led to arguments between the couple. Just like with Allan Krebs, Bob Jackson's work frustrations began to pile up, so did the abusive behavior.

Lecia recalled that Bob, just like Allan, used to smack Connie around. "He would hit on her," she continued, "throw her down, sit on her, just general abuse."

Similar to the Krebs household, the abuse of Connie often took place within earshot of her children, including Rex. "Most of the time I would make sure that Rex and my little sisters were with me," Lecia recounted. "We'd go in my bedroom or something and just close the door and pray that we would be safe and that he wouldn't hurt Mom."

Eventually Bob Jackson's cruelty went from Connie to her children. It started with the verbal abuse of Rex. Apparently, Jackson felt that Rex resembled Allan Krebs a little too much for his comfort, so he decided to take it out on the five-year-old boy. According to Lecia, Jackson was always picking on her little brother. He also enjoyed calling Rex "the little bastard" to his face.

Eventually the abuse of the children escalated from verbal to physical.

Jackson had taken over the disciplinarian chores in the household whenever the kids screwed up. If they so much as looked sideways at him, Bob would put them over his knee and spank their bottoms. Lecia recalled, "It didn't matter what you did, you got a spanking for it." Lecia also spoke of Bob Jackson's controlling ways when she stated, "He was generally abusive. He didn't usually hit me or anything, but I got grounded a lot. He was a real controlling person."

Bob Jackson seemingly began to lose control after Connie had a car wreck. She ended up in the hospital for six weeks. While she was bedridden, Jackson would visit her at the hospital during the day. He would spend his nights somewhere else altogether. Lecia claimed Jackson began to make late-night visits into her bedroom and they were not to console her during her mother's absence.

"He did sexually molest me. And he was just a real control freak," Lecia frightfully recalled. "I remember the first time he came into my room. I don't want to remember it." According to Lecia, Jackson's visits to her bedroom continued long after Connie returned home. She does not remember for exactly how long. She was only nine years old at the time.

Connie's accident became a financial burden for the family. They had to give up the Ranchos area home and move back into town into another small apartment. Once again Bob's frustration rose as he began to feel worthless. As was his pattern, Bob took out his frustrations on the children. He seemed to have a special place on his knee warmed up just for Rex.

Rex had a penchant for defecating in his underpants. Instead of cleaning the boy's bottom and potty training him, Jackson would take the boy across his knee and swat him repeatedly. As he punished the boy, he yelled at him and called him worthless.

Bob Jackson's corporeal punishment escalated. One time Rex soiled his underwear and Bob had decided enough was enough. Instead of spanking Rex, he was ready to teach the boy a serious lesson. He forced Rex to wear the dirty underwear on his head for one hour. He then forced Rex to sit on Marcia and Tracy's potty-training toilet. The experience, to say the least, was humiliating.

It only got worse.

Another time Rex dirtied his underwear. Bob Jackson, believing that Rex had done it on purpose, grabbed one of the toddler girl's cloth diapers and pinned it on Rex. He then forced the little boy to go to school wearing the symbol of infancy. Rex was again humiliated.

Two years later, things had not changed much. Bob still worked for the construction company and Connie ran a daycare center out of their tiny apartment. Another thing that remained the same was that Connie and Bob continued to get drunk. It became an even greater problem for the kids as their parents' alcoholic binges became part of their daily routine.

Jackson and his buddies from the construction crew would usually have several beers after a hard day on the job. Connie, who was in charge of baby-sitting several children, was at least conscientious enough not to drink until all of the children had gone for the day. As soon as the parents picked up the last child, she would crack open a bottle. By the time Bob Jackson returned home, the couple was already soaring and neither was ready to return back to earth. To keep the buzz going, Bob and Connie would pack the kids into their car and spend the rest of the evening at the local bar getting hammered. Sometimes they brought the children into the bars and casinos, such as Sharkey's Club in Minden or the Pony Express Bar. Eventually a manager would come and tell them they had to take the kids outside because they had been there for such a long period of time. Most times, however, children could not come inside. Rex and his three sisters sat outside, in the dark, until their mom and stepfather stumbled out early the next morning.

Lecia testified that it was a form of prison: "We weren't allowed to get out of the car if you had to go to the bathroom or anything like that. You weren't allowed any toys with you." Apparently, the wardens were not too keen on checking up on the prisoners either. "They would come out and check on us every so often, but usually not that regularly. So sometimes they'd bring out snacks for us."

At the time these events occurred Lecia was ten, Rex was seven, Marcia was three, and Tracy was two. Lecia was responsible for her three younger siblings while Connie and Bob would party it up inside the bars. Sometimes this responsibility entailed illegal activity on her part. If Bob and Connie were too intoxicated to drive, Lecia was determined to get everyone home alive. The precocious preteen received an early crash course in driving. Luckily, she did not actually crash on any of her ten-to-fifteen-mile sojourns behind the wheel.

More glycerin was mixed into the explosive environment when Connie and Bob started to take foster children into the household—as if four kids and six mouths to feed were not enough. Interestingly, all of the foster children were girls. Lecia does not recall if Bob Jackson ever molested any of the foster children or, for that matter, her own sisters.

"I always figured if he was bothering me, he was leaving them alone."

She did recall, however, that Bob, like Allan, would not allow the children or Connie to interact with other people while they lived under their numerous roofs. They were not allowed to have friends over.

They did receive a visit one evening from a police officer. Lecia believed that one of the neighbors called the cops to inform them of the abuse and neglect going on. When the officer arrived, Connie and Bob were gone. Lecia answered the door.

"He wanted us to go with him and I knew they were just going to take us away. And there was no way I was going to do that." Lecia feared the authorities would separate her from her brother and sisters.

"I still don't know why he didn't take them. I just pleaded with him not to. I don't know why he didn't, but he didn't."

In addition, no relatives or neighbors would stop by and visit. Rex, Lecia, and the other girls were on their own. One relative, however, did make a surprise visit.

Allan Krebs showed up in Nevada.

NINETEEN

Connie purposefully avoided her former husband for four years. She never informed him where they relocated. She felt safer knowing that he had no idea where she and the children lived.

One afternoon Rex and Lecia took a walk down to the convenience store two blocks from their residence. They bought some items, then headed back home. As was usual, Rex walked faster, while Lecia absentmindedly sauntered behind. She was startled when a dirty car pulled up alongside Rex. Instead of ignoring the driver and walking on, Rex stopped and began to chat with the man who rolled down the driver-side window. Lecia began to reprimand her brother. She and Rex were taught not to speak to strangers.

She was mortified when the car door opened and Rex jumped inside. The car took off.

Lecia, frightened as she had never been frightened before, ran home. She darted upstairs and found her mother. She frantically told Connie that somebody had kidnapped Rex. Connie shot out of bed, got dressed, and was about to run outside to find her only son, when a noise stopped her in her tracks. It came from the apartment parking lot. She pulled back the thin curtain and saw the same dirty car.

Suddenly a muscular man sauntered out of the car and headed toward the apartment staircase. Lecia watched the expression on her mother's face as it became ashen.

"I can remember the look on her face," Lecia recounted, "just mortified that he'd found us."

It was Allan Krebs. Rex followed his father up the staircase and opened the door.

Connie, frightened by the appearance of her former husband, called Bob Jackson at work. She told him to hurry home and help out. Meanwhile, Allan left the house to go pick up some dinner. Bob arrived and prepared to defend his wife.

He loaded up his rifle with ammunition.

Allan showed up and entered through the front door. He walked over to the couch and made himself comfortable. As he began to eat, Bob greeted him with the barrel end of his rifle.

Bob Jackson did not say anything. He simply held the gun directly at Allan Krebs's face.

Allan instinctively raised his bulky arms slightly above his head. He was in full protective mode. He quietly and calmly pleaded with Bob that there was no need to point the gun at him. He could sense that Bob was the more nervous of the two men. Allan did not make any sudden moves toward his ex-wife's new husband.

Instead, he moved closer to Rex.

Somehow Allan distracted Bob, who turned his head away. Allan stealthily grabbed Rex and pulled him in front of his body. He was using his own son as a shield. Rex began to cry—he was actually wailing in fear. He began to scream out at his father, "What are you doing, Dad?"

But Bob Jackson did not put the rifle down.

Finally Allan let Rex go. He grinned as he left the house.

TWENTY

Allan Roger Krebs was a New Year's Day baby. He was born on January 1, 1946, in the tiny town of Logan, Utah, near the northeastern portion of the state. He was the youngest of eight children born to Alfred and Florence Krebs. The Krebs family moved 666 miles northwest to Sandpoint, Idaho, in 1956, when Allan was ten. Alfred Krebs bought land on Colburn Culver Road and set up shop for a dairy farm. His father was a hard worker who often held down two jobs at a time to support the large family. He also worked in a nearby sawmill and for the railroad company.

Both Allan Krebs and his sister spoke highly of their early family life. Allan believed everyone in his family was close to one another. Katherine described their relationships as "pretty darned good."

Allan attended Sandpoint High School, where his favorite subjects were girls and playing hooky. He met Connie Howell at school and became infatuated with her. He was disappointed when Connie gave birth to Lecia in 1963 and married the father.

Connie's first marriage lasted only three months. Soon she was on the lookout for someone to take care of her and Lecia.

Her savior was Allan Roger Krebs—or so she thought.

In 1965 Allan impregnated her with Rex. Confused as to what to do next, he asked for her hand in marriage. Better yet, he did not want his first child to be born out of wedlock. The couple tied the knot on June 22, 1965, in Sandpoint. They moved into his mother-in-law's home in town. Rex was born just over seven months later.

Allan Krebs was not the brightest bulb in the batch. He was, however, a strong man who was good with his hands and capable of lifting heavy objects. These traits suited him well for a job on the railroad, just as his father had done on the side. From 1966 to 1969 he bounced back between Sandpoint and St. Paul, Minnesota, where he worked for the Northern Pacific Railroad.

After Connie, Bob Jackson, and the kids left, Allan withdrew inside himself even further. His sister Katherine felt sorry for her brother, who almost never got to see his own children. She claimed that Connie was manipulative and used the kids against Allan. To deal with the loneliness and bitterness, Allan found comfort in the arms of another woman. He spent four years, from 1972 to 1976, with Sandy Mondgan in a common-law "marriage." They never officially married, but everyone considered them husband and wife.

When Sandy could not please Allan, he sought solace in the bottle. He continued to drink more and more. To make matters worse, Allan also worked another job out of state. From 1973 to 1976 he labored as a pipe fitter in Rock Springs and Green River, Wyoming.

By the time he returned from the job, Sandy had already left him. At the same time Connie could not control Rex and decided to dump him off with Allan in Sandpoint. Allan had no idea why she would leave ten-year-old Rex with an angry, bitter, lonely man like himself.

Nevertheless, she did.

TWENTY-ONE

Back on the farm with his father was the last place Rex Krebs wanted to be. In 1978 Rex attended fifth grade at the Northside Bonner County School, which catered to the children in the rural areas of Sandpoint. Many of the kids, like Rex, rode a bus in to school from several miles away. There were at least 150 other students, most of them farm children from the valley area, and some of the poor kids from the area known as the Huckleberry Commune who also commuted to school.

Rex did not make many friends at Northside. He tended to be a loner and an outcast. Most of his fellow elementary school classmates would snicker at his clothes, which always seemed to be dirty or disheveled. Sometimes it appeared as if Rex did not bathe for school either. Most of the kids stayed away from him.

Anthony Poelstra met Rex Krebs in third grade at Northside Elementary. He had classes with him for five years. He recalled that Rex was a bit of a loner whom the other kids picked on. Sometimes the other kids would "antagonize him to fight," Poelstra recalled. However, he did not think the teasing toward Rex was harsher than what some other kids received. Poelstra stated that Krebs definitely reacted negatively when the bigger kids picked on him.

Another student who noticed Rex's outsider status was classmate Debbie Simmons, now Debbie Rogers. Debbie's best friend, Rebecca Wise, lived down the road from the

Krebs family farm. The two girls often rode their bicycles down to a creek near the Krebs farm. Many times they saw Rex standing out in the field by himself. Sometimes Rex would walk up to the road and speak to the girls. They tried to get him to come to the creek with them, but he always begged out. Debbie noticed that Rex usually looked nervous and constantly glanced over his shoulder back toward his house. He was making sure that his father did not see him speaking to the girls.

Debbie also saw Rex look nervous at school. Her impression was that other kids picked on him for his out-of-style appearance. "Whether it be he didn't have the right pair of shoes, or they didn't fit appropriately, or his hair wasn't clean enough or the right style," Debbie recalled that Rex just did not fit in.

"There were a couple of people that would often antagonize until they could get him to react and then they would step back," Debbie remembered. "It would look like he was the one doing the picking, or being the antagonizer, and then he would get in trouble and they would go laugh in the corner."

Debbie Rogers and Anthony Poelstra recalled seeing bruises on Rex. At different times they both noticed that Rex had big scrapes on his arms. Neither was sure if they were the normal scrapes and bumps of a young boy. Debbie Rogers had suspicions, however, about the black eyes that Rex occasionally sported.

Dorothy Thompson, Northside Bonner County School's principal, remembered that Rex made several visits to her office. It was not for disciplinary reasons, as may be expected.

"He seemed to be a lonesome boy for attention from adults," Thompson recalled. "He would come in, and our secretary, who had been there several years, so she knew him well, and he would come there and stand at the desk and just kind of want to talk to her. She would encourage him and so he was in the office very often."

Other than hiding out in Principal Thompson's office for

company, Rex did not fit in anywhere. His dad berated him and beat him at home. His classmates taunted him at school. Only one person became his friend. Jimmy Maddox. Unfortunately, Jimmy would only attend Northside for a couple of years, but when the two were together, they stuck together. As outsiders, they had to.

Principal Thompson recalled a specific incident where Rex and Jimmy stuck together. One gorgeous spring day Rex left Northside Elementary but did not take the bus home like he normally did. Instead, he decided to run away from home. The following day, when Rex did not show up for class, Mrs. Thompson called his father, but no one answered. She incorrectly assumed that Rex was with his father, so she did not press the issue.

When Rex failed to show up to school the next day, his classmates started to worry. All of the students began to talk about Rex. As the buzz built in the classroom, Jimmy Maddox spoke up and asked, "Mrs. Thompson, if I tell you where Rex is, you won't tell that I told on him, will you?"

Principal Thompson calmly stated, "No, I don't have to tell who told me, but I need to know where Rex is." She was also concerned because she had received a couple of phone calls from Allan Krebs and they were not of the expected nature. According to Thompson, she never saw Allan Krebs at any of Rex's school functions and never once at a parent-teacher meeting. The only time she ever heard from him was when Rex had gotten in trouble. He would always blame the school for Rex's transgressions.

This day was no different. Allan Krebs called earlier that morning and accused Principal Thompson of hiding his son from him. He was determined to go find Rex and bring his butt back home. He told her that he had a pack of dogs and was going to conduct a search-and-rescue mission for his son. And he was *not* happy that he had to spend his time with such a venture.

Thompson acted quickly. She believed that Allan Krebs

might harm his own son if he found Rex first. She intervened. She confirmed with Jimmy that Rex was one-and-a-quarter mile up Old Creek Road east of the school. He was hiding under a large, overturned tree root. It was cold, so she jumped in her car. She was going to get to Rex before Allan Krebs did.

"I knew where I was supposed to go," Principal Thompson detailed the retrieval. "It was an old rugged road. I was going very slowly and I did see movement out there." She had spotted Rex but did not want to scare him away.

"I didn't go out after him because there was a ditch there and a fence [between them]. And I spoke to him and he spoke right back. He said, 'I don't want to go back.'

"I said, 'Rex, there's two things you have to think about.'" The first was for him to go back to school. The second, and apparently more frightening proposition, was to call his father. If he did not do it, Thompson would.

To the first, he told her he had no desire to return to class.

As for calling his father, Rex replied, "I don't want to go back home. I have so much work to do."

TWENTY-TWO

From 1978 to 1979 Rex Krebs's behavior began to change. He began to lash out at his father for the abusive treatment. He got into a lot of trouble for it.

In 1979 he snuck out of the house without his father's knowledge. This time, instead of having nothing in his possession, Rex grabbed a ski mask and a butcher knife. He walked down Colburn Culver Road to twelve-year-old Roseann Littlejohn's trailer home, where she lived with her mother. As he walked up to the trailer, he noticed there were no lights on. He managed to jimmy open the door to the vehicle and silently slipped inside. Rex found his way into one of the two bedrooms, which turned out to be little Roseann's room. He crouched down in the closet, laid the knife beside his leg, and began to masturbate.

He was in this same position when Roseann and her mother returned home. The Littlejohns screamed in fear when they turned on the trailer light and found Rex in a compromising position holding the knife. Their screams terrified him. He thought he could get away with this peccadillo since no one was home. Frightened, he bolted out of the closet, streaked out of Roseann's bedroom, and ran out of the Littlejohn trailer home.

The following day, the police brought him in.

Roseann's mother, though terrified and upset, decided not to press charges on one condition: Allan Krebs take his son in for psychological counseling to determine why he committed such a horrible deed.

Krebs agreed.

The commitment was short-lived. Allan stopped taking Rex to the counselor after only one visit. He believed the psychologist tried to examine him and not Rex. Allan called Connie and told her he would not attend any more sessions with Rex. He informed her that it was her responsibility now. She refused and Rex never went back to counseling. Apparently, the Littlejohns were unaware of this.

One year later, in July 1980, when Rex was fourteen, he got into trouble for making obscene phone calls to a woman named Betty. He then called another woman and described the sexual things he wanted to do to her. This woman turned out to be his aunt. She told Allan what Rex had said and Allan beat the living tar out of his son.

Over the next year Rex continued to get into trouble and his father continued to beat him. He continued to get into fights at school with the other kids. Sometimes he started the fights, instead of being the one picked on. He also stole money from his father's secret cash stash. Allan Krebs claimed his son stole more than $1,000 that year.

The cycle continued until Rex screwed up one too many times.

On February 20, 1981, Rex stormed out of his home. He was "ticked off at his dad" and feeling rather feisty. He had taken a BB gun with him and decided to pay his next-door neighbors a visit. Rex did not like the patriarch of the Benda family. He believed Arnold Benda treated Rex's family with disdain and looked down his nose at them.

Rex walked up to the Benda home and opened fire with the BB gun. He shot out a window and then broke into the empty home. While inside, Rex grabbed a few items, including a bag of marbles, a calculator, a .22 pistol, and some other small items. As with his break-in at the Littlejohn trailer home, Rex claimed to be very nervous while inside the home.

He ran outside with the stolen goods and immediately tossed some of them across the road. He took some of the other items with him to school the next day. Rex gave the calculator to a classmate by the name of Jay Newton. He kept the .22 for himself.

Later the next evening, Arnold Benda contacted Allan Krebs and accused Rex of breaking into his home. When asked by his dad if he was involved, Rex denied having anything to do with it. Allan Krebs helped Benda look for the stolen items. He stated, "The whole family had combed his property looking for these articles," including Rex. Of course, they did not find anything.

Eventually the local authorities arrested Rex. He felt bad about the break-in and told Arnold Benda, "It was a stupid thing to do, and I won't do it again." It was his first official run-in with the law.

It would not be his last.

Less than two weeks later, on March 3, 1981, at 6:25 P.M., Rex was rushed to Bonner General Hospital emergency room by Allan Krebs. His father informed the nurse that Rex had fallen off the back of his truck. Dr. Fred Marienau examined Rex. Allan seemed annoyed at having to be at the hospital. He was also uncooperative with the nursing staff when he checked Rex in. According to the medical report, Allan refused to give Connie's name or contact information. He also claimed to have lost his insurance card.

Dr. Marienau performed a cursory observation of fifteen-year-old Rex. He noted that the teenager had an abrasion on his left shoulder, swelling and a laceration on his right cheek, a small amount of blood from his left ear, and several contusions on his body.

Dr. Marienau again asked Allan Krebs what happened to his son. Allan claimed that Rex fell off his pickup truck "while the truck was stopped and we were tossing out garbage." Krebs contended that Rex hit his head on the concrete when he fell.

According to Dr. Marienau, the various marks, lacerations,

and bruises seemed to indicate something unusual. The capper for him was the blood from Rex's left ear. He stated, "It usually signifies that the ear has suffered some kind of blow. You could make blood come from the ear by hitting it very hard on the outside and rupturing some blood vessels in there." The doctor assumed something untoward had happened to the teenage boy.

According to his notes, Dr. Marienau wrote "Verbal Advice." The elderly doctor did not recall specifically what, if anything, he said to Allan Krebs, but he knew "Verbal Advice" on a patient's chart indicated he had spoken to the parent about possible child abuse.

In a possible abuse situation, Dr. Marienau also made it a policy to ask the child how he or she obtained their markings. In this instance Rex, while in the presence of his father, reiterated everything his father said.

Exactly as his father had said it.

When Dr. Marienau asked Allan Krebs to leave the examining room, he again asked Rex how he got the cuts and bloody ear. Rex changed his story. He told the doctor, "I think—I think I fell in PE today. I think I hit it with a board. I think—I must have fallen in PE there too."

Dr. Marienau ordered X rays for Rex to make sure nothing was broken. The results were negative. Instead of following up further on what seemed like an abuse case, Dr. Marienau sent Rex home. He concluded that Rex had suffered a "Head trauma." He suggested "rest and observation at home." He did not file a child abuse report with the Child Protective Services Agency.

During 1981 fifteen-year-old Rex decided to escape his father's clutches one more time. He headed for the nearby train tracks, hoping to hop a train and get the hell out of Sandpoint. He waited around for hours, but no train appeared. Soon he became less excited about running away and more interested in causing some destruction. Rex spotted a loose metal rail in the area and grabbed it. As he did, he spotted a train repair car coming up the tracks by itself. There was a repairman on board on his way to fix one of the beaten-up trains. Rex dragged the metal rail across the train tracks.

As the repair car came down the tracks, Rex leaped over a small hill of rocks and watched the events unfold. In a case of the world's largest penny-flattening experiment gone awry, the train car ran over the rail and catapulted off the tracks, accompanied by a screeching symphony of scraping metal and crushed rocks. The repairman was tossed off the car into a heap of dust and blood.

Rex whooped it up with laughter at the site of the destruction. He took off from the accident scene, hoping to avoid capture.

Luckily, the repairman had not been seriously injured.

When later asked if he was concerned that the repairman may have died, Rex replied that he did not care.

The sheriff picked Rex up. He returned him to his father and ordered him to appear before a court. Less than one week later, Rex ran away again. Once again he was caught and returned to his father.

Allan Krebs had enough. He believed he could no longer control his only son and felt that Rex "needed some help." On May 1, 1981, Allan Krebs took his fifteen-year-old son to the Orofino State Hospital, a state-sponsored hospital that helps patients with mental illness or substance abuse problems. Rex remained in the psychiatric treatment unit at Orofino until May 28, 1981.

Dr. Leslie Gombus diagnosed Rex at Orofino State Hospital. Dr. Gombus attempted to define Rex's problems in his evaluation: "Diagnostically, this patient showed primary difficulties with adolescent, antisocial behavior and difficulties residing within the family situation. Within the confines of the Psychiatric Treatment Unit, the patient was able to improve his behavior and hold it within the confines of the limits placed upon him. Staff felt that appropriate treatment plan for this young individual to be removed from the confines of the family situation and be placed into a facility which could provide for educational and vocational training, along with a structured therapeutic setting."

Dr. Gombus recommended a transfer to the state juvenile diagnostic unit, where state-appointed caseworker Jean Bistline interviewed Rex. In conversations with Bistline, Rex let her know that he had no desire to return to his father's home. Allan Krebs let Bistline know that he had no desire for his son to return until he shaped up. Connie Jackson, Rex's mother, informed Bistline that Rex needed help and that "he does need to be away from here." Connie claimed that Rex was welcome in her home, but it might not be the best idea considering her husband's penchant for firearms and threats.

Social worker Kenneth Stucker, from the juvenile diagnostic unit, concurred that Rex should be placed in a group therapy setting. He stressed that Rex needed to "learn more appropriate ways to control his anger and hostilities toward others." Apparently, he believed Rex's anger to be so bad that if he did not control it, they might have to send him to Youth Center Services in St. Anthony, where "they can control his hostilities."

After her review of Rex's analyses, Bistline agreed to place him in an Idaho children's group home. She contacted the Idaho Youth Ranch in Rupert, Idaho; however, they had no vacancies until August of that year. She then contacted officials at the North Idaho Children's Home in Lewiston, Idaho, approximately 170 miles south of the family farm in Sandpoint. They had an immediate opening and were more than happy to take Rex into their program. Bistline also noted that the home was close enough to Sandpoint so "that the family can continue to be involved."

TWENTY-THREE

According to child-care worker Scott Mosher, the Northern Idaho Children's Home (NICH) was founded in 1917 as an orphanage and remained one until the mid-1960s. NICH drew up contracts with the state of Idaho to convert it from an orphanage to a private nonprofit residential treatment facility. The home accepts children in the custody of the state under the Children Protection Act, as well as the Juvenile Justice Act. NICH treats children with behavioral and/or emotional problems. The state compensates them for their efforts.

The main goal for NICH's employees is to have a positive impact on the wayward youths who enter through their doors. Many of the kids are serious troublemakers. The workers help students via "treatment modalities," such as individual therapy, group therapy, and a behavioral incentive program. The two former methods are self-explanatory. The third method is a system created by the counselors at NICH wherein the kids are responsible for their own personal list of chores and act responsibly with other students and staff members. There are five levels that the students must attain each with a greater amount of responsibilities attached to them. The students must meet their responsibilities before they move up to the next level. As the students make progress, they receive more privileges. The goal is for the students to reach the fifth level so they can return to their family.

Rex Allan Krebs, age fifteen, entered the Northern Idaho Children's Home in June 1981. Rex moved into South House.

It is one of three buildings with different groups of troubled children. The other two houses are Jewett House, which houses all girls, and Cedar House, which is less strict. South House handled approximately twelve to fifteen adolescent boys at a time. The building has several offices, a large common living area, a living room, and two long hallways with bedrooms on either side of the hallway, a kitchen, and a basement recreation area with games and a pool table. The kids received their schooling at an educational center at nearby Lewis and Clark State College.

South House remained under a constant twenty-four-hour watch by counselors.

This was Rex Krebs's new home.

Scott Mosher was Rex's child-care worker at North Idaho Children's Home. His job was to make sure that Rex's (as well as a number of other students in South House) needs were met. That meant food, clothing, and shelter. It also meant working with Rex and other staff members to develop a suitable treatment plan to help Rex reintegrate into normal society. Mosher worked with Rex every day for almost a year.

Mosher noticed right away that Rex Krebs was different from the other kids. In recalling Rex's initial time at South House, Mosher noted that Rex seemed to be a "real needy kid, in need of a lot of attention, a lot of nurturance." Mosher also sensed that Rex was afraid of something. It turned out that Rex was afraid of his father. He let Mosher know just how much he did not want to go home.

Mosher noted on an acceptance form for Rex—Presenting Problems at Admission—that this was a troubled kid. He had "poor impulse control, not being truthful, substance abuse, problems with school, at school with teachers." Indeed, these personality traits flared up when Rex arrived at South House. He had difficulty, at first, warming up to the other kids. He also lied and stole from some of the other kids early on. Rex also got angry whenever he got into trouble. He would usually throw a tantrum or yell out in anger at someone.

Rex tended to gravitate toward the counselors and other staffers at NICH. He felt more comfortable speaking with people in positions of authority rather than kids his own age with similar problems and concerns.

Mosher also realized that Rex had serious issues with anger. "He had a pretty short fuse," Mosher reflected. "He would be prone to temper outbursts." The counselor developed a specific program for Rex to try to help him solve his anger management problems. Over time the program seemed to work for Rex. He made noticeable progress in controlling his frustrations and anger. Mosher noticed that instead of lashing out at the other kids or staff members, Rex eventually learned how to talk things over. He eventually stopped having temper tantrums and he quit making threats at the other students.

Art teacher Frederick Deibel also noted a marked improvement in Rex during his first year at NICH. Deibel watched as Rex worked his way into the structure of the treatment program and how he interacted with others. He felt that Rex often stayed away from the other kids and the staffers at first. It was as if the boy was assessing the situation to see where he fit and how others would treat him. At first he would get into fights with some of the other boys. Moreover, he would usually be the one to start them. He would also argue with the counselors about trivial matters. Over time, however, as he became more comfortable in the environment, he came out of his shell. He joined the other boys in activities and worked positively with his counselors. He also took a shine to athletics. Rex, despite only being 5'1" and 123 pounds soaking wet at the time, had a certain athletic prowess. He seemed especially adept at basketball. Deibel noted that almost nine months after his initial processing into NICH, Rex Krebs was becoming a respected participant in the program.

Rex did so well that he became Mosher's "model resident." He received the prestigious Gentleman of the Month award on March 9, 1982, while in South House. Mosher noted that they did not give out the award lightly. It was a certificate of achievement for exemplary behavior by one of the home's students. Each month the NICH staff and students voted on the award. It truly was a special recognition by both peers and authorities. One month later, Rex received another accolade. This time on the basketball court. On April 7, 1982, he received a certificate for Best Ball Handler.

After nine months of steady progress, Rex attained Level Four. Mosher believed that Rex had become a leader in South House and earned a ticket to Cedar House. Mosher also noted that not one person from Rex's family came to visit him during his stay at South House. He believed they would have been proud of the efforts Rex made while at NICH.

Cedar House had far fewer restrictions than South House. The concept for Cedar House was born out of "emancipation living." Students who wanted to transfer to Cedar House had to show true personal growth while at South House. They were required to act like responsible young adults who could function in normal society. As such, they had more freedom. They were able to leave the facilities and travel downtown to the grocery store or movie theater without supervision. They attended Lewiston High School instead of Lewis and Clark State College. Cedar House students were also allowed to obtain jobs in town as part of their privileges. Rex participated actively in all three of these endeavors.

Rex enrolled at Lewiston High School and seemed to mingle well with the other high school students there. The kids at Lewiston did not pick on him. He did not necessarily make any lifelong friends, but he went about his day with little or no problems with the students and teachers. Rex even improved on some of his more difficult courses, such as math and science.

Rex also got a job working for the city's transportation division. It was a grease monkey position that allowed him to muck it up. Each weekday, at the end of a long day of school followed by work, Rex would come home to Cedar House covered in dirt and grease. It appeared as if the grime were a badge of honor for Rex.

In addition to making a concerted effort at school and holding down a solid job, Rex also tried to enjoy himself while at Cedar House. One of his favorite things to do was to walk to the downtown corner store. One day Rex was walking to the store when he spotted a girl standing in her yard. He stopped and looked at her, then quietly approached. He asked her her name and she told him it was "Donnie." It was a nickname for Adonia. Adonia Krug. She had been watching him for several days as he walked past her mother's house on the way to the store. She thought Rex was cute. They chatted about the usual teenage fascinations of the time, but mainly they just liked being in each other's company.

Rex made it a point to stop and talk with Donnie every time he went to the store. He seemed to want to go to the store more and more often. Each time he met up with Donnie, their conversations would last a little bit longer and get a little bit deeper. After a while she gave Rex her phone number and soon they were staying up until all hours of the night talking. Their topics became more serious as Donnie began to see in Rex someone she could confide her innermost thoughts and fears. She spoke of how her parents' divorce shattered her life. Rex listened intently and asked her just the right questions. He let her know he was interested in what she had to say.

Rex never told Donnie about his parents.

Donnie began to make trips outside of her home to see Rex. She would meet him at the park near Cedar House, where Rex played basketball. It was almost three miles away from her home. They would usually spend hours talking about her problems.

Eventually their relationship blossomed into something more than a friendship. Rex began to call Donnie his girlfriend. Nothing had really changed for a while as they simply continued to have long talks. Rex would give Donnie advice on how to handle rough situations and help her not to worry about things she could not control.

After a month of this, however, Rex discovered information that changed things.

On Donnie's birthday Rex called her to extend his warmest wishes. Donnie's mother, Diana Krug, answered the phone. Krug liked Rex, but she was getting a little concerned about the close relationship he had with her daughter. After all, there was a problem.

"Rex, do you know how old Donnie is?" Krug asked.

"Yes ma'am, she turns sixteen today," he innocently replied.

Krug hesitated before she responded, "No, Rex, she just turned twelve."

Rex was speechless. Donnie Krug had lied to him. He had been trying to make time with a twelve-year-old, while he was seventeen. He was not happy. He apologized to Diana Krug and hung up the phone.

A few days later, Rex called Donnie. The topic of conversation was her age. Rex was upset and said it could not be true. He could not be with a girl who was so young. He told her that he was breaking up with her but that they could remain friends.

Deep inside, he could not believe that another person he cared for had lied to him.

Rex and Donnie did remain friends, just as he promised. She continued to cry on his shoulder and he continued to give her advice. However, he never pursued her in a romantic fashion after the revelation.

During March 1983 Rex received approval to terminate his stay at North Idaho Children's Home. There was reluctance on behalf of Scott Mosher and Jean Bistline about releasing Rex back into his father's custody. In the end both social workers decided Rex could return to his father. They believed Rex was ready to make a difference in the world. If anything, he was ready to make a difference in his own life.

Everyone at North Idaho Children's Home was optimistic for Rex Krebs.

They had high hopes.

TWENTY-FOUR

Any hopes of Rex holding on to what he learned while at North Idaho Children's Home faded almost as soon as he returned to Sandpoint. Allan Krebs had not changed for the better over the two years while Rex was away. If anything, he had become even more vile and temperamental.

Allan met an attractive woman by the name of Janice Grabenstein during the summer of 1982. Janice was a single mother who lived with her seven-year-old daughter, Debbie. Allan and Janice hit it off fabulously and, within months, Janice and Debbie moved in with Allan and Rex. On the surface they had a seemingly idyllic relationship. Upon closer inspection, however, everything was far from normal.

Janice noted that the Krebs family farm was far from a thing of beauty. Its structure was in disrepair and the home was filthy. There were holes in the ceiling where rain poured through. Several walls needed repairs, as did most of the floors. There was no running water in the house. Someone would have to drive a quarter mile to Alfred Krebs's house to fetch drinking water in two large milk jugs.

Janice Grabenstein's first chore when she hooked up with Allan Krebs was to clean this pit. She did it, all by herself. In the process of the cleaning, she learned a bit more about her boyfriend.

He liked guns.

He liked guns so much that he actually kept a gun in every single room in the house. He kept several in the living room.

Each gun was loaded and ready to use. It was a veritable militia compound inside the Krebs home.

Despite this initial turnoff, Janice was determined to make the relationship work. She also noticed that Rex and Allan actually seemed to get along well. They would go swimming together down at the nearby creek or ride horses out on the land behind the house. Janice also spoke very highly of Rex. She saw him as a polite young man who treated her daughter with nothing but respect. He helped Janice with a plethora of chores around the house: cleaning, hauling water from Grandpa Krebs's house, baby-sitting Debbie when Janice had to step outside the home. Rex even taught her how to ride a horse. In her mind he was a great kid.

Even though Janice saw Allan and Rex getting along, to her it seemed as if Allan was always trying to control Rex. He constantly denigrated his son by telling him how worthless he was. He called Rex "bastard" and "asshole." Soon the controlling behavior went from verbal abuse to physical abuse.

Janice recalled a specific instance of physical abuse between Allan and Rex Krebs. One night Rex attempted to cook a pasta dinner for the family, but he got caught up in reading a book. Before he knew it, the pasta had burned and there was nothing for dinner. Allan did not take too kindly to his son's absentmindedness. Upon smelling the burning dish, Allan marched into the kitchen with a full head of steam and unleashed a torrent of punches on seventeen-year-old Rex. He slapped him in the face and punched him in the stomach.

"He backhanded him," Janice said years later, "and then just took his fist and would slug him and kind of knock him back and keep going at him."

Over burned spaghetti.

Janice recalled more incidents of abuse between Allan and Rex. One night Rex went out drinking. When he returned, Allan was waiting. He could tell his son was drunk, but he also smelled something funny on Rex's breath. He accused Rex of smoking marijuana and then punched him several

times in the face until he bled. Janice was in their bedroom
when she heard Allan scream at the top of his lungs that Rex
was a "worthless, fucking, piece of shit." She also heard his
fist land on Rex.

Allan went inside the bedroom and asked Janice to look
at Rex. When she entered Rex's room, she saw that he looked
horrible. Blood covered his face and his lips swelled up right
before her eyes. Allan angrily asked Janice if she could smell
marijuana smoke on Rex. Janice, fearful for Rex's well-being,
claimed that she did not smell anything. Years later, she admitted she smelled marijuana on Rex, but she wanted to save
him from another beating.

Allan did not save his abusive behavior for just Rex. He
also directed some of his more cruel treatment for Rex's
youngest sister, the mentally challenged Marcia. By the time
Janice had moved into Allan Krebs's home, his biological
daughters, Marcia and Tracy, spent the weekends with him.
He constantly berated the girls whenever they stayed. Janice
recalled that he often used cruel language in front of Marcia.
He referred to his emotionally disabled thirteen-year-old
daughter as a "bitch," a "whore," or a "cunt," and called her
"stupid" or "retarded." He would also make fun of her buck-
teeth. Marcia had difficulty using a fork due the combination
of oversize teeth and her disability. He would mock her as she
spilled food all over the table and all over herself.

Allan also physically abused Marcia. Janice recounted the
time when the family all went out for a horseback ride. Marcia had been riding in a rocky creek when her horse panicked
and tossed her facefirst into the water. She scraped her face
on some rocks and suffered a great deal of pain. She arose in
a wail of tears. Allan would not tolerate such behavior. He
screamed at his daughter to "get back on the fucking horse,"
which only made her cry more. She would not budge. Allan
dismounted and walked up to his youngest daughter. He
screamed at her again to get her butt up on that horse. She responded with more tears. Allan reached over and grabbed

Marcia by the back of the hair, turned her around so that her backside was facing him, and literally kicked her bottom. The force of the blow was so strong that she actually went airborne and landed on top of the horse.

Janice Grabenstein believed that alcohol and drugs usually set off Allan Krebs's behavior. He drank often, and when he did, his temper flared. His propensity to snort methamphetamine compounded his behavior. Janice claimed that Allan began taking speed quite frequently within a year of her and Debbie moving in.

Despite Allan's reprehensible behavior during that first year together while Rex lived there, he never once directed it toward Janice. He would save his physical abuse for her later, after Rex no longer lived there. He did humiliate Janice in front of Rex. He often called her a "whore" and grabbed her in inappropriate ways. Allan also spoke derisively about women in front of his son.

He also expressed contempt for Debbie. He often called her a "cunt," a "bitch," or a "rectum." Debbie seemed to recall Allan enjoyed the humiliation. His abuse was not limited to words. He would also spank his stepdaughter for the slightest infraction.

"The majority of the time he spanked us," Debbie recalled several years later, "he sent us out to the woodpile for a stick to get us prepared for our spanking." Like digging their own graves, the kids had to fetch a stick that was "big enough that you knew you were in trouble." Allan was not always satisfied with their selection of switches, according to Debbie. "If you brought one back that was too small, he'd send you back." One time Debbie grabbed a piece of wood that was too big—it was a two-by-four.

"I figured the bigger the stick, the happier he'd be."

It only served to make Allan Krebs angrier.

His punishment was not limited to sticks. Debbie claimed that he also used his hands on her. Allan slapped her across the mouth for seemingly innocuous things. For instance, the young girl had a nervous habit of twisting her hair. It drove Allan crazy, so he smacked her for it.

Years later, after Rex had moved out, Debbie had a vicious encounter with her stepfather that indicated what he could do to her.

It happened the day after her fifteenth birthday.

Debbie had finished vacuuming the living room. The vacuum she used required water to hold the dirt and she went outside to empty it. As she walked out the front door, she almost bumped into Allan. Instead of moving aside and letting her pass, Alan Krebs shoved the skinny teenager out of his way. He grumbled as he walked inside his house.

Debbie kept her head down and did not look up at him. She was furious, but continued to walk to the sidewalk to unload the dirt from the vacuum. As she dumped the mess, she glanced over her shoulder back at the house and muttered, "Fuck you" under her breath. Allan was standing in the kitchen, staring at her through the kitchen window. He saw her mouth move. He could read her lips. He was enraged.

Allan dashed outside and asked Debbie what she said. When she begged off, he called her a "lying whore." She turned and walked away when out marched Janice, who stepped in between them. Allan told Janice everything was fine and that he was not angry. Janice believed him and moved out of the way. As soon as she did, Allan lunged at Debbie with his fist, punching her square in the face. He hit her so hard that her lips imbedded into her braces. When she later removed her lips from the metal, she could see large chunks of tissue torn out from inside her mouth.

The attack on her daughter was the last straw for Janice. She packed up her bags and made a late-night getaway, just as Connie had done several years earlier.

TWENTY-FIVE

One year after Rex returned home, his life would change forever. So would the life of an innocent twelve-year-old girl.

Rex hated to stay at his father's house. If his dad was not beating up on him, he was smacking his sisters around or cussing out Janice. Rex started to get away from the house more often so he would not have to deal with his father's bullshit. He actually made a couple of friends in Sandpoint. His running buddies were two local boys, John Lowry and Alex Black.

On February 3, 1984, a chilly winter evening, Rex headed to the downtown video-game parlor known as the Electric Horseman, located at First Street and Pine Street. He pumped a handful of quarters into games such as Defender and Tempest, but soon got bored. He wanted something more exciting.

As Rex walked down the icy downtown street, he noticed his friend John inside the Kentucky Fried Chicken. He went inside and told John that he had a surprise, something his father had given him, he claimed. Rex pulled back his long winter coat and revealed a shiny new bottle of vodka. John's eyes lit up. They blazed out of the restaurant.

After a few swallows of the clear liquor, Rex and John went back to the Electric Horseman, where they met some of John's other friends. The young men hid out behind the parlor and continued to drink from Rex's bottle of vodka for about fifteen minutes. They were then joined by two young girls, Karen James, aged fourteen, and Jennifer Everwood (pseud.), who was only twelve years old.

Karen and Jenny had been out on the town for the night. They were supposed to go to the Panida Theater to catch a movie, but they spent all of their movie money at the Electric Horseman. After they left the game room, the girls started to head over to the Pastime Café, but instead made a beeline for the Cedar Street Bridge, which crosses over Sand Creek, where they ran into John, Alex, and Rex. The guys were well on their way to getting drunk. They encouraged the girls to join them.

Rex offered his bottle to Karen, who proceeded to drink a few large gulps from it. She then passed the bottle to Jenny, who took a few swigs. Rex insisted that they drink more. The girls did as requested. Soon they were feeling no pain.

Rex turned to Karen and asked her, "Who, in order, is the most drunk from most to least?"

The teenager replied, "You, John, Alex, me, and Jenny."

Rex turned his attention to twelve-year-old Jenny and said, "You need another drink." He handed her the vodka. Jenny accepted it and took another swig. Rex told her he would finish it off for her, so she handed the bottle back to him.

Everyone felt in great spirits by now. The drunken partyers decided to try their hand at some shoeless ice-skating on the frozen creek under the Cedar Street Bridge. They clumsily slipped about on the ice, but had a grand old time. After about fifteen minutes of this foolishness, they decided to go back into the Electric Horseman to get out of the cold. They left the bridge area and began walking to the parlor when Rex turned off the road toward the Panida Theater. Alex and Karen, who were getting cozy together, joined him. Jenny stopped for a moment. She did not know what to do. She decided she did not want to be without her best friend, so she tagged along. John continued on to the Electric Horseman. That left two couples. Alex and Karen. Rex and Jenny.

Behind the theater sat a 1960s blue pickup truck with its tailgate down. Karen and Alex claimed the tailgate and immediately cuddled up together and began to kiss. Rex and Jenny walked toward the front of the truck. Rex attempted to put the moves on Jenny, but she rebuffed his advances. He attempted to kiss her, but she told him no. She let him know that she was only twelve years old, but that did not stop him. He told her that he was going to kiss her "nicely." She said she did not want him to kiss her at all. She jumped up to get Karen.

When she went around the front of the truck, Karen and Alex were not there.

According to her statement to the police, Rex grabbed Jenny again and started kissing her. She resisted and they both fell to the ground of the parking lot. Rex got up and Jenny tried to trip him with her feet. He fell to the ground and then rolled on top of the young girl.

"Do you want to have sex with me?" Rex asked the twelve-year-old girl.

"No," Jenny replied, "I'm not interested in kissing you and I certainly don't want to have sex with you."

Rex was not pleased with her response. He forcefully pulled down her denim blue jeans, then her panties. Somehow he also managed to disrobe himself from the waist down. Next thing Jenny knew, Rex had mounted her and "tried fucking, but didn't succeed." Jenny begged and pleaded for Rex to get off her, but he would not listen. She tried unsuccessfully to knee him in the groin. Finally, after several attempts, she connected, then scrambled away from Rex and rose to her feet. She hurriedly pulled up her underwear and pants. She began to run away from the older, bigger boy, but he tripped her. Jenny sprawled to the parking lot, her Walkman headphone wires pulled taut around her neck, choking the preteen.

Rex angrily jumped back on top of Jenny.

He clasped his hands around the young girl's throat. Jenny, however, continued to fight back. She also grabbed for his throat, albeit with much tinier hands and far less strength. The two of them yelled at each other while in the throes of a mutual death grip. Finally Rex released his hands from her neck. He did not relent, however, in his attack. Instead, he balled his right hand into a fist, reared it backward, and thrust it toward Jenny's face. He connected with a brutal ferocity that rocketed the young girl's head backward so hard that it smacked the concrete beneath her. He then punched her in the forehead and in the eye. He reared back one more time and connected with the girl's fragile jaw. He hit her so hard that she bit through her tongue.

The final blow sent Jenny plummeting over the curbside embankment and down the dirty hillside onto the frozen creek. She was not alone as she had grabbed Rex's shirt and pulled him over the side. As Jenny helplessly rolled down the hill, she bumped her head against a large rock embedded in the ground. Despite feeling woozy, Jenny grabbed Rex's hair and continued to scream at him to leave her alone. Rex turned to her and, without warning, apologized.

"I'm sorry," he sincerely intoned. "Please don't tell anyone."

Jenny somehow managed to bolt upright, found her footing on the hillside, and took off running. She made it up the embankment in no time and was over the side. She saw a couple walking hand in hand and headed directly toward them. She asked for their help and told them that someone raped her. They did not believe her and laughed in her face. Nonplussed, the adolescent continued on to the Sandpoint police station, one block away from the theater.

Jenny arrived at the police station and hustled inside to the front desk. She frantically told the dispatcher Sandra Maben what had happened and that all she knew was the young man's name was Rex. Maben called Detective Andrew "A.D." Anderson. He arrived at the police station within five minutes. He spoke with Jenny for a few minutes in the front lobby and then brought her to the back, where she could have more privacy. Detective Anderson noted that her speech was slurred and he had difficulty understanding what she said. He asked her to write down the events that had just transpired; however, she was not able to scrawl down more than two or three words. She was either too upset or too intoxicated, the detective concluded. He contacted her parents to come to the station and then advised them, when they arrived, to take their daughter to the local hospital and have them perform a "sex crime kit" exam on her.

Just before midnight Detective Anderson telephoned Allan Krebs. The officer told him about Jenny's accusation and asked him to bring Rex to the police station.

Rex did not arrive at the police station until 4:00 P.M. the following day. Detective Anderson confronted him with Jenny's story and asked Rex to recount his whereabouts from the previous night. Rex told the officer that everything Jenny said was true up until the attack. He even admitted that Jenny did not want him to "kiss and pet" her. He also claimed that he was too drunk to remember what had happened from that point on except that he got sick and fell down several times on the way to his grandmother's house.

Rex was arrested and locked up in the Sandpoint Jail. The charge was attempted rape. One month later, on March 8, 1984, Rex Krebs pleaded not guilty to the charge and was held over to the Bonner County District Court to set up a trial date. On March 19, 1984, Joe Jarzabek, Kreb's attorney, convinced the court to downgrade the charges to a misdemeanor assault. The prosecutor agreed and Rex pleaded guilty. He was remanded back into the custody of the sheriff's department and forced to serve out the remaining thirty-six days of his ninety-day sentence.

Rex Krebs received a slap on the wrist for the attempted rape of a twelve-year-old girl.

TWENTY-SIX

Rex Krebs walked out of the Sandpoint Jail in May 1984. Less than two months later, he was in trouble again. On the night of July 17, 1984, Rex broke into a car, which belonged to Mike Smolinski, near Eleventh Street, by the Snake River in Lewiston, Idaho. The theft took place near Rex's former residence, the North Idaho Children's Home. Rex claimed that he dumped the car beside the local police station so the owner could find it the next day.

But he was not done yet.

He next headed over to Eighth Avenue and broke into a 1973 Toyota Landcruiser, which belonged to Dennis Murphy. It was only a few blocks away from Smolinski's car. The police captured Krebs and arrested him later that night.

On July 19, 1984, a complaint was filed against Rex Krebs in the Nez Perce County District Court for first-degree burglary and grand theft. He was not represented by an attorney at the time and was assessed a $10,000 bail. The judge also set Krebs's preliminary conference for six days later, July 25, 1984, at which time he obtained counsel, Owen Knowlton. Krebs's arraignment date had been set for Wednesday, August 1, 1984. The judge also found sufficient cause to hold him for trial.

Krebs stayed locked up until September 5, 1984, when he pleaded guilty to two charges of grand theft for the stealing of the automobiles of Mike Smolinski and Dennis Murphy.

Rex Krebs, who only served three months for the attempted rape of a twelve-year-old girl, received a three-year sentence in the North Idaho Correctional Institution for steal-ing two cars.

The North Idaho Correctional Institution is a former mili-tary radar station located just north of the quaint town of Cottonwood, Idaho. It is located just below the Nez Perce Na-tional Historical Park. Most people refer to the prison as Cottonwood.

According to the Idaho Department of Corrections, Cot-tonwood is a "program-specific prison designed for male inmates sentenced to a retained jurisdiction commitment by the court. It provides a sentencing alternative for the courts to target those offenders who might be, after a period of pro-gramming and evaluation, viable candidates for probation rather than incarceration. The retained jurisdiction inmates participate in a boot camp program which instills confidence and self-esteem."

It is a minimum-security prison, where the inmates are not locked down behind the security fence. There are no bars on the windows and the inmates are free to roam the grounds. In-mates of Cottonwood are not considered escape threats.

This would become eighteen-year-old Rex Krebs's newest home.

According to Correctional Officer Daniel Werline, Cotton-wood uses a two-tiered rehabilitation program: the rider program and the timer program. The rider program takes first-time offenders and observes their behavior, gives them an education, offers counseling for psychological problems, as well as alcohol and drug abuse prevention programs. Staff teachers, as well as correctional officers, supervise the inmates.

New inmates must proceed through a 120-day program of observation, education, and counseling before they can be deemed fit to be allowed back into society. As part of their program, they are required to speak with counselors and se-curity staff members about their issues. Inmates are monitored as to how well they communicate with other in-mates and other staffers, how they act around those same people, and if they show remorse for the crimes that got them incarcerated in the first place. Staff members and officers then evaluate an inmate's progress and write up a summary report that gives an opinion as to how well that person has done in the program.

The timer program consists of minimum-custody prisoners or "timers" brought in from other prisons. Timers are usually prisoners up for parole. They participate in jobs at Cottonwood to earn a little money, which will help them upon their release from prison. Some of the work includes construction, kitchen duty, and laundry detail.

Timers are usually older and savvier criminals than riders.

The breakdown of inmates at Cottonwood during Krebs's imprisonment, according to Werline, usually consisted of 60 to 70 timers and 150 to 200 riders. A large security fence separated the two groups.

The correctional officers at Cottonwood placed Rex Krebs into the rider program.

Officer Werline watched over Krebs every day. He observed his mannerisms as well as his interaction with prisoners and staffers, his cleanliness, and whether or not he took his education seriously. Prisoners were on a twenty-four-hour watch, even when they slept. Officer Werline spoke highly of his newest charge.

"Other than some immaturity," Werline noted, "I thought he had an excellent attitude for the program." Werline further noted that Krebs acted polite and treated him with respect.

After 120 days, Werline wrote an evaluation for Krebs. He gave him a "go," which meant that the inmate had passed the program. This one recommendation, combined with other recommendations from other staffers, could determine whether the inmate would be released from the program. Despite Werline's glowing praises, Krebs did not leave the program.

Judge John Maynard of Lewiston apparently took a hardline stance on riders who screwed up while on the program. The judge rubber-stamped all inmates who received a single negative evaluation. In other words, if the inmate did not do everything and please every staffer, he would not be released from the rider program. Instead, Judge Maynard would ignore the reports and not write a recommendation. After a two-week extension passed with no word from the judge, the Department of Corrections would automatically change an inmate's status from rider to timer.

This happened to Rex Krebs. He was moved from Dorm Three over to Dorm Two. According to Officer Werline, when Rex was upgraded to a timer, his attitude sank.

"He was a little depressed at first, but he was a minimum-security case. We had no problem with him." Indeed, Krebs even earned a position in the administration building working among the female secretaries of the prison.

"You had to be trustworthy in order to work with the secretaries," Werline conceded.

As far as Krebs's stay with the timers themselves, he apparently kept his nose clean by staying out of the way. Werline recalled that Krebs did not seem to be a leader. He also did not appear to be a follower.

"He wasn't outgoing. He wasn't the bullying type or tough or anything like that."

In 1987, after three years behind bars, Rex Krebs stepped outside the gates of Cottonwood Prison. His father did not pick him up. His mother did not pick him up. Instead, Diana Krug picked him up and took him back to her and Donnie's home in Lewiston. Rex lived with the Krugs for one week, when he received a phone call from his mother. She informed him that she had remarried and moved to Oceano, California. It is a small coastal town about fifteen miles south of the town of San Luis Obispo. She wanted to start a new life with her fourth husband and wondered if Rex wanted to come along.

Rex had the choice of going out on his own, moving back in with his dad, or moving to the coast of California.

The choice was obvious.

He told his mother he would be there in a week.

PART V

CALIFORNIA

TWENTY-SEVEN

Connie divorced her third husband, Bob Jackson, while Rex was in Cottonwood. Soon thereafter, she married a kind gentleman from Sandpoint named John Hollister. It was his second marriage. They lived in a small house on A Street on Pack River.

In 1987, before Rex Krebs's release from Cottonwood, Connie and John Hollister decided to pack their bags and head for greener pastures. John was unemployed at the time and his brother-in-law had recently opened a welding shop in Arroyo Grande, California, just sixteen miles south of the town of San Luis Obispo. The brother-in-law told John's sister that he needed some help, she called her brother, and he agreed to relocate. John moved first, followed by Connie one week later. The couple set up in a small yellow rental home on the corner of Mentone Avenue and Eighth Street in Oceano, less than a mile-and-a-half from Grover City (now known as Grover Beach) and the Pacific Ocean. Their house was easy to spot due to the massive palm tree that reached well over thirty feet high in the front yard. The street they lived on seemed a bit run-down; however, the houses were clean and the neighbors were all relatively well mannered.

Things seemed to be looking up for Connie and John in Oceano. John enjoyed working at the welding shop. Connie enjoyed decorating the small home and looked forward to another addition to the household. Her younger brother Calvin Howell planned to move down from Idaho to work at the welding shop. Soon after Calvin moved in, Connie received word that Rex was out of Cottonwood. She contacted him at Diana Krug's home in Lewiston, Idaho, and suggested that he come to California and move in with them.

Rex readily agreed.

Upon arriving at his mother's home in Oceano, Rex asked her if he could convert a room attached to the garage into his own personal living quarters. She thought it would be a great idea and agreed. She let him know that he could use the bathroom and shower inside the house. She also offered to cook Rex's meals for him and wash his clothes.

It seemed like the perfect setup for the ex-con.

Rex set about installing wires for his electricity. He took hammer and nails and erected some wooden walls, which he sealed and painted. Rex did all the labor himself.

He looked forward to having his own space.

In less than two weeks, Rex landed a job at the local Wendy's hamburger restaurant. He enjoyed the job because it gave him a sense of responsibility, which he had been lacking most of his life. He made enough money to buy his own clothes. He even made enough to purchase a used white Volkswagen Bug, which made getting to work much less of a hassle.

He also made friends.

One of those friends was Leisl Turner. The attractive seventeen-year-old Arroyo Grande High School senior and Wendy's coworker caught Rex's eye immediately. After getting to know her better, Rex and Leisl spent much of their work time cutting up together. Soon they were spending time together outside of work.

Rex began to learn more about his new friend. Leisl had come from a difficult family background. She was born and raised in Colorado. Her mother and father were divorced, and Leisl never got along with her mother. She moved out of her mother's home for three months. Then, in June 1986, she moved halfway across the country to live with her father and his girlfriend in a tiny apartment. Due to the cramped environment, that did not work out either, so she moved out again.

Leisl was on her own until she met Rex. Given his past, he did not seem to mind. In fact, he enjoyed driving her to school and to work. He even let her borrow his car so she could run errands, go to her job, or shop at the nearby mall.

In a short period of time, Rex and Liesl began to date. On their first official date, Rex took her to Taco Bell. He became enthralled with his younger coworker. He often wrote her love letters and romantic poems and secretly delivered them to her. Rex invited Leisl over to the Hollister residence for a romantic candlelit dinner. Rex even cooked the meal. The teenage girl fell for the gestures and soon the couple moved in together into Rex's garage bedroom.

Rex, not wanting to mess up a good thing, asked Leisl to marry him.

She agreed.

The young couple engaged in an intimate relationship immediately. According to Leisl, Rex had a predilection for kinky sex. He constantly pestered Leisl to perform anal sex with him. She refused his requests. He also asked the seventeen-year-old girl if he could tie her up with a rope when they had intercourse. He told her he wanted to bind her wrists together, as well as her ankles. Again she refused. She did not worry that he would get angry at her. She saw him get upset at work if things went wrong, but she did not fear for her own safety.

Not until she saw the picture.

Rex kept a framed photograph of a beautiful blond young woman on his nightstand, next to his bed. Leisl wanted to know more.

"Who's that girl, Rex?"

"Her name was Lisa."

Leisl noticed his emphasis on the word "was."

"She was my fiancée. She and I were engaged to be married back in Idaho," Rex wistfully recalled. "She had been raped and murdered. That's why I stole those cars."

Leisl did not know what to make of this statement. "What do you mean, Rex?"

"I stole those cars so I could be put in jail and kill the person who raped and killed her."

Leisl looked at Rex in shock. Maybe he thought this would make him look heroic. Unbeknown to Rex, what he told Leisl repulsed her.

"Did you do it? Did you kill the guy?"

"Yep," he replied rather nonchalantly. "I found him and I killed the son of a bitch."

Leisl tried to hide the look of fear on her face. All this time she thought her fiancé had merely stolen a couple of cars and had a run of bad luck. Now she had no idea what to make of Rex Krebs. All she knew was that she wanted to get out of that garage.

Leisl did not understand why Rex had told her that story. Did he do it to intimidate her? If so, it worked.

A few days later, Leisl ran into her stepmother on the Arroyo Grande High School campus. They spoke for a while and both agreed that it was fine for her to return to her father's apartment. Leisl wanted to move out of Rex's garage, but she had no idea how to do it without incurring his anger.

Leisl returned to the garage. Rex had not come home from work yet. She rummaged through his dirty work clothes when she came upon a tiny scrap of white paper in his blue jeans. It contained a girl's name and telephone number.

For Leisl, it was her ticket out.

When Rex returned later that evening, she confronted him. She wanted to know who the girl on the piece of paper was and how Rex knew her. She accused him of cheating on her and she let him know, clearly, that they were through. She stormed out of the garage door that Rex had installed and out of his life forever.

The date was May 17, 1987.

TWENTY-EIGHT

May 24, 1987
B Street, Oceano, California
10:00 P.M.

Shelly Crosby (pseud.), a twenty-one-year-old mother, separated from her husband, felt restless as she sat alone in her comfortable duplex apartment. Her roommate, Lisa Wood, worked the night shift at Farm Boys restaurant in Pismo Beach and would not be home until 6:00 A.M. the next day. In fact, Shelly hardly ever saw her roommate because she worked the day shift at Farm Boys. On this particular evening Shelly's daughter and Lisa's two children were with a baby-sitter. Shelly had no kids to worry about, but she also was bored out of her skull. She grabbed her coat and headed out the side door.

Shelly ended up at Harry's Cocktail Lounge, located on the pier over the Pacific Ocean in Pismo Beach, around 11:30 P.M. She sat near the bar and ordered a tequila sunrise. She chatted up a couple of guys in the bar, but just to keep her company. She headed out the door as the cries for "last call" rang out. She still felt restless.

Shelly decided to pay Lisa a visit. She hopped into her car and drove down the main street in Pismo Beach to Farm Boys. As Shelly walked in to her place of employment, she passed a young man, about her age, with stringy brown hair and nondescript facial features. He looked up at her as if to get her attention; however, she focused only on Lisa. She walked by the young man without acknowledging his presence. The man seemed to recoil as if struck with a forceful blow to the abdomen.

Shelly pulled up a chair and ordered a stiff black cup of coffee.

The young man rose from his chair and glanced at Shelly. She still did not notice him. He opened his mouth as if to say something to her, then turned around suddenly and slightly stumbled on his way out the door.

Shelly was blissfully unaware of the young man.

She spoke animatedly with her roommate as the night seemed rather slow. She would not get Lisa in trouble. The two women spoke of nothing important, just Shelly's desire to get out of the apartment. Lisa tended to three customers, who straggled in late, and Shelly ordered more coffee. After another ninety minutes Shelly felt exhausted. She informed her roommate that she had to go back home and gave her a hug good-bye. Shelly turned for the exit and passed through the large doors. She walked up to her car, pulled out her keys, unlocked the door, and slid into the vinyl front seat.

She did not see the young man from the restaurant. He sat in the front seat of his beaten-up white Volkswagen. His car lights were off. He had his eye on her.

He was planning to teach her a lesson. Never look down at another man again.

Shelly started the ignition in her car, checked her hair in the mirror, and pulled out of the Farm Boys parking lot. She was ready to crawl into bed and get some shut-eye. She was only five miles away. As she drove home, she pulled into the Grover City 7-Eleven. She had no idea that someone had been following her for three miles. She purchased a pack of cigarettes and a bottle of Pepsi.

Shelly jumped back into her car and pulled out onto Grand Avenue. By the time she got to Thirteenth Street, she felt strange. She looked up in her rearview mirror and saw two bright headlights staring back at her. The car behind her had practically parked itself on her rear bumper. She pulled away from the stop sign and kept an eye on the car. She tried to get a glimpse at what kind of car it was, but the dark streets made it difficult for her to get a good look.

Shelly drove for several more blocks, taking several turns that she normally would not take, to get home. The car continued to follow her. The headlights seemed to track her every move. It was still too dark to see what kind of car it was.

Finally Shelly arrived at her street. Eighteenth Street.

She drove about fifty yards up the street and took a left turn up the concrete incline drive-in, past the brown wooden fence, which did not fully surround her house. The driveway remained open at all times, since there was no gate. She pulled up the small hill, turned off her lights, and sat in her car. She wanted to see what the other car would do next.

Shelly glanced up in her rearview mirror and watched as the car slowly drove past her driveway. This crazy fool had definitely gone out of his way to follow her. She started to get a little scared, until the car eventually accelerated and continued down Eighteenth Street. Shelly felt safe enough to get out of her car and hurry inside to the safety of her ground-level, one-story apartment. As she leaped out of the car, however, she noticed that the driver had turned the car around and headed back toward her. The car did not stop, but rather drove back down the street the way it had entered.

Shelly did not feel comfortable yet. She kept on eye on the vehicle. Sure enough, the driver pulled the car back around and headed toward her. It slowly crept up the narrow asphalt road until it came to a stop beside a field about one hundred yards from her apartment.

Shelly darted behind the six-foot-tall wooden fence and peeked through a four-inch round knothole. She easily spotted the car. The driver had turned off the lights and seemed to be looking directly at her. She sensed that the driver could see her through the tiny knothole.

Shelly pulled back, but not before she got a decent look at the vehicle.

It appeared to be a beaten-up old Volkswagen.

Even though she was nervous, Shelly felt safe enough to go inside. After making sure she locked all the doors, she turned on the living-room lamp and headed to the bedroom. She felt safe in her nice and dark cave of a bedroom. She and Lisa had pinned up blankets over the windows to keep the sunlight from coming in. Despite the initial adrenaline rush, Shelly was not afraid. She stripped out of her clothes, except for her panties, and threw on her comfortable old gray sweat bottoms and a lavender tank top. She crawled into bed and immediately fell asleep.

Forty-five minutes later, she woke up.

A man's smooth hand covered her mouth.

Shelly had no idea what had happened. Suddenly, as if from behind a curtain, a man's voice warned her: "Don't say anything louder than a whisper."

She lay completely still. In fear, but quiet. She glanced up at the intruder and noticed that he stood over her and had one knee on the bed. Her movement caused a reaction in the man. He aggressively placed a sharp blade on the left side of her throat. It was a ten-inch knife with a seven-inch blade. It appeared to be almost three inches wide. The man made sure that the sharp edge grazed against her cheek. Shelly stifled a scream. She had no idea what to do.

The man added to the tension when he leaned into her face, his breath smelling of liquor and cigarettes. He asked her in a hushed tone if there were any kids in the house.

"Yes," she lied in a voice lower than a whisper.

"What did you say?"

"Yes."

The man did not pursue that line of questioning any further. He seemed more interested in tormenting the young mother.

"Do you have any sharp kitchen knives?" he inquired.

Shelly looked up at him with pleading eyes. She did not want to answer.

"Sharp enough to cut your throat with?"

Shelly closed her eyes and began to cry. She did not want to die here. Not like this. "I don't know," she replied.

"Don't worry, mine is."

He then dropped the knife, which landed with a loud *thud* on the carpeted floor. Instead of letting her go, however, the man grabbed another, even bigger knife, and thrust it toward her throat. He finally removed his hand from her mouth and again reminded her not to speak above a whisper. He turned her over onto her stomach and pulled back the covers. He grabbed both of her arms behind her back and reached into his pocket. He pulled out a smooth white nylon rope. It looked like rope used on outdoor laundry clotheslines. He clasped her wrists together and bound them with the rope.

Shelly struggled for a brief moment, but stopped when she felt the intruder harshly grab her right ankle. He then inserted the massive blade inside her sweatpants leg and sliced upward. He slit the sturdy fabric with a fluid motion all the way up to the inside of her thigh. After he finished the right side, he repeated the process on her left leg. He then ripped the tattered sweat bottoms off with his free hand, leaving Shelly lying on her stomach, clad only in her panties and tank top. She remained tied up with the rope the intruder had brought with him.

He slowly moved toward her panty-clad bottom. He ran his hand over the smooth, silky fabric before viciously grabbing and slicing it with the knife. Her backside was now exposed for the man to gawk over.

He methodically repeated his slow torture with her tank top. He started from the bottom of the shirt and slit it all the way to the top. Right up the middle. He then clutched the material and pulled it out from underneath her like a magician's tablecloth.

Shelly lay nude on her bed. Tied up in ropes. Shivering.

The intruder grabbed the top of her head and began to shove a piece of cloth into her mouth. He wanted to gag her.

"I promise I won't say anything," she pleaded with the man. He stopped his attempt at gagging her and instead tried to use the cloth as a blindfold.

"I—I won't look at you," she cried out. He did not blindfold her either.

The man moved away from her head, roughly grabbed her ankles, and yanked her toward him. She still lay on her stomach, but now the bottom of her legs dangled over the edge of the bed.

It got very quiet in the room. Suddenly the silence was shattered by the sound of a zipper being pulled down. Next thing she knew, the man jerked her legs apart. A sharp pain followed as he roughly penetrated her vagina with his penis. He continued to rape her. He pulled out and reinserted himself into her anus. The torture continued for what seemed like hours.

The intruder pulled himself out of Shelly, stood up, and grabbed her by the arm. He yanked her still-bound body up toward the top of the bed. She remained on her stomach, unable to see who had just violated her body. He grabbed her ankles and bound them together with a second rope. He then connected the rope around her wrists with this second rope around her ankles. He cinched the ropes together and had her in a hog-tied position.

The man climbed back onto the bed, slowly moving toward Shelly.

"Where's your purse?" the rapist demanded.

Suddenly a loud noise disrupted him. It rumbled through the neighborhood like an angry locomotive. The sound came from Lisa's car. It had a hole in the muffler, which she had been meaning to fix. It seemed to rock the entire neighborhood as she pulled into the driveway.

Lisa usually arrived home from work at 6:00 A.M. For some reason, she was home early.

Shelly did not know what to do. She feared that the man might attempt to attack Lisa as well. The man rose from the bed and then faced Shelly.

"Is that your roommate?" he asked.

"Yes," Shelly whispered. She felt even more scared than before.

The man walked closer to her, but she still could not see his face. He leaned in and, with his smoke-filled and liquor-saturated breath, said something eerily grotesque to her: "Have a nice day."

He turned around and headed out the way he came in. Shelly rolled off the bed and managed to squeeze her hands out of their restraints.

Less than one minute later, Lisa walked into the house. She dumped her purse and keys on the coffee table and slowly made her way into her bedroom. The room was too dark to see anything. She tried to keep quiet so as not to wake Shelly. Instead, she screamed when Shelly stumbled out of her bedroom half naked.

"Is he still here?" Lisa asked, scared out of her wits.

"I don't know," Shelly responded.

She remembered that the rapist had dropped the first knife under the bed. She grabbed it and cut the rope off her ankles. Lisa bundled her up and took Shelly to her mother's house in Arroyo Grande. From there, they called the police, who suggested that she go immediately to the hospital for a rape exam.

Shelly had no idea how the man had gotten into her house. She also had no idea what he looked like.

TWENTY-NINE

June 14, 1987
Trader Nicks Restaurant, Pismo Beach, California
3:30 P.M.

Thirty-one-year-old waitress Anishka Constantine (pseud.) called it an afternoon. The Colombian-born Constantine's shift at the Trader Nicks restaurant ended and she looked forward to going home and seeing her seven-year-old daughter, Adina. She put away her food-stained smock, grabbed her purse, and said good night to her coworkers. Normally, Anishka would stop by the San Luis Obispo gym for a brisk workout between 5:00 P.M. and 6:00 P.M. This particular day she opted to go straight home.

Nine days earlier, June 5, 1987, someone had broken into Anishka's cozy three-bedroom, two-bathroom home located on Fair Oaks Avenue. Her house was situated in a flag lot off the main street, along with four other homes, in a cul-de-sac. The intruder apparently snuck in through her partially opened bathroom window. Anishka and her daughter were not home when the break-in occurred; however, Anishka could tell someone had been inside her home. She noticed her clothes had been rearranged in her closet, so she contacted the Arroyo Grande Police Department and filed a report.

After the break-in, Anishka took extra safety precautions around the house. She wanted to make sure nothing would happen to her or her daughter. Each night she locked every door and made sure every window was sealed shut. She turned on the outside lights in her backyard, and flicked even more lights on inside her house. She also locked her bedroom door so no one could easily walk through.

On June 15 Anishka came home and spent a quiet evening with her daughter. Anishka and Adina's father had been recently divorced and the daughter split time between Oceano and Nipomo, where her father lived. When she stayed in Oceano, Adina slept in her mother's bed with her. The mother and daughter fell asleep around 10:00 P.M..

At 1:00 A.M., Anishka jumped out of bed. A noise startled her, so she decided to look. Her neighbors across the way owned a cat that would sneak out and terrorize the neighborhood. Anishka thought the cat might be the cause of the racket outside, but she wanted to make sure. She went to her bathroom, which had been broken into only a week-and-a-half earlier. She pulled back the thin curtain and peered outside. Darkness stared back at her. She could not tell what made the noise. Nor what may be outside her window.

She backed away from the window and let the curtain drop back into place. She turned toward the bathroom wall and flicked on the light. She walked out of the tiny bathroom and left the light on so it would shine in her bedroom. She tiptoed back to bed.

Adina slept like a mouse.

Anishka stealthily slid under the covers and pulled them up to her chin. Her daughter looked like an angel sleeping beside her. After fifteen minutes of listening, Anishka could not hear anything else. She fell asleep.

Without warning, a crash sounded as her bedroom door rocketed forward. Anishka bolted upright, but before she could get out of bed, someone grabbed her by the throat and told her to be quiet. He gripped a screwdriver in his fist with the metal end pointing at her eye like a knife. Adina, startled by the intrusion, looked up at her mother and began to scream. Anishka tried to calm her down.

The scene was total chaos.

"Please don't hurt us. Here, take my money," Anishka pleaded with the intruder. "I will give you money, jewelry, anything, just leave us alone. Please don't hurt us."

"I don't want your money." The man breathed in her face with the stench of marijuana. "I just want you."

Anishka knew what he was after. She heard Adina screaming at the man to leave her mommy alone. Anishka turned to her daughter and cried, "Get under the bed, baby. Get under the bed, now."

Adina did as her mother told her. She pounced off the bed and crawled underneath, squeezing under the coiled springs that strained close to the floor due to the extra weight of the intruder. Adina noticed the Princess telephone receiver and cradle had been knocked off the nightstand during the scuffle. She picked up the receiver to dial 911. The line was dead.

As soon as her daughter slipped under the bed, Anishka began to fight. This man did not break in to steal anything. He wanted to rape her. She knew she must defend herself. Anishka lashed out at the man with her hands, striking him squarely in the face. She clawed at him with her long nails and scratched him repeatedly. The man fought back and thrust her down hard on the bed. He continued to poise the screwdriver toward her face with his right hand.

He then managed to unbuckle his belt and unzip his pants with his left hand. As he did this, Anishka spotted something ominous on his belt. It was a large Buck knife, encased in a black snap-on sheath. She reached for the case and somehow flipped up the button enclosure. The man pushed back at her and they continued to scratch and claw and slap one another. In the process Anishka successfully struck the sheath and the knife fell to the floor, two feet from the bed.

In a flash she stopped fighting.

She looked at the intruder and said, "Why don't we go into another room?" She glanced down, as if to acknowledge the presence of her daughter. The intruder fell for the ruse and stood up to get off the bed. He gently grabbed Anishka by the arm and pulled her up from the bed. Anishka, however, managed to squirm free from his clutches and dropped to the floor. She spotted the knife and grabbed it. The man, unaware that she had armed herself, violently jerked her other arm and dragged her out of the bedroom.

Once in the hallway the man told her to stop and turn around.

"I want to tie you up," he said quietly.

Anishka did not comply. Instead, she fought the man. He was fed up with her antics so he grabbed her by her long, thick black hair and thrust her head into the wall. Not once, not twice, but three times. The dazed woman, however, still had some fight left in her. Fearing that he would increase the ferocity of his attack, she opened the retractable 7 ¾" blade. She haphazardly thrust the knife upward, then down toward the man's right arm.

She connected.

Unfortunately, she only nicked his belt buckle. The man was furious. He grabbed her by the right wrist and inched her hand toward his face. He opened his mouth and clamped down on one of her fingers with his teeth. Anishka, her hand bleeding, screamed and dropped the knife. In a state of panic, she lurched for the front door. She thrust it open so hard it left a door handle impression on the entrance wall. She screamed and tore off outside.

Adina remained inside underneath the bed.

The man took off to the back of the house. He struggled to open the sliding glass door, which led to Anishka's backyard. He escaped by climbing over her six-foot-high wooden fence.

Anishka scrambled to the house across the street and banged on the front door. No one answered. Frantic, she ran up to the front window and smashed in the louvered glass. The resultant cacophony awoke her neighbor, who, along with his brother and a friend, ran outside to see what was going on. The neighbor saw the tiny woman shivering with fear. He also noticed a man running down the street in a big hurry. Two of the neighbors set out on foot after the man, but they were too late. The attacker jumped into what looked like an old white Volkswagen Bug parked along the main portion of Fair Oaks Avenue. The man hurled himself into the car, cranked the engine, threw it into gear, and sped out making a U-turn. Dust and the smell of burned rubber were the only things left behind.

Arroyo Grande police officers Steve Harris and Barry Bridge received a call for a break-in on Fair Oaks Avenue in Oceano, at 1:36 A.M. Officer Harris arrived first. He spoke to seven-year-old Adina Constantine, who told him about the intruder and how she attempted to call for help. The officer then spoke with Anishka's neighbor, who saw the man flee the scene just minutes before. Officer Harris made a call to the Grover City Police Department and gave them a description of the vehicle that left the scene. He told them to be on alert as the crime had just occurred. Officer Harris walked inside the Constantine residence and found Anishka Constantine lying down on the carpeted floor in her den. He contacted paramedics, who arrived in no time and whisked Anishka off to Arroyo Grande Community Hospital emergency room.

Officer John Tooley, Arroyo Grande crime scene investigator (CSI), received a call from Lieutenant William Andrews to check out a report of an attempted rape and burglary. He arrived at the Constantine household at 2:15 A.M. Officer Tooley conferred with Officers Harris and Bridge, who updated him on the attack. Harris informed Tooley that he confiscated a black Mini Maglite flashlight from Adina. She picked it up from the bedroom during the scuffle between her mother and the man.

Officer Tooley walked around the perimeter of the house and began to take notes. He walked up to the west side of the house, next to the garage. He glanced down and noticed a plastic white bag of fertilizer on the ground next to the wooden fence. The intruder probably stepped on it and used it to hurdle over the front gate. Tooley noted that this gave the suspect access to the Constantine backyard. The suspect must have then walked over the dry soft sand and weeds that covered the area that led to the garage. Tooley walked up to the west side of the garage and directed his flashlight toward the door handle. He instantly noticed scuff marks on the bolt and striker plate. He noted that the marks were made with a pointed instrument, possibly a slotted screwdriver. He also noted that the door remained open. It appeared as if this was where the man entered the home.

Officer Tooley continued to peruse the perimeter of the residence. He also noted a window screen that lay in the grass of the backyard. He wrote down that someone had recently opened the sliding glass door. He also noted a cut screen window over the master bathroom from the prior break-in.

Officer Tooley continued his observation of the exterior of the house. He walked around to the driveway and entered the house through the front door. As soon as he walked in, he spotted a large black Buck hunting knife. Officer Bridge walked up and informed him that the brown Princess phone in the kitchen had its coiled vinyl cord cut. Someone slit it with a sharp knife.

Officer Tooley headed back out the front door. He returned to the garage and found that the door from inside that led into the house also had marks on the bolt and striker plate. Again it appeared as if a slotted screwdriver was used to gain access. He continued to observe the garage area when he came across a bundle of colored wires near the back wall. It was an assortment of severed television cable wires and phone lines.

Officer Tooley noticed a small spatter of blood on the front-door threshold. The blood markings indicated to him that whoever bled in this spot was leaving the house, not coming inside it. He also noted the impression left in the wall by the door handle when Anishka slammed it open during her escape.

Officer Tooley proceeded to the master bedroom. He noted

someone forced the door open, not with a kick of a foot, but rather with a shoulder. It appeared as if the intruder rammed the door so hard that he knocked off the striker plate and two of its screws. The striker plate actually flew a couple of feet into the entrance of one of the other bedrooms.

Officer Tooley walked through the damaged door into Anishka Constantine's bedroom. As he slowly looked around the room, he scanned for additional pieces of evidence that might lead him to the person responsible for the attempted rape. One clue jumped out at him. He spotted a brown corduroy snap-bill cap on the floor in front of the mother's closet. Officer Harris, who followed Officer Tooley into the bedroom, informed the CSI that the hat did not belong to the Constantines or anyone they knew. Adina stated unequivocally that it belonged to the suspect.

Officer Tooley continued to scan the bedroom, where he spotted a large clump of thick black hair. Officer Bridge informed Officer Tooley that the suspect had grabbed Anishka's hair during the struggle. Tooley noted the "messed-up condition" of the sheets on the bed. The bottom fitted sheet had been pulled up from the mattress. He then knelt down on his knees to observe underneath the bed. He found a black Buck hunting-knife sheath with no knife.

THIRTY

At 2:47 A.M., an Arroyo Grande reserve officer received a 415 PC call, disturbing the peace, at the 7-Eleven food store at Halcyon Road and Grand Avenue in Grover City. The store is located only one-and-a-half miles from Anishka Constantine's home. Twenty minutes later, at 3:07 A.M., Officers Vasquez and Sweeton spotted a man stumbling along Thirteenth Street and Grand Avenue. He stood out quite conspicuously with his pink long-sleeve shirt. He was more than ten blocks west of the 7-Eleven; however, he appeared to be heading back east in the direction of the store. The officers pulled up alongside the man and got out of their car. Officer Maria Vasquez walked up to the man and asked him his name.

"Charles Ervin," the man replied.

"What are you doing out here this late at night, Mr. Ervin?" Officer Vasquez inquired.

Ervin looked down at the ground and hesitated before he responded, "If you want to talk to me, you'll have to walk alongside of me."

This response did not please Officer Christopher Sweeton, who lunged at Ervin and tackled him to the wet grass. Sweeton pulled Ervin to his feet, placed his hands in cuffs, threw him back to the ground, and placed him under arrest.

The officers transported Ervin to the San Luis Obispo Jail and deposited him there for the night. The next morning, at 10:00 A.M., Officer Tooley began to ask him a series

of questions about the disturbance outside of the 7-Eleven.
Ervin denied being anywhere near the store or even in Arroyo Grande, for that matter. He claimed that he and his
friend Alan Hammon and Alan's friend Laurie Nielson had
all driven out to Harry's Cocktail Lounge in Pismo Beach.
The same bar that Shelly Crosby went to the night of her
rape only three weeks earlier.

Ervin stated that he and his two friends had a few drinks
before he and Neilson got separated from Hammon. Nielson
offered to take Ervin home, so they stuck around until closing time at 1:45 A.M. and continued to drink. Ervin believed
he drank eight beers that night. By the time they left, he was
thoroughly intoxicated and quite obnoxious. Nielson piled
him into her gray Camaro and drove home down Highway 1
toward Grover City. He argued with Nielson. She got fed up
with him and pulled off the highway and onto Grand Avenue.
She pulled up to the 7-Eleven and told him to get out. He said
this occurred around 2:00 A.M.

Officer Tooley then switched gears and began to ask him
questions about the attack on Anishka Constantine.

"Do you drive a white Volkswagen Bug?" Officer Tooley
started.

"I don't drive a car. Just my Triumph motorcycle," Ervin
responded.

"Do you wear a hat of any kind?"

"My hair is receding so I never wear hats," Ervin replied.

"Where did you get that scratch on your cheek?"

"The police handcuffed me and threw me on the ground,"
he responded. Ervin also showed Officer Tooley a scratch
on the left side of his neck, as well as a rug-burn-like mark on
his left shoulder. There were also bruises on his arms, which
Ervin claimed came from the one-sided scuffle with Officer
Sweeton.

"What about the clothes you wore tonight?" Officer Tooley
continued the interrogation.

"You see 'em. Gray pants, pink shirt with the sleeves cut off, and tan loafers."

"Why aren't you wearing a jacket?"

"Because I didn't plan on doing any walking outside tonight."

"Do you carry a knife with you?"

"Never."

Officer Tooley asked Ervin if he could take his clothes for evidence collection and comparison. Ervin readily agreed. Tooley then took photographs of Ervin's various marks and scratches. One of the photos showed a cut on his finger.

"Did you cut your finger when you broke into that woman's house?" asked Officer Tooley.

"I don't remember how I got that cut," pleaded Ervin. "But I know I wouldn't break into someone's house. Not unless I blacked out."

Later that same morning, Officer Tooley showed Anishka a photo lineup with six photographs, including one of Charles Ervin. She gasped when she spotted the photo of Ervin. "It is very close. It was somewhat dark at the time I saw him," the young mother replied. For some reason, though, she was not completely convinced that the man in the photo was the one who attacked her. Some similarities existed, but she just was not sure.

After he interrogated Ervin, Officer Tooley placed him under arrest. Based on the victim's identification through the photo lineup, scratch marks on his neck, and his location near the crime scene, Officer Tooley read Ervin his rights, drove him to the San Luis Obispo Sheriff's Office, and booked and fingerprinted him. Correctional Officer Jack Nix removed and cataloged all of Ervin's clothes with the suspect's consent. Ervin also agreed to take a polygraph examination.

Officer Tooley made several phone calls to family, friends, and associates affiliated with Charles Ervin. Alan Hammon's mother claimed to have known the suspect since he was thirteen and stated that he never wore a hat. She also noted that he did not drive a car of any kind, much less a Volkswagen Bug. Bud Wheeler, Ervin's boss at L&K Liquor, believed that he saw Ervin wear a snap-bill baseball cap once, but not recently. Alan Hammon informed Officer Tooley that he got separated from Ervin and Nielson at Harry's Cocktail Lounge and that she probably drove Ervin home. He also described what Ervin wore that evening and that Ervin never wore a hat. Finally Laurie Nielson, who had returned to her home in Boise, Idaho, claimed that she did indeed drive Ervin to the 7-Eleven in Grover City after their argument. She remembered the time: 2:00 A.M.

He also showed the photo lineup to Adina Constantine. The seven-year-old did not recognize Charles Ervin. She said that she did see the suspect's face, but Ervin was not the right one. She remembered the attacker had "greasy hair."

Officer Tooley realized he might not have the right man in custody.

He sent a teletype message to the San Luis Obispo Sheriff's County Jail to release Charles Ervin. The reported time of the break-in and attempted rape was 1:30 A.M. Laurie Nielson confirmed that Ervin could not have been at the Constantine residence at that time.

Charles Ervin became a free man.

On June 17, 1987, Officer Tooley asked Anishka Constantine to come to the Arroyo Grande Police Department to look at another photo lineup. When she met the officer, she told him about a man she met about a month or a month-and-a-half earlier. The man installed garage doors and had been working on her neighbor's door one day. She thought he seemed rather unusual because he came up to her and asked if she was married. He said that if she did not have a husband around, he could help her with her garage door if it needed some repairs. She told the young man that she was not married and lived alone in the house with her daughter. She also mentioned that the garage door did not close all the way. She noticed that the man wore a snap-bill baseball cap.

Officer Tooley went back to the evidence room to retrieve the hat that he found at the scene of her attack. When he asked her if it looked like the same hat, she replied that it appeared to be the same one.

Anishka told Officer Tooley that the man worked on her garage door right then and there. When he finished, he gave her his business card. She did not have it with her, but she told the officer that she knew where it could be located. Officer Tooley told her to go get it.

Anishka returned to the police station minutes later with the business card in hand. It said, *Grover City Door and Supply Company*. There were four names on the face of the card. The man had circled one with a black pen: REX KREBS. On the back of the card, the man wrote in black ink, "I will be back first thing Thursday morning. To finish your door. Rex Krebs GCDC."

Anishka Constantine looked up into Officer Tooley's eyes. "I am almost certain that this is the man who attacked me."

THIRTY-ONE

Officer Tooley ran a quick check of the name Rex Krebs through the Department of Motor Vehicles. He matched a Rex Allan Krebs as the registered owner of a 1967 Volkswagen. The driver's license information listed Krebs's address as 817 Mentone Avenue in Oceano, California. He jumped into his squad car and drove over to the Mentone address. Unfortunately, 817 Mentone Avenue did not exist. Officer Tooley then drove to his boss's home in Arroyo Grande, north of the 101 Freeway. When he pulled up, he spotted an off-white Volkswagen Bug parked in the street in front of the house. Officer Tooley stepped out of his vehicle and slowly walked to the front door. He knocked for several minutes. No one answered.

Later that night, on June 17, 1987, Officer Tooley, joined by Detective John Ferdolage, drove back to Mentone Avenue in Grover City. When they arrived, they spotted Krebs's Volkswagen parked in front of a house on Mentone Avenue. The 817 address number had been incorrect.

The two officers parked their cruiser across the way from the quaint house. They stepped out of their vehicle and edged up the concrete sidewalk to the front door.

The time was 8:54 P.M.

Officer Tooley knocked on the front door. John Hollister, Rex's stepfather, answered it. Connie Hollister, Rex's mother, stood behind Hollister. Rex Krebs followed behind, wearing a faded blue denim jacket and a blue-and-white snap-bill baseball cap with a HELLWIG LOAD PRO logo on the front. He also had a fresh cut on his right nostril.

Officer Tooley cut straight to the chase. He informed Krebs that he suspected him to be involved in a burglary from two nights before in the neighborhood.

"I need for you to come in and submit some fingerprints," Officer Tooley informed the suspect. "We'd also like to take your picture."

"OK," Krebs replied with a seeming lack of concern.

Connie piped up, "He's just been released from parole."

Officers Tooley and Ferdolage looked up at Krebs. The young man nodded his head and informed them that he did two years for grand-theft auto in Idaho. He claimed that he stole a car for a joyride and drove it eight blocks before the cops pulled him over and arrested him.

"Do you have any other arrests?" Officer Tooley wanted to know.

"None to speak of," Krebs responded.

Officer Tooley told Rex Krebs to drive his car to the Arroyo Grande Police Department. The officers followed close behind. When they arrived at the police station, Officer Tooley wasted no time in reading Krebs his Miranda rights. Upon completion, Officer Tooley asked if he understood these rights.

"Uh-huh," Krebs grunted. "I understand my rights, but I haven't heard your questions yet." Krebs paused for a moment before continuing. "I'll answer your questions, but I will let you know if I feel endangered."

Officer Tooley led off with the scratch on Krebs's face. Krebs told the officer that he went to the Red Fox Bar in Grover City on the night of June 14, 1987, by himself. He drank two Miller beers in a bottle and two martinis. He stayed at the Red Fox Bar from about 9:00 P.M. until 1:30 A.M. When he finished for the night, Krebs grabbed his jacket and keys and headed out to the parking lot toward his Volkswagen Bug. As he approached his car, he spotted a man leaning against it.

"It looked like he was waiting for me."

Krebs claimed that he did not recognize the man. He asked him if there was anything he could do for him. The man responded, "No," so Krebs asked him to get off his car. The man responded by throwing a fist, according to Krebs, that landed square on the left side of his jaw. The two men then wrestled to the ground and the unknown assailant must have scratched Krebs's face.

He did not say how the fight resolved itself.

Krebs took off in his car, but did not report the assault to the police.

"Were you in Arroyo Grande on June fourteenth?" asked Officer Tooley.

"Yeah, I stopped by Sharon Shelly's apartment over on Ash and Elm around eight-thirty P.M." Ash Street and South Elm Street are located two blocks away from Anishka Constantine's residence. "When I did not see her car," Krebs continued, "I kept going." He then mentioned that Sharon Shelly sang at Trader Nicks, the restaurant where Anishka worked.

"Do you ever go over to Trader Nicks?"

"Off and on. But I don't eat there."

"Rex, do you remember working on a garage door in the eleven hundred block of Fair Oaks Avenue about one-and-a-half months ago? Just down from Elm Street Park in a cul-de-sac? A little blue-and-white remodel job?"

"I don't think so."

"Does this help you remember?" Officer Tooley asked as he showed Rex his Grover City Door and Supply business card.

"Oh yeah, yeah, now I remember. I worked over on Buzzy Bower's house."

"Do you remember speaking to the lady next door to Buzzy's? Did you ask her if she needed some help with her garage door?"

"Yeah, I remember this woman came outside and asked me

if I could help her out. I think her door was stuck or something like that. I don't remember everything that we said, but I did fix her garage door so it wouldn't rub on the sides or catch on the bottom."

"Did you go back to that house on June fifteenth?"

"No, no, not at all. I never did go back there."

Just then, a phone rang. Officer Tooley picked it up and heard Detective Ferdolage on the other end. The detective informed Officer Tooley that both Anishka and Adina Constantine positively identified Rex Krebs as the intruder and potential rapist from a photo lineup. Officer Tooley excused himself for a moment. He returned with the brown corduroy hat that the suspect left at the scene.

"Rex, have you ever seen this hat before?" Officer Tooley inquired.

"Yeah, that's mine," he replied incredulously. "Where'd you get that?"

"Where did you lose it?"

"It was in my car."

"Do you know what size it is?"

"Nah, I just picked it up at Kmart and put it on."

Suddenly Krebs snapped to and realized what he had done. He became visibly nervous and fidgeted in his chair. His answers were shorter and less forthcoming.

"When did you last see the hat?"

"Can't recall. Had it on the night of the Red Fox."

Officer Tooley then reached into a paper bag and pulled something else out. It was the Buck hunting knife.

"Is this yours too?" Officer Tooley asked.

"Uh-huh," Krebs dejectedly answered.

"Remember where you lost it?"

"Uh-huh. It was under my front seat of my car."

Officer Tooley had nailed him. Krebs's face turned redder than a Texas fire ant's behind. He acted nervous and upset.

"I get the feeling I should quit answering your questions," Krebs despondently replied.

"Fine, if that's what you want to do," replied Officer Tooley. "You can invoke your rights and I'll stop asking you questions. If that's what you want."

"I don't know. I feel endangered."

"Do you want to quit answering my questions?"

"No. I don't know." Krebs fumbled his words.

"Rex, you have been positively identified in a photo lineup by the victim and her daughter." Officer Tooley also mentioned the fact that he had the cut on his nostril, that he wore a blue denim jacket, and that he himself had identified his own hat and knife—which were recovered from the crime scene—all of which proved to be enough evidence to place him under arrest for the burglary and attempted rape of Anishka Constantine.

"Rex, I think you are lying. I believe you were there on Fair Oaks Avenue that night." ·

"I've told you the truth," he insisted.

Rex Krebs did not persuade Officer Tooley. The detective arrested Krebs and booked him into the Arroyo Grande Police Department Jail. He asked Krebs for consent to search his vehicle and his home. Krebs agreed and handed his car keys to Officer Tooley.

At 11:30 P.M., on June 17, 1987, Officer Tooley walked outside the police station. Krebs's Volkswagen Bug remained out front. The officer located a small slotted screwdriver with a yellow handle on top of the passenger seat. He also discovered a pair of wire cutters with green rubber handles and a pair of needle-nosed pliers with red rubber handles on the passenger seat. He grabbed and bagged them and booked them into evidence.

The following morning at 11:00 A.M., Tooley received a phone call from Krebs's stepfather, John Hollister. He informed the officer that he and Connie were home and the officer could stop by and search the house.

Tooley arrived within five minutes. The Hollisters greeted him at the front door. The officer asked Hollister if he could search Krebs's room. Hollister explained that his stepson lived rent free in the attached portion of the garage behind the house. Tooley informed him that Krebs had given written consent to conduct a search. Hollister had no problem allowing the officer to conduct the search.

He did not believe Rex Krebs could commit such a devious crime.

Officer Tooley mentioned to Hollister that a hat and knife had been found at the Constantine residence. Hollister explained that Krebs owned two brown corduroy baseball caps. He also informed the officer that Rex possessed an 8" fixed-blade Buck hunting knife with a black handle and a black leather sheath. He also mentioned that Krebs used to carry around a black Mini Maglite flashlight on his key ring.

Officer Tooley walked toward the back of the house with the Hollisters. He began the search of Krebs's room in their presence. He gathered up two pairs of boots in case there were footprints at the scene, a MARSHALL SUPPLY baseball cap, and a bundle of white cotton rope. Tooley mentioned the hat in his report and seemed to recall a similar cap worn by the suspect in the Shelly Crosby rape from three weeks earlier. He also remembered that the attacker had used a slightly different type of rope, almost like clothesline rope about ¼" in diameter. Tooley turned to John Hollister and asked if Rex Krebs had access to such a rope.

"I keep around thirty feet of that kind of rope out back."

"Do you mind if we go take a look?"

"Not at all," Hollister replied.

The three walked to the backyard. The rope, however, could not be located. Dumbfounded, Hollister began to search for it. After a few minutes he found the rope in the garage by a window on the east wall. It lay on top of a toolbox. Someone had re-coiled and secured it. Hollister did not recall doing either.

Tooley bagged a few more items, booked them into evidence, and headed back to the Arroyo Grande Police Department.

While Officer Tooley searched Krebs's garage, Detective John Ferdolage paid a visit to Nipomo, California, just eleven miles south of Grover Beach. He met with Anishka Constantine at her boyfriend's home. He carried with him a new photo lineup, which included a photograph of Rex Krebs. She scanned the six new photos for several minutes. Finally she pointed at the photo of Rex Krebs. She felt almost sure he attacked her; however, she feared she might send an innocent man to jail.

Detective Ferdolage then headed over to Adina Constantine's father's, also in Nipomo, to have her look at the lineup. Adina looked at the photos and within ten seconds pointed at number five on the chart: Rex Krebs.

"That looks like him," she said.

"What about photo number six?" Detective Ferdolage asked the little girl.

"No, his hair is too light."

She looked at photo number five again and repeated, "That looks like him."

Adina's father asked if she was certain. The seven-year-old vigorously nodded her head. "Yes, Daddy, I'm certain that's him."

Detective Ferdolage contacted Officer Tooley on the telephone and let him know the results of the lineups. Both parties made positive identifications of Rex Allan Krebs.

Detective Ferdolage headed over to the San Luis Obispo County Jail. On the way over, he remembered certain details of the Shelly Crosby rape from the month before. Something nagged at his brain about Krebs and the Constantine attack. His thoughts were interrupted by a phone call from Officer Tooley, who informed Detective Ferdolage that he located nylon rope in Krebs's garage similar to the one used in the attack on Shelly Crosby.

Detective Ferdolage arrived at the jail and headed for the "fish bowl," a small interview room with windows all the way around, to speak with Krebs. He introduced himself and took a seat directly across from the twenty-one-year-old ex-convict. He informed Krebs that he wanted to talk to him about the burglary and attempted rape of Anishka Constantine, as well as an earlier rape in Oceano.

"Do you recall the rights Detective Tooley read to you yesterday?"

"Yes," Krebs replied.

Detective Ferdolage proceeded to repeat those rights to Krebs, just to avoid any legal entanglements down the line if the case went to court. When he finished, the detective told Krebs that two people had positively identified him.

"Why did you go into that house?" Detective Ferdolage asked.

"I wanted to steal her stereo."

"Why did you go into the bedroom to steal her stereo and not the living room?"

"I thought it was in the bedroom."

Detective Ferdolage and Krebs continued to talk about Anishka Constantine. Krebs told the officer that he met her about a month ago while fixing her neighbor's garage door. He then told Ferdolage that he pried open her garage door with a screwdriver. Once inside the garage, he managed to get inside her house. He silently moved around the house and crept into the two bedrooms. In the second room he spotted the woman and her little girl in bed. He startled the woman and she fought with him instantly. He stated he lost his hat, knife, and flashlight in the ensuing scuffle. He did not realize he had lost his knife until he looked down at his pants and noticed that his belt had somehow come undone and the sheath had fallen off. He stressed that he had only gone to her house to steal her stereo, not to rape her.

Detective Ferdolage decided on a new tactic. He began to ask questions about the rape of Shelly Crosby in Oceano on May 24, 1987. He wanted to know if Krebs had attacked the young woman. Krebs repeatedly denied involvement in the case.

"I don't think you're telling me the truth, Rex." Detective Ferdolage was exerting more pressure.

"I'm telling you, I had nothing to do with that. I don't know anything about that."

Detective Ferdolage could sense that Krebs was ready to break. He put more pressure on him. He talked about the importance of telling the truth, of clearing one's conscience, and understanding the value of remorse. Detective Ferdolage also talked about the benefits of psychological counseling.

After several minutes, Krebs glanced down at the floor. He slowly lifted his head in Detective Ferdolage's direction. The detective waited patiently, not wanting to blow an opportunity.

"I want the counseling, but I am afraid of the time," he pathetically pleaded.

"Rex, there's obviously going to be some jail time with this kind of crime. I can't tell you how much, but our judicial system is set up so you are gonna have to do some time."

Krebs's eyes were downcast. He looked defeated.

"Why did you do this, Rex?" Detective Ferdolage desperately wanted to know.

"I don't know why I did it," Krebs sullenly replied. He tried to explain what happened with Shelly Crosby. He had been drinking at the Red Fox Bar in Grover City that night. He consumed four martinis and several beers and was intoxicated. He drove over to Farm Boys for some coffee in hopes that it would wake him up. He stated that a cute woman caught his eye as she entered the restaurant. He hoped to catch hers and maybe have a late-night rendezvous; however, she walked right past him.

"She looked down on me like I was trash," Krebs bitterly recalled.

Shelly Crosby's nonacknowledgment of Rex Krebs angered the young man, so he decided to take out his frustrations on her. He followed her home in his Volkswagen Bug, waited until she entered her home, and then waited an additional thirty minutes before he entered through an un-locked living-room window. He walked into the kitchen and grabbed a large knife from a drawer. He had a large coil of nylon rope with him. He looked around the house and found her asleep in her bedroom. He tied her up and attempted to rape her for thirty to forty-five minutes, but could not get an erection.

Krebs stated that he could not tell him any more. He began to cry.

"What's going to happen to me?" he worried aloud to Detective Ferdolage.

Rex Krebs eventually plea-bargained in the rape of Shelly Crosby and the attempted rape of Anishka Constantine. San Luis Obispo County Superior Court judge William B. Fredman sentenced Krebs to twenty years in prison. Judge Fredman, however, gave Krebs an additional admonishment.

"You're going to be in prison for a substantial period of time," Judge Fredman warned Krebs. "And you will be getting out when you will not be so old that your predisposition might not rise again and you may be tempted to commit similar offenses."

Judge Fredman encouraged Krebs to participate in as many treatment programs as possible while behind bars to avoid becoming a repeat sex offender.

"And if you get into that program," Fredman continued, "I think it will assure you that when you get out, you won't be going into the community and committing the same kind of offense again and spending the rest of your life in an institution."

THIRTY-TWO

After Rex Krebs's conviction, the courts transferred him to Chino. Chino, now known as Wasco for the Central Coast of California, is a designated intake prison. It is a holdover prison for persons convicted of crimes whose eventual prison has not yet been determined. While there, the prisoner undergoes a rigorous ninety-day evaluation. Prison officials determine whether the prisoner-to-be has gang affiliations, drug problems, or is prone to violence. Psychologists and psychiatrists check the prisoner out to determine his mental-health status.

All of these factors are weighed together to determine a "point" value for the prisoner, which then helps to determine what level of security is needed for that prisoner. This, in turn, lets officials know in which prison the convict will spend his time.

On November 5, 1987, Krebs received an administered psychological evaluation from the Chino Guidance Center. It consisted of two questions on drug and/or alcohol use and/or abuse; seven questions about mental hospitals and/or treatment; four fill-in-the-list questions concerning self-examination; a description of the offense that led to the incarceration; forty-nine questions where the respondent filled in the missing part of a sentence; and a Draw-a-Person segment, both male and female.

Concerning the drug and alcohol questions, Krebs listed that he used heroin and that he occasionally drank alcohol.

As for the mental-health questions, he did not mark either yes or no when asked if he had ever been to prison or a mental hospital for a sexual offense. He did mention, however, his stay at North Idaho Children's Home. He also stated that he often felt the need to speak with a psychiatrist, that he often felt inferior, and that it bothered him to think of what he did to "those people." He also worried about "being hurt both physicly and mentaly (*sic*)." He feared that people would not accept him as a person. Finally he requested that he would like to receive regular psychological counseling while in prison.

"I'm not sure exactly what my problem is," Krebs wrote on the form, "I hope I can be helped to realize and deal with it while I'm here."

In the fill-in-the-list portion of the evaluation, Krebs described his ambitions, who he was as a person, his personality, and how he wanted to change while in prison. His ambitions were to lead a successful and productive life, get married, have two children, and make money.

He described himself as a farmer's son who was open-minded, yet scared. He relayed that his personality was that of a fair-minded person who liked sports and the outdoors. He was a hard worker. He seemed somewhat unsure what his personality was, but he knew he liked people and people liked him. He also stated that he liked to be alone. Finally Krebs stated that he hoped to find out why he did things a certain way and to change that part of himself while in prison.

Krebs's description of the crimes that caused his imprisonment was brief. It took up only ¾" of a 7 ½" sheet of paper. The instructions stated that the prisoner could write the rest of his story on the back of the page if necessary. Krebs wrote the following:

I am not sure how I feel right now. I know I feel badly abought (*sic*) it But I don't know quiet (*sic*) how to put words to it. Im (*sic*) not sure why I did it. I Know I've had I guess fantasies abought (*sic*) Rape since I was abought (*sic*) 15 years old, I don't Know why!

Krebs also filled out all forty-nine fill-in-the-blank questions. Among them included:

#7. I don't like girls who <u>Flirt alot</u>.
#9. I could not love her because <u>she is to (*sic*) mean</u>.
#15. Sometimes sex <u>is scary</u>.
#24. Marriage <u>is what I wanted most with Liesl</u>.
#27. I almost lost hope when <u>Liesl left me</u>.
#33. My father annoyed me <u>when he beat me</u>.
#44. If I fail <u>in life it is my own fault</u>.
#49. I want my doctor to <u>help me if he or she can</u>.

Finally Krebs drew a picture of a man and woman. The man is a twenty-six-year-old standing on the beach, thinking about how he failed his family and himself. The man is at his wit's end and cannot stand himself.

The woman is a twenty-year-old who just got off work. Krebs wrote about her that she "thinks she'll go home." He described the woman as extremely tired.

Upon completion of Krebs's evaluation, California Department of Corrections officials determined that he would be best suited for the Correctional Training Facility (CTF) in Soledad, California. CTF is located approximately 26 miles southeast of Salinas, California, and approximately 150 miles southwest of Fresno. It consists of three sections: CTF South, CTF Central, and CTF North. South provides outside minimum-custody workers and offers academic, vocational, and industrial assignments for the inmates. Central is a training facility used to teach inmates life and work skills. North provides the same as Central.

The prison opened in 1946 on 680 acres in the town of Soledad when the South facility acted as a camp for San

Quentin State Prison. Central opened in 1951, followed by North in 1958. The prison added an additional dormitory to the Central building in 1984.

CTF is the largest of all the California prisons. According to the 1997 to 1998 Fiscal Year reports, CTF's budget stood at $105 million and its annual population consisted of 7,100 inmates, 213 percent more than its designed capacity.

CTF houses Security Level I and II inmates, the least likely candidates for violence. The South house is a Level I facility, while Central and North are Level IIs. The Central facility also houses a protective custody wing known as Administrative Segregation. "Ad Seg," or "the Hole," is an area where they keep certain prisoners separated from the rest of the prison population. Average time served at CTF is three to five years. Fifteen percent of the population, however, is serving a life sentence.

A number of factors determine a prisoner's security level in California: charges, sentence length, education level, military background, marital status, and family history. Prisoners at CTF receive annual reports that monitor their progress behind bars. These reports offer a numerical charting system that calculates points for or against the inmates. For instance, they may receive good time credits for work or classroom accomplishments. Prisoners will have points deducted for rule infractions, such as engaging in fights or smuggling drugs into the prison.

The prison architects designed CTF cells to be single-prisoner cells, but now they must double up. The cells are 6' x 8' and consist of a two-tiered bunk bed and a toilet.

CTF offers its inmates several educational and vocational opportunities. The goal here is to help set these criminals on a path to improve their lives upon release so that they can function in normal society. To accomplish that goal, the prison offers numerous activities: carpentry, appliance repair, printing, upholstery work, welding, landscaping, toy repair, and clothes making.

The population does not fluctuate drastically at CTF. A monthly average of seven hundred inmates are transferred to and from CTF. These include parolees and prisoners released to the Immigration and Naturalization Service (INS).

Krebs received a room assignment in the North Facility at CTF, Level II security. The North building consists of two units, one on each side of the building. Unit One is two prisoner halls and one dormitory. Unit Two is two prisoner halls. It is an open-air facility surrounded by armed guard towers.

The North Dormitory, a former gymnasium, consists of eighty double bunk beds for 160 inmates. It resembles a military barracks unit, with one big hall lined with several beds on either side.

The dormitory has a community shower area, community rest room area, two television rooms near the back of the building, and two pay phones on the back wall. Correctional officers oversee the dormitory perched on top of a podium located at the front of the room. An armed sharpshooter keeps watch at all times to make sure prisoners stay in line.

This became Rex Krebs's new home.

The inmates assigned to the North Dormitory were revered in CTF. They had the plum assignment in prison. They were the day-shift textile workers. They were allowed to leave their barracks every weekday to go and work for eight hours in a building behind the Unit One yard. They made blue jeans. They also received more pay than the other prisoners did. Seven-and-a-half cents a day.

Krebs's bed assignment was 80 Lower, located directly underneath the gunman. The other inmates considered his bed to be prime real estate. Located next to a wall, the bed only had one neighbor to the right of it. He also had a direct sightline to the podium, so he could keep an eye on the guard. Eighty Lower also provided a perfect vantage point for the rest of the dormitory, perfect for keeping your eye on other, more volatile inmates.

Krebs, however, seemed to get along with almost everyone in the North Dormitory. The prisoners respected him and went to him if they had a problem. He listened intently and made good suggestions on a myriad of problems. The prison staff liked him as well. He usually stayed out of trouble and worked hard.

Rex's hard work paid off with his ordination as the Caucasian representative for the Men's Advisory Council (MAC). The MAC adviser is an exalted position in the prison system. The MAC adviser acts as a liaison between the prison staff and the ethnic group represented. If there are problems between certain ethnic groups, the MAC adviser can approach the prison staff and attempt to work out the problem. In addition, if there is a problem between a particular prisoner and a specific guard, the MAC adviser can approach the prison representatives without fear of reprisal and attempt to solve the problem. The purpose of MAC is to open up the channels of communication among the prisoners and between the prisoners and the guards. In addition, the hope is that by opening up these channels, prisoners will use violence less often to resolve conflicts.

Krebs loved his role as the MAC adviser. One had to be elected by the other inmates in his dorm, which meant he had to have a good relationship with others in the building. Krebs held the position for three years. He liked that he had a responsibility to keep the attitude in the dormitory calm. He also liked being in charge when it came to informing the other inmates when a lockdown occurred.

Krebs considered anything that drew attention away from his actual crimes a good thing. The prison system has an internal pecking order among its inmates. There is a hierarchy of acceptable and despicable crimes in prison. It is a bizarre code of cell ethics.

The lowest of the low are the rapists and child molesters.

A certain machismo seems to exist among hardened criminals. The predatory sex offenders do not rank on that scale of macho crimes. Other prisoners look down on sex offenders as scumbags who are too weak to pick on someone their own size and who must attack defenseless people for their personal gratification.

If a prisoner finds out that one of their cellmates or dorm mates is a child molester or rapist, the response is usually not pretty. Gang rapes in the shower are common. Male rape by prisoners inflicted with AIDS assures a death sentence for some. Others have slits across their faces made with a homemade shiv. It marks their true nature, that way if a sex offender is transferred to a new prison, the new prisoners will know what crime he committed.

Rex Krebs managed to keep his crimes a secret from the rest of his dormitory mates. He did this by claiming that he was a "lifer." A lifer is someone in prison for life, usually for murder. It is common knowledge among prisoners not to mess with lifers because they will kill you in the blink of an eye. They have nothing to lose.

The ruse also kept Krebs from participating in any psychological counseling while in prison. He did not attend meetings for sex offenders because the other inmates would then know that he had raped women and attacked little girls. He kept his mouth shut and stayed away from the shrinks.

Krebs's time in CTF seemed rather unremarkable. He kept his nose clean, stayed out of fights most of the time, did a good job with the MAC, did his job in the textiles department, and kept up a good working relationship with the correctional officers. He also spent much of his spare time working with leather or jewelry crafts.

He also had an affinity for belt buckles. He would sit for hours in his cell making sketches and designs for unique belt buckles. His favorite buckle contained the infinity logo, or the number 8 on its side. Apparently, the number had a significant meaning for Rex. According to sources, he had a fascination with Egyptian numerology and the number 8 specifically. Anja Heij's report on the meaning of the word "infinity" comes up with an interesting description: "Progress or change is accomplished by walking both sides of the spectrum, usually named opposites, switching over once a critical mass has been reached, thus finding a new balance time after time."

Some numerologists view the number 8 as a symbol of death and resurrection. It has also come to symbolize the masculine and feminine sides of an individual. In sexual terms infinity is a form of sexual congress between a man and a woman.

The circle represents the purest form of life. When the two circles join in harmony, they make the perfect symbol of infinity. Unfortunately, the circles can create a negative reaction, throwing everything into a state of flux. Regardless of the outcome, the number 8 ultimately represents the concept of total responsibility for one's life.

According to numerologists, the number 8 also deals with everyday practical matters. It requires hard work and attention to detail. The bottom line with the number 8 is that in order to get what you want out of life, you must reap before you sow.

People with the number 8 as their key number tend to be team leaders, but not the ultimate boss. They keep the ship running. Eights also view intimacy as a waste of time. There are more important things out there that need tending, they seem to think.

Others interpret it to signify death and resurrection: the infinite cycle. The infinity symbol can be both masculine and feminine energies that comprise a harmonious synergy between the two. It may represent karma or the repayment of karma.

Possibly the most bizarre read is of the Ogdoad—eight deities who were the basis of the creation of Egypt. They were comprised of a masculine/feminine pairing and represent an "aspect of the primordial chaos out of which the world was created." The gods are men with the hair of snakes, while goddesses have the heads of frogs.

Correctional Officer Concepcion Aguilar believed that Krebs owned a round black key chain with the number 8 on it.

Despite Krebs's seemingly good behavior, he was no angel.

He was busted for having "pruno," prison-generated alcohol, in his cell. He had an altercation with one of the female correctional officers. Some of the other guards mentioned that Krebs sulked quite a bit. If he got into a verbal disagreement with one of the guards or one of the other prisoners, he would avoid a physical confrontation. Instead, he would dejectedly walk back to his bunk bed and begin to fiddle with his belt buckles.

In 1996 Krebs moved out of the textile job into an even better gig. He became Officer Aguilar's porter, or personal janitor. Every inmate wanted to be a porter. It was an easy job and one got to work alone.

Krebs's hard work and good behavior would ultimately be a huge benefit to him.

THIRTY-THREE

On September 2, 1997, the California Board of Prison Terms granted parole for Rex Krebs. He had only served ten years of his twenty-year sentence.

The California Board of Prison Terms, according to its Web site (www.bpt.ca.gov/home.html), "conducts parole consideration hearings for all inmates sentenced to life terms with the possibility of parole, establishes terms and conditions for all persons released on parole in California, and conducts parole revocation hearings for violations of the terms and conditions of parole."

The Board of Prison Terms also conducts hearings for prisoners who suffer from mental disorders and prisoners or parolees in "revoked status who meet the criteria for sexually violent predator status." The Board of Prison Terms also has the power to resentence some prisoners if they believe their sentencing duration is not fair or is not harsh enough.

The Board of Prison Terms is comprised of nine commissioners appointed by the governor of California. Commissionerships are full-time positions that allow commissioners to travel around the state and participate on parole-hearing panels comprised of three representatives, two of whom must be commissioners.

According to the California Board of Prison Terms Web site, the board's mission statement is "to protect and preserve public safety through the exercise of its statutory authorities and policies, while ensuring due process to all criminal offenders who come under the Board's jurisdiction."

This seemingly innocent, progressive mentality must be viewed under the harsh light of the reality of Rex Krebs's potential for recidivism at the time of his parole. According to the Center for Sex Offender Management organization's study entitled "Recidivism of Sex Offenders," Rex Krebs would have been a perfect candidate for *not* being released back into society. The center's study describes a process whereby the criminal justice system can determine whether a sex offender who is up for parole should be set free. The fear is that a paroled sex offender may commit a similar offense once faced with the temptations of the modern world.

The report cites a 1980 study, conducted by John Taylor and Vikki Henlie Sturgeon, which is a five-year follow-up on a 1973 study of mentally disordered sex offenders released from the maximum-security Atascadero State Hospital in San Luis Obispo, California. Their study indicated that ten of the fifty-seven rapists who were under supervision for the study were reconvicted of rape within five years.

Nineteen percent.

Most within the first year of their release.

Prisoners with no mental disorders were even worse. Nineteen of the paroled sex offenders, or 28 percent, were reconvicted of rape within the next five years.

Moreover, these are just the reported rapes.

Another study, conducted by the National Crime Victimization Surveys, also spotlighted in the center's study, pointed out the seriousness of underreporting the crime of rape. According to the results, only 32 percent of all sexual assaults are reported to the police. An additional study cited by the center showed that in a group of 4,008 women studied, of the women who reported that they were rape victims, 84 percent of them did not report the attack to the authorities.

According to the center's study, there is a plethora of reasons why rape victims do not report:

- Further victimization by the offender
- Other forms of retribution by the offender or by the offender's friends or family
- Arrest, prosecution, and incarceration of an offender who may be a family member or friend and on whom the victim or others may depend
- Others finding out about the sexual assault (including friends, family members, media, and the public)
- Not being believed
- Being traumatized by the criminal-justice system response

Such underreporting of rape would possibly skew the Sturgeon and Taylor numbers even higher that a paroled rapist will rape again. This information was available to the Board of Prison Terms when its commissioners released Rex Allan Krebs.

The Center for Sex Offender Management also offers a concise checklist to determine whether to parole a sex offender. A twelve-question checklist could easily provide information about the potential parolee to a parole board and help them make a clear, reasonable choice before granting parole. The characteristics to consider, according to the center, include:

- Multiple victims
- Diverse victims
- Stranger victims
- Juvenile sexual offenses
- Multiple paraphilias (or sexual fetishes)
- History of abuse and neglect

- Long-term separations from parents
- Negative relationships with their mothers
- Diagnosed antisocial personality disorder
- Unemployed
- Substance abuse problems
- Chaotic, antisocial lifestyles

Rex Krebs's name could appear beside almost every single one of these criteria. Apparently, the Board of Prison Terms failed to use such a checklist when they decided to free Krebs.

The Board of Prison Terms made an egregious error ten years earlier in the case of Lawrence Singleton, convicted in 1979 for the kidnap, attempted murder, and brutal rape and maiming of fifteen-year-old Mary Vincent. Singleton hacked off both of Vincent's arms at the elbow with a hatchet after he raped her. He left her to bleed to death in a ditch off the side of Interstate 5 in Del Puerto Canyon, California. Vincent somehow managed to crawl to safety and later acted as chief eyewitness against the sadistic rapist.

Singleton only received a fourteen-year-and-eight-month sentence for his crime. Incredibly, the Board of Prison Terms released him for "time off for good behavior." The main reason the "good behavior" system is in effect is due to prison overcrowding. California prisons, such as Correctional Training Facility in Soledad, are overflowing with nonviolent drug offenders. As a result, the parole board in California—inexplicably—occasionally releases potentially dangerous recidivist criminals and rapists.

The decision by the Board of Prison Terms to release Singleton proved to be a fatal one. On February 19, 1997, less than seven months before Rex Krebs would go before the board, Singleton stabbed to death Roxanne Hayes, a prostitute from Tampa, Florida, his new home. The police found the nude geriatric Singleton covered in blood as he stood over the mutilated body of Hayes.

The Board of Prison Terms knew they were under scrutiny. Armed with the knowledge of the rate of recidivism among rapists and the negative publicity because of the Singleton case, the board would make its decision on Rex Krebs.

Should they release the sex offender or make him serve out his twenty-year sentence?

Their final decision proved, again, to be fatal.

THIRTY-FOUR

On September 2, 1997, Rex Allan Krebs met with David Zaragoza, his parole officer, for the first time at the California Men's Colony (CMC) in San Luis Obispo.

The former inmate stepped outside of confinement for the first time in ten years.

Krebs had $375 in his pocket and an escort to boot.

Zaragoza drove to downtown San Luis Obispo, where he pulled into the dusty parking lot of the Motel 6, located on Calle Joaquin, off Monterey Street. He exited his Jeep Cherokee and marched firmly to the motel lobby. He noticed the motel manager behind the counter and informed him that he needed a room for a paroled felon. Zaragoza glanced down at Krebs, who stared forlornly at his feet. His bald head stared back at the manager, who checked the register, spotted an open room, and informed the parole officer that he had one room available for one week. The cost would be $150. Zaragoza proceeded to room 101, checked it out from top to bottom for contraband, and gave it his approval.

Rex Krebs had a new home. Only for a while.

Within less than two weeks, Rex Krebs also had a new job. He answered an advertisement in the local newspaper for 84 Lumber, a national lumber company that sells wood products used for home building by exuberant do-it-yourselfers. Krebs filled out an application, hitched a ride to the store on South Higuera Street, and scored an interview with the store manager, Greg Vieau. Apparently, Krebs impressed Vieau enough to warrant a callback interview. Krebs also met with another store manager and the area manager. The three bosses were so impressed with Krebs that they asked him to come back for a second round of interviews, along with two other candidates.

Once again Krebs impressed Vieau. He got another callback. This time it came down to between him and one other applicant. The yard person position entailed brutal work. Whoever was hired would have to unload heavy stacks of wood early in the morning, place them on forklifts, and then transfer them to the company's trucks for delivery later that same morning. Vieau believed Krebs to be a viable candidate because it appeared as if, physically, he could take care of himself.

The scrawny teenager from Idaho had bulked up in prison.

Krebs took to weight lifting in Soledad like a baby to candy. He was proud of his physique and could handle any physical chore. His biceps seemed to bulge out another five inches and his broad shoulders and flat abs were comparable to a *Rambo*-era Sylvester Stallone.

Vieau knew about Krebs's criminal history. He did not care. He believed Krebs would be the right man for the job and called him in to offer him the position. When Krebs entered Vieau's office, he believed he would receive bad news.

"I know why I didn't get the job," Krebs dejectedly and prematurely stated to Vieau.

"No, you got the job," Vieau informed the parolee.

Krebs said nothing. Ten seconds later, a broad grin began to stretch across Krebs's face.

That grin faded when Krebs arrived at his new job for the first time, on September 15, at 6:45 A.M. Not because he was not excited about getting a job so fast, but because he knew it would be tough work. Nevertheless, he was up to the task.

Indeed, he began to enjoy the long twelve-hour workdays in the perpetually sunny climate of Central California. The strain on his body made him feel strong. The lifting of the bulky wood tested his muscles to their maximum capacity. The sweat flowed liberally from every pore in his body. He felt free again.

Alive, for the first time.

THIRTY-FIVE

Rex Krebs took the San Luis Obispo Transit bus to get to work in the beginning. One day he hopped on the bus and looked up at the female bus driver. Her name was Carol Nunes. She smiled at him and went on her way. After a few more encounters, she finally struck up a conversation with him. Nunes related to Krebs that one of her coworkers might be interested. "I know a girl who you might get along with. She's real cute, about twenty-one years old. Her name is Roslynn Moore. We call her Roz."

"When can I meet her?" Krebs asked with a sense of excitement in his voice.

"Where do you live? I'll bring her over."

"Motel 6, Room 101."

Carol was as good as her word. She brought Roz with her to meet Rex at his motel room. Krebs immediately noticed the creamy coffee color of her mixed-heritage skin. The frail, bespectacled Moore appeared demure but inquisitive to Krebs. She weighed all of one hundred pounds soaking wet and stood 5'2".

Much smaller than Rex.

This pleased him to no end.

Unlike Krebs, Moore had an education. Her interests as a young teenager were dance and visual arts. She dreamed of becoming a professional ballerina. She graduated from a creative/performing arts high school. Unfortunately, Roz permanently injured her knee. Dancing was no longer an

option. She turned her focus to illustration. After she graduated from high school, she attended the Academy of Art
College in San Francisco. She became disillusioned with
the San Francisco art scene and made the decision to relocate to San Luis Obispo in July 1997. Some of her friends
had bought a house in San Luis Obispo and invited her to
join them. She agreed, packed her bags, and hit the road.
As soon as she arrived, she found work with the San Luis
Obispo Transit Authority as a bus driver.

A little over a month later, she met Rex Krebs.

That mid-September, Carol Nunes hit Roz up to go out
with her. "C'mon, Wayne's going to the football game," she
referred to her husband, Wayne Nunes. "We need to hit the
town."

"I don't really want to do anything tonight," Roz demurred.

"C'mon, we'll have a good time."

"All right," Roz relented.

The two women drove over to Tio Alberto's, a local Mexican-food restaurant, for dinner. As soon as they settled into
their chairs, Carol began to talk about a man she met, whose
name she could not remember. Carol explained to Roz that
the man rode on her bus several times a week and that he had
just gotten out of prison. Roz blanched at the mention of
prison. Carol went on to explain that she had not seen the man
in quite a while and was concerned.

"I remember he told me he lived in the Motel 6," Carol
continued.

"Which one—the one by Margie's Diner?" Roz inquired.

"I don't know, but we can check it out."

The two women headed over to Motel 6, the one next to
Margie's Diner. Once inside the lobby, they asked the manager if he knew their man. He told them he did not, so they
decided it must not be the right Motel 6.

They jumped into Carol's car and moseyed over to the
Motel 6 located next to the Denny's restaurant on Los Osos
Road on the southernmost tip of San Luis Obispo. Once

again they asked the manager about Carol's mystery man. The manager informed them that the man did indeed stay at the motel. He phoned the man up, told him there were two women looking for him, and asked if he wanted to speak to them. The manager hung up the phone.

"He'll be right down."

Sure enough, two minutes later, Rex Krebs appeared in the lobby. He said hello to Carol and nodded in Roz's direction.

"Ya'll want to come back to my room?" he plaintively asked.

Once back at Krebs's room, Carol and Roz stood outside of his door and spoke with him for the next ninety minutes. Carol expressed her concern over not seeing him on the bus and that she was just looking out for him. Krebs told her he was doing fine. He appreciated her concern. The three spoke about themselves, their jobs, their hobbies. The girls gave him their phone numbers and told him to call if he ever needed any help. Again Krebs expressed his gratitude. He smiled at Roz as she walked away from in front of his room.

The next day, he called her.

"Hi, Roz, it's me, Rex Krebs. From last night. How are you?"

"I'm fine, Rex. What's going on?"

"I just wanted to see if I could come over and see you?"

Roz began to worry. She knew he recently got out of prison. But for what charges? "How about we meet for lunch instead?"

They agreed to meet at Taco Bell downtown. They spent the next two hours talking about their lives.

One week later, they began to hang out together even more. Soon they were in an intimate relationship. The skinny, mixed-race, artsy twenty-one-year-old bus driver and the muscled, short, white, bald thirty-one-year-old paroled rapist did not seem to be your usual pairing.

THIRTY-SIX

On September 19, 1997, Rex Krebs informed David Zaragoza that he found a place to stay. He felt it was time to vacate the Motel 6 and set up more permanent digs. Carol and Wayne Nunes offered to let Krebs move in with them.

Twenty-five-year-old Wayne Nunes worked as a press operator. Carol mentioned to Wayne that Krebs might make a suitable roommate for their newly purchased condominium in Atascadero, a small community approximately twenty-five miles north of San Luis Obispo. Their two-bedroom, one-and-a-half-bathroom condominium had plenty of room for a third person, and the Nuneses needed the money. Wayne, however, had concerns about Krebs's prison history. He wanted to know what crime Krebs committed to warrant imprisonment for ten years. Krebs told Wayne he went to prison because of a date rape. He explained that he and his girlfriend at the time were strung out on drugs; he wanted to have sex with her and she did not; he then forced himself on her.

Apparently, this explanation satisfied both Wayne and Carol. They made Krebs an offer to move in, which he readily accepted.

Rex Krebs moved into his new home in the Vista del Norte Condominiums on El Camino Real during the first week in October. Krebs usually rose before the sun came up, headed out to his job five days a week, and oftentimes worked ten-to-twelve-hour days. Though usually exhausted, he also made time for Roz.

As part of Krebs's parole, he had a curfew. He was required to be home every night by 9:00 P.M. and could not leave. He also could not drink alcohol. These restrictions limited the couple's options for entertainment. They would usually head over to the Thursday-night farmers' market on Higuera Street and pick over the vegetables.

Krebs told Roz everything about his sordid past. He told her why he went to prison. He told her about the rape and the attempted rape in 1987. He also told her about his conditions for parole. Despite this new information, Roz found him charming. She liked that he brought her a flower one time when they went out. She liked that he had manners and treated her like a lady. She liked that he carried her backpack full of books or that he bought her dinner. She loved the attention that he showered upon her. She did not care that he had sexually molested other women years before. He belonged to her.

Krebs was doing everything he was supposed to do. He stood out at 84 Lumber as one of the best workers. Greg Vieau even hired him to help with personal chores. Krebs also reported to John Blum, his new parole officer, on a regular basis with no problem. He also kept up his relationship with Roz. The ex-convict's life definitely seemed to be in turnaround.

By the time 1998 arrived, Rex Krebs appeared to be living a blessed life. Good job, good relationship, and good relations with the authorities. On January 21 Parole Officer Debra Austin was assigned to Krebs's case.

His third parole officer in five months.

To maintain a sense of continuity on parolees, the State of California Department of Corrections requires that parole officers keep a record of supervision, or parole packet. The parole packet is a progress report of sorts used to record the meetings that take place between the assigned parole officer and the parolee. Officers are to log in their observations of the parolee, work patterns, and contact with any individuals—such as roommates, relatives, love interests, neighbors, etc. It is used to detail the parolee's current work status and to track if the parolee is adhering to the conditions of his/her parole. In Rex Krebs's case, for example, Austin made a notation in Kreb's parole packet as to whether or not he had maintained his 290-registration requirement. It is a requirement for all paroled sex offenders to sign up with the local police department stating that they are sex offenders.

Parole Officer Austin noted that Krebs had difficulty registering in February 1998. Krebs claimed that he attempted to reregister at the San Luis Obispo Sheriff's Department; however, the clerk responsible for maintaining the record books was not available. This irritated Krebs because he had called the station before he arrived to make sure someone would be there to register him. Subsequently he had not registered since. Austin informed him to return to the sheriff's department and register. He complied.

Krebs also complained to Austin that he never received his hobby craft items from CTF. He added that he had mailed a money order to the prison, but he never received a package. Austin picked up the phone and contacted Soledad hobby craft manager Danny Ybarra to ask for Krebs's crafts. She wanted her parolee to know that she would gladly help him out.

When it comes to recently released convicts, help is usually hard to find.

Rex Krebs, however, seemed to have people falling over themselves to help get him back on his feet. In addition to Parole Officer Austin, Krebs also received additional support from Greg Vieau. His boss helped Krebs establish a bank account at 84 Lumber's bank by personally asking the clerk to set Krebs up with his own personal checking account.

Vieau also aided Rex with the purchase of a well-kept 1993 blue Ford Ranger extended cab pickup truck. Vieau noticed a neighbor of his in Los Osos had the truck sitting outside for a long period of time and it had not been used in a while. He approached the neighbor who informed him that the truck belonged to his son. Vieau asked the neighbor if his son would be willing to sell it because he knew someone who could use it. Vieau called Krebs up to take a look at the vehicle. Krebs noted that the truck needed some work, but Vieau convinced the neighbor to sell it to Krebs for next to nothing.

Vieau also hired Krebs to do work around his house. He once asked Krebs to come over and help him assemble his children's swing set. Vieau also owned a house next door to his rental house. The house he owned was not in great condition. According to Vieau, fleas had infested the house. The previous owners smoked a plethora of cigarettes and covered the inside with smoke smell and tar stains on the walls. Vieau had been renting the Los Osos house and his rental contract was close to expiration. He needed a rush job on the cleanup of the house next door and asked Krebs to be his man. He had two weeks to complete the job, but Vieau had total faith in his employee.

Krebs did not disappoint. The two men worked together during the day at 84 Lumber, then went over to Vieau's property in the early evening. The two men thoroughly cleaned up the filthy site and hauled all of the trash out to the local dump. They spent every night for the next two weeks working until midnight or one in the morning. They scrubbed floors, painted, and tore carpets out—anything to rid the place of the stench and bugs. Somehow they got the job done and Vieau was able to move into his new home.

Krebs worked hard for Greg Vieau. He wanted his boss to know that he truly believed he could reform himself, that he could contribute positively to society.

Vieau rewarded him with a steady job, a dependable truck, and extra income on the side. The two even became friends. Sometimes they would go out to grab a bite to eat. Vieau also invited Krebs and Moore over for cookouts. Everything seemed to be rolling along smoothly.

Krebs, however, did get tired of the twenty-five-mile commute to and from Atascadero. He and Roz decided to move

into San Luis Obispo with four of Roz's friends from Cal
Poly—Isreal Peña, Christopher Amos, Jeff Bell, and Bell's
wife, Luisa Jamesbravo. The six roommates cloistered together
in a tiny rental home near campus.

It was not long before Roz's friends found out about
Krebs's criminal history.

On April 21, 1998, Parole Officer Austin contacted Bell
and told him about Krebs's violent past. After hanging up,
Bell contacted his wife, Peña, and Amos and let them know
that he wanted to hold a meeting to discuss Krebs's living status at their house.

That night Bell informed everyone that Krebs had raped
two women more than ten years earlier and that he had been
paroled from prison only eight months earlier. Without hesitation the other three roommates agreed that both Rex and
Roz had to go.

They even changed the locks on the door the next day.

Krebs and Moore went their separate ways after they
moved out, yet they remained a couple. Roz moved into a
room of a coworker's house in Los Osos. They shared the
home with a third female roommate. Krebs, meanwhile,
stayed at a local hotel. Roz's roommate made it clear that
Krebs was not welcome in her home. Krebs barely saw Roz
during that first month. Roz lived with the two women until
her coworker moved out one month later. That is when Krebs
started to visit.

"I could tell he was a real shady character with a mean look
to him," Roz's remaining roommate told the Cal Poly *Mustang Daily* school newspaper. "He seemed friendly in
conversation. But, he was kind of a creepy guy. He just wasn't
a clean-cut guy; he got into fights at the bar. . . . He had kind
of a mean look to him."

Roz's roommate never felt comfortable when Krebs came
over. "I like to think I can defend myself," she continued, "but
I know I couldn't defend myself against this man."

She noted that Krebs would tag along with her and Roz

whenever they would head downtown to the local college bars, in direct violation of his parole conditions. Roz's roommate did not like being seen with Krebs.

"He wasn't somebody I really wanted to know."

At times Roslynn Moore wished she had never known Rex Krebs. The two lovers were constantly at odds with one another. They would fight over the smallest issue. By February 1998 their relationship had hit a sour note. They broke up after a nasty fight outside of the Nuneses' condominium in Atascadero. One month later, they were back together. By April they were fighting again. This time, because they were both in the process of moving to new places and barely saw one another. This, of course, raised the tension level in their relationship.

Roz's friends also began to whisper in her ear. They believed Rex Krebs was cheating. Roz blew up when she heard this and angrily confronted him. He denied the accusations, but Roz did not believe him. She screamed, "Go to hell!" and broke up with him again.

Krebs decided he needed to deal with the tension with Roz in some way. He decided the best way was with alcohol. Krebs began to frequent the biker bar in Atascadero known as Outlaws. The restaurant/bar was also home to a poker room known as the Card Parlour. Krebs usually dressed up in a pair of blue jeans, a white muscle T-shirt to show off his massive biceps, and an oversize black cowboy hat. He attempted to portray an imposing figure in the rough crowd—someone with whom you did not want to mess, someone who could take care of himself.

In late February 1998 Krebs found an unusual way to make a friend at the bar. One night a fight broke out between an African American male and a Hispanic male. The two men were throwing down right in the middle of the bar—haymakers were flying. Dan Thomspon, the Outlaws bouncer, all 6'5", 290 pounds of him, jumped in and grabbed the Hispanic man in a giant bear hug. Thompson recalled,

"I put my arms around him. He was out of the fight then, but that's when I realized the fight already ended." Thompson continued, "It's common practice for me, when I wrap my arms around somebody, I'm telling them the whole time, 'I'm a bouncer, don't turn around and try to swing at me.' This time was odd because I had said, 'Man, who are you fighting?' and the guy said, 'Man, he's right down here by my feet.'" Thompson looked down at the floor and saw Rex Krebs. The short, bald ex-convict had subdued the black man. "It was completely over. And Rex took him out one door and I took my guy out another door and made sure they went their separate ways."

Thompson dusted off his britches, turned toward Krebs, and stuck out his huge hand. Krebs accepted the offering and said, "My name's Rex."

"I'm Dan, nice to meet you."

It was the unusual beginning of a close relationship.

Thompson described their friendship as something bigger than the usual bullshit male bonding. "We seemed to have a kindred spirit as far as when I look into—when he spoke to me, he looked into my eyes and I looked into his and I knew he wasn't hiding anything." Thompson's praise of Krebs's character increased as he spoke about his new friend: "It's just, what's up? How are you doing? Face value. And he shot from the hip and in between the eyes." He mixed his metaphors. "It was pretty easy to talk to him."

Thompson and Krebs began to see each other every weekend at Outlaws. Despite the fact that Krebs clearly violated his parole conditions by stepping foot into the bar, Thompson added that Krebs stayed sober—for a while. Krebs mainly hung out to lend Thompson a hand when any of the Outlaws patrons became a little too unruly. As the two bonded over bouncing, Thompson began to open up to his new friend. He let Krebs know that times were tough financially and that he needed a second job. Krebs told Thompson about his job at 84 Lumber in San Luis Obispo and that he happened to be very good friends with the store manager. He assured his new buddy that he would see what he could do for him.

When Krebs talked, things happened. Within a matter of weeks, Krebs hooked Thompson up with a job at the lumber company stocking drywall. By this time Krebs ran the entire outdoor lumberyard at 84 Lumber. One of the tasks in the yard was loading drywall. Krebs convinced Greg Vieau that Thompson's size would benefit the company. Vieau trusted Krebs and told him to hire his friend.

Krebs's kindness toward Thompson did not stop at getting him a job. He also picked up Thompson and took him to work every day in his Ford Ranger. Thompson attempted to repay Krebs's kindness by inviting him into his personal world. Thompson introduced Krebs to his girlfriend, Jamie Beth Prisco. Jamie and Dan invited Krebs over to their place for dinner. Eventually, Rex and Roz would get back together and Dan and Jamie asked Krebs if they could meet her. He agreed and brought her over to their house for dinner. Jamie and Roz hit it off instantly and became fast friends. Soon the two couples spent every weekend together at Outlaws while Dan worked and Krebs had his back. Eventually Krebs started to partake of the alcoholic beverages that the bar had to offer.

He preferred Jack Daniel's and Coke.

THIRTY-SEVEN

Rex Krebs briefly stayed at Greg Vieau's house in Los Osos. In less than two weeks, on May 9, 1998, Rex found a quiet, tiny studio apartment located on Bajada Avenue near Traffic Way in Atascadero, the same town where he lived with Wayne and Carol Nunes. He lived in an attachment to a larger house out front. According to Parole Officer Debra Austin, Krebs's apartment was excruciatingly small. It consisted of one room, which acted as his bedroom, living room, and kitchen, and a small bathroom. Austin paid Krebs a visit to his new domicile on May 19, 1998, at 8:40 P.M.

"Hello, Rex," Parole Officer Austin intoned after Krebs answered his front door.

"Hello, Ms. Austin," he courteously replied while opening the door to let her in.

"Rex, I just want to take a look around and make sure everything is in order here."

"No problem."

"Are you still working at 84 Lumber?" Austin inquired as she began to walk around the studio apartment. Nothing seemed to catch her eye.

"Yes, ma'am."

"How is Roslynn?" Austin wanted to know if their relationship was holding up.

"Ummm, not so hot. She needs some serious growing up to do."

Rachel Newhouse, 20.
*(Courtesy of the
San Luis Obispo
County Superior Court)*

Rachel Newhouse and family at her brother's high school
graduation. *(Courtesy of the San Luis Obispo County Superior Court)*

Aundria Crawford, 20, leans against her Mustang.
(Courtesy of the San Luis Obispo County Superior Court)

Aundria Crawford, proud graduate of Clovis High School.
(Courtesy of the San Luis Obispo County Superior Court)

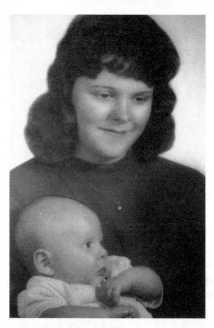

Connie Krebs holds her infant son, Rex.
(Courtesy of the San Luis Obispo County Superior Court)

Sixteen-year-old Rex Krebs sits on the lawn outside
the Northern Idaho Children's Home in Lewiston, Idaho.
(Courtesy of the San Luis Obispo County Superior Court)

Krebs after his 1984 arrest for attacking a 12-year-old girl in Sandpoint, Idaho. *(Courtesy of the San Luis Obispo County Superior Court)*

Allan Krebs with his teenaged son, Rex. *(Courtesy of the San Luis Obispo County Superior Court)*

Krebs after his 1987 arrest for attempted rape in California.
Notice the cut on his nose caused by his victim.
(Courtesy of the San Luis Obispo County Superior Court)

San Luis Obispo
parole officer David
Zaragoza suspected
Krebs after reading
about Aundria
Crawford's abduction
in the local paper.
*(Courtesy of
David Zaragoza)*

Krebs's garage apartment located deep within the woods of Davis Canyon. He repeatedly raped then killed Aundria Crawford in his bedroom. *(Author's photo)*

A smiling Krebs poses for a photo for his father during Allan Krebs's visit to San Luis Obispo in January 1999, less than two months after he murdered Rachel Newhouse. *(Courtesy of the San Luis Obispo County Superior Court)*

Aundria Crawford's 8-ball key chain was discovered inside a wooden box that belonged to Krebs.
(Author's photo)

Primary Investigator Larry Hobson elicited confessions from Rex Krebs.
(Courtesy of Larry Hobson)

Krebs confesses to the murders of Rachel Newhouse and
Aundria Crawford to primary investigator Larry Hobson.
(*Courtesy of the San Luis Obispo County Superior Court*)

Rachel Newhouse was last seen alive outside of Tortilla Flats
after an argument with her roommate. (*Author's photo*)

Jennifer Street Bridge, where Rex Krebs attacked Rachel Newhouse and then abducted her. *(Author's photo)*

The battered, dilapidated A-frame house where Krebs raped and later killed Rachel Newhouse. *(Courtesy of the San Luis Obispo County Superior Court)*

The blood-stained couch in the A-frame house where
Krebs raped then killed Rachel Newhouse.
(Courtesy of the San Luis Obispo County Superior Court)

Aundria Crawford's
condo, where she was
abducted by Rex Krebs.
(Author's photo)

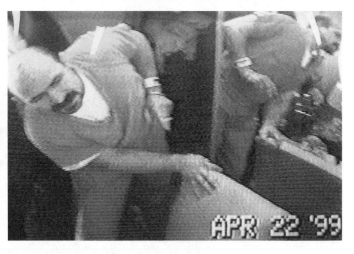

Krebs during a walk-though of his apartment after his confession.
(Courtesy of the San Luis Obispo County Superior Court)

FBI agents begin the excavation of Rachel Newhouse's body
approximately 100 yards away from Krebs's apartment.
(Courtesy of the San Luis Obispo County Superior Court)

Location of Aundria Crawford's burial site behind Krebs's apartment.
(Courtesy of the San Luis Obispo County Superior Court)

District Attorney John Trice
(Courtesy of San Luis Obispo Tribune)

Defense attorneys
James Maguire III and
Patricia Ashbaugh.
*(Courtesy of James Maguire III
and Patricia Ashbaugh)*

Judge Barry LaBarbera.
*(Courtesy of
Jeff Greene/ImageWest
Photography)*

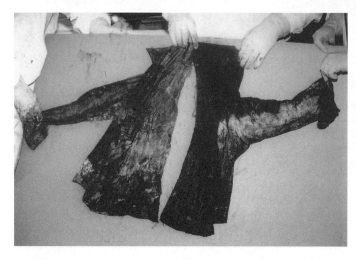

Rachel Newhouse's shirt which Krebs slit up the back before he raped her. *(Courtesy of the San Luis Obispo County Superior Court)*

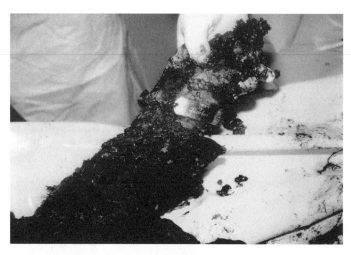

Medical examiners hold the mud-encrusted arm of Rachel Newhouse. Her bracelet with her name is visible. *(Courtesy of the San Luis Obispo County Superior Court)*

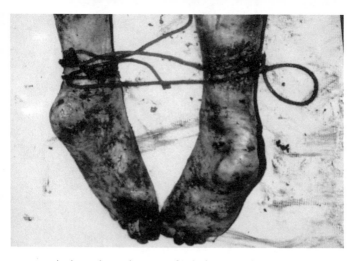

Rex Krebs bound Aundria Crawford's legs together at the ankles.
(Courtesy of the San Luis Obispo County Superior Court)

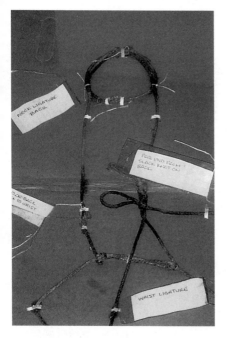

A portion of the rope Rex Krebs used to hog-tie Aundria Crawford.
(Courtesy of the San Luis Obispo County Superior Court)

Memorial plaque located on the Jennifer Street Bridge.
(Author's photo)

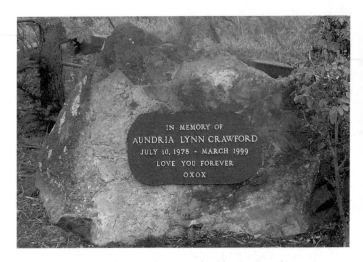

Memorial stone for Aundria Crawford located on the campus
of Cuesta College. *(Author's photo)*

"What do you mean, Rex?" Austin sidled her way into the kitchen, where something finally did attract her attention. Several oversize, gleaming kitchen knives lay out on the kitchen counter.

"She's only twenty-two, immature. You know how young girls can get," Rex said in a light yet exasperated tone.

Austin stepped up to the counter and grabbed one of the sharp instruments. "Rex, we need to talk about these. I think you better start putting these away in their proper drawers and not leave them out on the counter."

"Yes, ma'am. I'll make sure to do that."

"One more thing, Rex," Austin continued, "I have some good news for you. I am deleting two of your parole conditions. You no longer will have the nine P.M. curfew. You can stay out as late as you want. Also, you do not have to report to me on a weekly basis anymore."

Krebs slowly began to smile. It quickly spread from ear to ear as he reached out to grasp Austin's hand. He began to pump it furiously and stated over and over, "Thank you so much. That's wonderful news. Thank you so much."

Nothing good would come of the decision.

One month later, everything began to fall apart for Rex Krebs.

Rex and Roz's relationship had been on the downward spiral for months, ever since they moved out of Jeff Bell's house. Roz, however, attempted to patch things up, even though she was supposedly mad that Krebs had been seeing other women. He vociferously denied her accusations, but she did not seem convinced. That June, Roz stopped by to see what Krebs was doing. He seemed somewhat perturbed by her unannounced appearance but let her inside anyway. Their conversation started friendly enough but soon evolved into a full-blown argument.

"Rex, you can't go to Outlaws. It's against your probation requirements," Roz pleaded with him. "I don't want to see you get hauled back into prison."

"I ain't gonna get put back in prison," he replied. He threw on his light coat and grabbed the keys to his Ford Ranger.

"But you're not supposed to be around any alcohol of any kind," she continued.

"I'm not gonna drink any," he angrily retorted.

"Rex, you need to stay home and out of trouble."

"No, I'm going and that's final!" he yelled at her, tearing out through the front door of the apartment and slamming the door behind him.

Roslynn began to cry. Then she went looking for something to drink in Rex's refrigerator. She hit the jackpot when she discovered several bottles of Jack Daniel's wine coolers. She found a bottle opener, popped the top, and began to toss back the bitter concoction. Her slight body size made it easy for her to become quickly intoxicated. Her depressed mental state slipped down a few more notches as she continued to imbibe. After a couple of hours of knocking back the booze, she realized that Krebs would not be back anytime soon. She decided she would let him know how she felt about him.

Roslynn rifled through Kreb's desk and found an Allweather Wood Treaters notepad and a pen. She tearfully began to write. Twenty-one pages later, she felt worse than when she had started. She had poured out her soul on these pages and the process had drained her. Her words revealed an insecure young woman under the thrall of a more charismatic elder man:

> I love you Rex.
>
> I wish you could see that I would never hurt you. The only person I'd want to hurt is myself.
>
> I think you're fine the way you are.
>
> I wish I could be like you friendly & fun you always know what to say or do.
>
> I wish I weren't such a horrible person.
>
> I am so afraid I am going to kill myself.
>
> See if I were dead you wouldn't have to worry about me & could be happy w/whatever you dated.

For twenty-one pages she laid bare her self-piteous feelings on the page. Reading the letter, it is apparent that she worshiped the ground upon which Rex Krebs walked. However, she felt disgusted with herself because Krebs would seemingly have nothing to do with her.

Roz's note continued, "I'm such a looser (*sic*) I have no friends & have been dumped by an ex-con. Yippee! All I want is to die but I know that'll never happen because I never get what I want."

She went on to add that "all I've ever wanted to be was someone's mom but that'll never happen cause I can't have kids. That's probably a good thing. I mean who'd want a pscopath (*sic*) for a mom."

Despite her obvious need for Krebs in her life, Roz also feared him as well. In her letter she addressed his physical strength: "When you grabbed my arm today it scared me because I thought I'd done something bad. You forget how strong you are."

Not only did Rex treat her bad in a physical way, he apparently lashed out at her verbally as well. "Sometimes when you talk to me it sounds the same as when you discipline a dog," Roz inscribed, yet she still played the abuse victim, "but I understand how you are and somewhat the way you were raised.

"It's pathetic to see the dog & I in your room both crying & staring at the door waiting for you to return."

Roz told Krebs that she felt that he could never love her and that she would run into her previous boyfriend's arms—a boyfriend she claimed beat her.

"All he wants to do is fuck me & then say see you later. I'll probably let him because hopefully I'll feel needed."

Roz went on to babble about her African slave ancestry, French Canadians being kicked out of Canada, and the Seminole massacre, claiming these were all reasons why everyone hated her. Or the fact that she was not into that "Jesus Bible stuff" and she wanted to know why the pope wore that "Klans

member outfit." She also believed Krebs did not love her because of her skin color.

"Why does everyone want to be as white as the lamb of
god," she wondered on the page. "Am I ugly should I not be
this dark is that why you hate me?" she wanted to know. "I'm
so tired of being this color sometimes I forget That I am black
& Then I look at myself in The mirror & yell oh shit! Who
The fuck is That? Oh yeah, I'm black I forgot!"

Roz's plea/diatribe/cleansing continued for several more
pages. Eventually, around page 20, she decided to wrap
things up and let Krebs know how much he meant to her.

"I love you so much," she noted in her closing, "that if you
asked me to cut out my heart & give it to you I would."

She signed her full name, then postscripted the letter with
the tag line "the most depressed little girl you ever had the
awful time meeting."

She added a caricature of herself with a morose smile.

She placed the notepad with the letter on the dresser near
Krebs's front door. She wanted to make sure he picked it up
when he returned from Outlaws.

THIRTY-EIGHT

Rex Krebs felt trapped in a corner. He sensed pressure from Roslynn to come back to her. He knew she could be a pain with her immaturity and clingy nature. He liked being around her, but she also drove him crazy. Not literally, of course.

To make matters worse, Rex heard from his father again for the first time in years on June 9, 1998. Allan Krebs contacted his son to let him know that police had arrested him in Montana a week earlier on June 2. He related the story of his arrest to his son. He told Rex it was set up. A bogus drug deal. The official sheriff's report painted an entirely different picture of Allan Krebs's arrest.

According to Lincoln County detective Steve Hurtig, on June 2, 1998, at 1:35 P.M., in Libby, Montana, he had staked out a position in the Venture Inn Motel parking lot. While sitting in his police cruiser, Detective Hurtig looked up and spotted an older white Volkswagen. He had seen the same vehicle earlier that day at Hardoms West Trailer Court, where there had been a report of a drug deal going down. While Hurtig did not spot any suspicious activity at the trailer court, his day would soon change.

A female sat in the driver's side of the Volkswagen. She parked the car next to the Fireman's Park Playground, directly adjacent to the motel. Soon after spotting the Volkswagen, Hurtig made note of another vehicle that pulled up alongside it. It was a maroon GMC truck. Hurtig noted that the vehicle might have been used in other drug deals in town. Hurtig watched as the truck pulled up next to the Volkswagen. The detective noticed a man in the driver's seat of the truck. He kept a close eye on the exchange between the people in the two vehicles. Instead of talking to one another from their vehicles, the man got out of his truck, walked away from the white car and into the dead brush-filled area in the playground. Hurtig watched as the brush shifted. The man returned to his truck.

The woman in the vehicle followed the man's lead. She got out of her car, walked into the brush, and shook things around. She emerged with a look of unease on her face. She jumped back into her vehicle, fired the engine, and pulled out of the motel parking lot. She followed the man in the GMC truck around Fireman's Park playground until he pulled up to a nearby campground area, which had seen better days. The man and the woman got out of their vehicles simultaneously and walked toward a beaten-up picnic table.

Detective Hurtig's first inclination was to call for backup. He believed the couple was ready to engage in a drug transaction. He contacted a Detective Martin, from the Lincoln County Sheriff's Office, who arrived at the motel. The two officers inspected the brush. Detective Martin discovered a Ziploc Baggie. Further analysis concluded that the Baggie contained methamphetamine and marijuana. When the officers emerged, Detective Hurtig saw that the couple had driven away. He headed back to the sheriff's office. While there, Detective Hurtig looked up information on one Allan Krebs, the owner of the GMC truck. Detective Martin, meanwhile, conducted a field test on the substance in the baggie.

Detective Martin's Narcotics Identification Kit (NIK), confirmed that the powdery substance in the plastic Ziploc bag was indeed methamphetamine. Detective Hurtig also discovered some interesting information on his new suspect. He spoke with officials from Sandpoint, Idaho, who informed him that Krebs had a violent history and should be considered dangerous. He also found that the Volkswagen belonged to a woman named Sines, a well-known drug dealer from Montana.

After gathering the necessary information to make a bust, Detectives Hurtig and Martin returned to Fireman's Park Playground. When they arrived, the two vehicles were gone. The officers hopped back into their vehicle and drove around town. Detective Martin spotted Sines's Volkswagen at a business called DeShazer Realty. He spotted Sines outside the building and pulled their car beside her.

"Hi there, ma'am. Would you mind telling us who you had lunch with today?" Detective Martin calmly asked.

"I'm not eating lunch," Sines replied.

"I know you're not eating now. I'm talking about earlier."

"I didn't eat lunch with anybody today."

"Who was that man I saw you with over by the motel? That short, stocky fellow?"

Sines looked nervous. "I don't think I should be talking to you. I'm not so sure this is a good idea."

As Detective Martin spoke with Sines, Hurtig radioed for more help in the search for Allan Krebs. He informed the officers of Krebs's potential for violence. Within minutes Hurtig received a transmission that police had spotted Krebs's truck at Jon's Auto Repair on Crossover Road. Detective Martin drove to the repair shop and kept an eye on the front door. Suddenly, the 5'6", 200-pound, green-eyed, baldheaded Allan Krebs stepped outside the business establishment, oblivious to the fact that someone's eyes were trained on him. Detective Martin pulled his cruiser up closer to the shop. Krebs meandered about in the parking lot. He did not appear to be in a hurry as he ambled up to his maroon GMC pickup truck. Martin parked his car, exited his vehicle, and withdrew his gun.

"Police officer, hold it right there!" he screamed at the top of his lungs.

Krebs looked over at him, rather nonchalantly. He hesitated.

"I said, 'Police officer,' don't move!" Martin ordered again.

Krebs looked up and noticed several more officers standing nearby, their guns drawn as well. Police had him surrounded. No sign of panic entered his face. He merely stared at Detective Martin.

"Goddamnit, I said, 'Don't move!'" Martin barked again. The other officers began to yell at Krebs as well.

"Get down on the ground!"

"Don't move!"

As the cacophony rose, Krebs appeared disinterested. He listlessly stared Martin directly in the eyes. He did not hit the ground as ordered. Instead, he opened the door to his truck. He did it with a measured assuredness. Martin was furious.

"You son of a bitch. Don't move," he hollered as he moved toward Krebs's vehicle.

Krebs looked up at him one more time, grabbed the keys from his pocket, and stuck them in the ignition. The defiant roar of the engine starting rose above the den of noise coming from the belligerent cops. Krebs threw the gearshift into reverse and stepped on the gas. Gravel flew on the officers like rice at a wedding.

Detective Martin began to chase after the truck. Krebs was about to escape.

That is, until his truck died.

Ten feet away, the GMC petered out and the mad chase ended. Krebs tried to start the truck up again, to no avail.

Detective Martin rushed up to the driver's side of the truck, his weapon poised at Krebs's head, and yelled at the attempted runaway: "Get your ass out the vehicle."

No response.

Detective Martin decided he could no longer wait. He yanked open the driver-side door, grabbed Krebs by the shirt, and threw the hefty criminal to the ground. It took a fight to accomplish the task. Detective Martin and the two other detectives were able to restrain Krebs with handcuffs. They also removed a fanny pack Krebs wore around his waist, fearing it may contain a weapon. One of the detectives discovered a plastic Ziploc Baggie that contained two "chunks of methamphetamine." He continued to rifle through the pack, where he also discovered a pager, sheets of paper with names and phone numbers beside them, a white container with drug paraphernalia inside, and eight individually wrapped strips with methamphetamine in each. The detective placed the evidence back in the pack, tossed Krebs into his car, and drove him to the sheriff's headquarters. They also impounded Krebs's truck.

The total haul of Allan Krebs's drug possession included 150.1 grams of meth, 28.54 grams of marijuana, and 1.68 grams of psilocybin mushrooms. The officers conducted a search of Krebs's truck after they obtained a search warrant. The search led to the discovery of a .38-caliber two-shot Davis brand derringer gun in a pocket in a black leather vest owned by Krebs. They also retrieved an electronic scale, a police scanner, two plastic Ziploc Baggies with .38-caliber and .44-caliber bullets, a red nylon pouch with more .38-caliber bullets, lists of various drug users and sellers in Libby with their phone numbers, and a pair of brass knuckles. A suitcase inside the cab of the truck contained an Interarms .44-caliber revolver.

Detectives Hurtig and Martin knew they had plenty of evidence against Allan Krebs. They arrested the fifty-two-year-old hooligan.

One week later, he contacted Rex.

It came as a surprise to Rex that his father would call him while in dire straits. He had not spoken with his father since he went to Cottonwood Prison.

No love was lost between them.

Rex also had no idea just how much trouble his father had gotten himself into since the last time they saw one another. Allan Roger Krebs's rap sheet, just in Sandpoint, Idaho, alone, looked like programming code for a new video game—it had so much information on it. Allan had become more than just another familiar face to the local authorities. In the short span of eight years, he had been arrested five times for various crimes from manufacture and delivery of a controlled substance, to assault and battery, to malicious injury of property.

Allan Krebs also caused several public disturbances, which usually consisted of fights down at the local bars. He had been nailed for illegal drug possession with the intent to sell. In addition, police brought him in for the unlicensed possession of weapons, mainly guns.

Allan Krebs sometimes scooted under the Sandpoint Police Department's radar. He had been their main suspect in various crimes from domestic abuse to burglary to rape. The police usually did not have enough evidence against him to prove guilt.

The most interesting incident on Allan Krebs's police record, as it pertained to his son, occurred on the night of July 29, 1994. According to the Sandpoint Police Department report, Allan Krebs worked as a bouncer at a local bar known as the Roxy. His job description included checking identification cards of customers, making sure no underage patrons entered the establishment, and keeping an eye on any unruly types that might cause trouble. In the event that a problem existed with a customer, Krebs had permission to toss them out unceremoniously on their ass. Krebs, despite his small stature, played the role of the tough guy well. He had plenty of experience. His appearance lent an air of danger to his persona, what with his gleaming bald dome and oversize bushy mustache.

Little did anyone know it would be Allan Krebs who allegedly engaged in the unruly behavior that evening.

According to Sandpoint police officer John Smith, twenty-four-year-old Martha Neumann entered the Roxy and began to drink alone. She had been to the club a few times—the bald guy at the front door had caught her eye. She wanted to get to know him. A friend of hers named Crystal knew Allan Krebs. Crystal said he was a nice enough guy but a bit possessive. As Neumann slowly nursed her drink, Allan Krebs

strolled over to her table. They engaged in some mild flirta-
tious chitchat and then Allan returned to his post. She
continued to drink; he continued to walk over to her. He eventually bought her a Bud Light, which she eagerly accepted.
Like two leopards in the jungle, they continued their time-
honored mating ritual. After five beers Neumann hinted to
Allan that she wanted to go for a walk. Feeling the effects of
the beer, but not wasted, Neumann and Allan Krebs headed
out the back door of the club and into a dark alleyway. They
talked about nothing important, just a private continuation of
the ritual. They walked for almost ten minutes and then
turned around to head back into the club.

As they neared the back of the club, they steered themselves over to a nearby apartment complex. There, next to a
cement mixer, Neumann and Allan Krebs began to embrace.
The kiss had passion and urgency, yet remained gentle. It
continued for a number of minutes, their labored breathing
masked by the pulsating music emanating from the club.
They eventually pulled themselves apart from each other,
straightened their shirts just a tad, and Neumann made sure
her coiffure looked sharp.

They went back inside. Neumann continued to drink.
Krebs resumed his work duties.

When closing time arrived, Krebs did not see Neumann.
He looked around the club one last time as he grabbed his
jacket. He experienced a twinge of disappointment as he
walked out the front door. Disappointment quickly turned to
excitement as he spied his new friend sitting in her 1988
Dodge two-door in the Roxy parking lot. She had been waiting for the man she called "Al." She waved Al over and told
him to get in the car. They began to talk and laugh some
more, and the next thing you know, they were having a sword
fight with their tongues. Hopped up on saliva, they agreed
to go somewhere more secluded. Neumann fired up the engine to her Dodge and took off for the nearest beach.

The slightly intoxicated woman tooled out of the parking

lot and blindly drove on the poorly lit streets. When they arrived at the beach, she drove around until she found a secluded area. She recalled that weeds and thick brush surrounded it. She could not hear the waves crashing on shore. She did hear several frogs croaking in the background. The area was pitch black, so dark that she could not see the downtown lights.

In darkness, talk turned to intimacy. Neumann, however, complained that she felt nauseous. That did not stop Allan Krebs as he quickly stepped up his efforts and began to kiss the much younger woman. Within seconds he began to fondle her breasts, to which she did not resist. As Krebs manually stimulated Neumann, she reciprocated by stroking with her right hand his erect penis, which unknown to her had escaped from his denim jeans. Their breathing escalated as the friction between their bodies increased.

The windows began to fog up.

They decided to get out of the car for more air and more room for maneuverability. They both tumbled out of the passenger-side door onto the sandy beach. Krebs leaned down to pick up the young woman. She complained that she felt "woozy." At the time she wore a white Victoria's Secret tank top shirt, a tan sports bra, black Rio jeans, and black Hanes Her Way underwear.

The next thing Martha Neumann recalled is that she lay on the hood of her Dodge with no pants on and no underwear. When she opened her eyes, she saw the grinning visage of Allan Krebs as he began to mount her.

"It'll be OK," he tried to reassure her as he stuck his penis inside her.

Neumann struggled underneath the bulky bouncer. She began to get nervous. "Please stop," she asked rather timidly at first.

"OK," Krebs complied and removed his manhood. After a few seconds he climbed back on top of her and this time inserted his penis in her rectum.

"Stop it!" Neumann shouted, this time truly frightened. She scrambled to get away from him.

Again Allan Krebs complied and retreated from within Neumann. Once again he went back for more. This time he went for the vaginal insertion.

"Relax. It'll be OK," he reiterated. He began to switch out from her vagina to her anus. At this point he did not seem to care whether she enjoyed it or not.

"Stop it! Stop it!" she screamed emphatically at Krebs.

He continued to pull out and then reinsert himself. As he entered her vaginally one more time, she figured out how to get him to stop.

"I'm going to be really sick."

Boom. That did it. He pulled out of her for the final time and zipped up his pants.

"I want to go home," she begged. "Please take me back to the Roxy."

Amazingly, Krebs agreed. Neumann did not recall much of the ride back. When they arrived at the club, Krebs pulled up alongside a small car.

"That's my Omni," he calmly stated as he glanced out of Neumann's car window. He then turned to the young woman and sincerely asked her, "Are you going to be OK? I'll drive you home if you want me to."

Neumann incredulously replied, "If you're that concerned, call me tomorrow." Krebs got out of her ride and into his Omni. She took off before he could even get his car started. She headed for Bonner General Hospital in Sandpoint. She slowly ambled to the counter in the emergency room and told the bored attendant about the rape. After a short wait she was ushered into emergency room 4, where a doctor gave her a cursory glance. Simultaneously someone notified the police. Sandpoint police officer John Smith came in to question her. His initial reaction was that someone definitely raped her. He contacted his sergeant, advised him as to his opinion, and requested that a matron come in to perform a rape examination on Neumann. Sandpoint Police Department dispatcher Kathy Stoddard came to the hospital. Smith and Stoddard met the victim in ER4 along with the doctor. After Officer Smith interviewed her, she consented to a sexual assault kit, or rape kit.

Two days later, at noon on August 1, 1994, Martha received a strange phone call.

"Hi. How are you doing? I was thinking about you this weekend."

She recognized the man's voice. Allan Krebs.

Martha hung up the phone and called the police.

Detective A.D. Anderson showed up at her residence on Schell Road on the northwest corner of Highway 95 South in nearby Sagle at approximately 1:35 P.M. She informed the detective of Krebs's phone call. He then asked her to look at a six-person photographic lineup he had prepared. She immediately picked out Allan Krebs as her attacker. Detective Anderson then asked her to give him the details of the attack.

Upon conclusion of their conversation, Anderson informed Neumann that he would submit her statement and a copy of the lineup with Allan Krebs's photo to Sandpoint County prosecutor Tevis Hull. Hull would take the case on and move forward with charges against Allan Krebs.

Martha Neumann seemed to dwindle upon hearing this. "I was under the impression that I would not have to testify. Officer Smith told me I did not have to go to court for this."

"Ma'am, it is highly unlikely that this case will go forward without your direct involvement and testimony," stated Detective Anderson. "It is very important as to where you want to proceed at this time."

Neumann bowed her head, took the officer's business card, and said nothing more.

After two weeks with no word from the authorities, Neumann got nervous. She contacted Anderson to see if he had received word on lab results from her assault kit samples.

"I'm sorry, Ms. Neumann, but we do not have those results

yet," he replied. "Is there anything specific you are looking for?"

"AIDS!" she hollered at him through the phone.

"Unfortunately, Ms. Neumann, we do not have any samples from the suspect at this time. Basically, I am waiting until you decide whether or not you want to press charges."

Neumann informed Detective Anderson that she would be out of state until September. She claimed she would file charges as soon as she returned.

She never did.

On April 26, 1995, Detective Anderson received notice from attorney Tevis Hull that stated that he would not seek to prosecute Allan Krebs in the alleged rape of Martha Neumann. He gave the following three reasons:

- Reluctance of Martha to testify
- The intoxication level of Martha
- The mutual fore-play (*sic*), intercourse seemed consensual at times

"Very difficult to prove beyond a reasonable doubt."

Rex Krebs did not welcome the return of Allan Krebs into his life. Rex's relationship with Roz also hit another sour note. The couple had another one of their furious verbal altercations about something inconsequential in the big scheme of things. Roz decided to take her frustrations out on Rex's Ford Ranger. She grabbed a baseball bat and swung with all of the force the tiny woman was capable of and smashed his taillight.

Another fight took place in front of Wayne and Carol Nunes. Roz became mad with Krebs because she feared he would soon violate his probation. She told him she was angry about his many trips to Outlaws and consumption of alcohol. She also pointed out that he kept a load of beer in his refrigerator, again a direct violation of his probation conditions.

"If you don't stop going to that damn bar and getting drunk, I'm gonna report you to your parole officer," she threatened Krebs while they sat at the dinner table in front of the Nuneses.

Krebs became furious.

"You do that and I'll kill you and your entire family," he calmly warned her.

Rex and Roz eventually made up after that fight. Krebs's downward spiral, however, continued to unravel one layer at a time.

THIRTY-NINE

Krebs's presence in the Atascadero neighborhood where he resided stayed largely unnoticed. That is, until one day Diane Morgan decided to head down to the San Luis Obispo County Sheriff's Department to check out their new Megan's Law CD-ROM. The CD-ROM provided names and locations of all known and reported sex offenders in the county and was available for viewing by the public.

Diane Morgan made the trip to San Luis Obispo because she had her suspicions about the man who rented an apartment from her next-door neighbor Sue Peterson. She found out from Peterson that his name was Rex Krebs. According to *Fresno Bee* reporter Michael Krikorian, Morgan described Krebs as "really creepy." As she pored over the Megan's Law records of San Luis Obispo County, she was at first horrified by the large number of sex offenders that were listed in the county: more than 650. The fear hit home when she scanned the expansive list and zeroed in on one name in particular—Rex Krebs. Her intuition was right. As she read the details of his sordid past, she "felt disgusted and afraid." She now knew that she lived next door to a man who raped women and sodomized them at knifepoint. Morgan and her friend Shelly Dye informed Sue Peterson of Krebs's sexual-offender status. The landlord was shocked by the news.

"During the summer of 1998," Peterson told the *Fresno Bee*, "Rex Allan Krebs lived in an apartment behind my house in the city of Atascadero. Upon application I checked his credit and work references. Finding no problem and with no knowledge or information of his criminal record, I rented the apartment to him."

Peterson had absolutely no problem with Krebs. "During the period of time he lived in the apartment, I found him to be a model tenant, quiet, paid on time, clean and pleasant."

Despite the glowing praises from his landlord, his neighbors had other, less pleasant things to say about Rex Krebs. His new nickname in the neighborhood had become "Old Rex the Rapist." Even more people were getting involved with trying to get rid of him. Former San Luis Obispo police officer Glenn Jordan lived in the neighborhood. He told the *San Luis Obispo Tribune* that Krebs seemed like an "ordinary man" who "kept to himself while living there." His opinion changed dramatically when he learned of Krebs's criminal history as a sexual predator.

Just five days after Krebs heard from his father, trouble struck in Atascadero. An irate neighbor contacted Sue Peterson and claimed that Krebs had slashed the tires on his vehicle. The neighbor was furious and screamed at Peterson. She claimed to have no knowledge of any wrongdoing on Krebs's part but assured the neighbor she would address the matter with him. The man continued his tirade at Peterson and asked her how she could put up a man who was a known rapist. Peterson called Krebs first. She then called Debra Austin and told her about the problem.

On June 16, 1998, Peterson again contacted Austin about the Krebs situation. According to Krebs's parole packet, Peterson claimed that "she has no problem with him" and that their neighbor Linda Pacheco "knows about subject's history and has no problem with it." She did mention, however, that a "cop who lives in a condo two doors down" had started the brouhaha. Peterson also related to Austin that she received an anonymous letter addressed to "Homeowner," which detailed the information of Krebs's parole for rape. Despite the letter, she had no intention of "kicking the subject out." Peterson also wanted Austin to know that the "so-called cop" upset her by yelling at her about Krebs in front of her five-year-old son.

Austin decided to look into the problem further before confronting Krebs. She contacted Peterson's neighbor Linda Pacheco. Pacheco stated that she also received a letter that detailed Krebs's sexual-offense history. She approached him about the matter. She replied that he was very frank with her and he admitted that he had been released from prison and that he was a convicted rapist. Pacheco then proceeded to tell Austin that the neighbors did not like Sue Peterson and that the Krebs situation "is just adding fuel to the fire." She continued to claim that Peterson "is probably an alcoholic" and that she is "somewhat a neglectful parent as she lets her five-year-old son roam too freely." Pacheco concluded by saying that the slashed-tire incident probably could be blamed on people at a rambunctious party thrown by some neighbors.

Austin absorbed all of the information. She paid Krebs a visit on June 16 and informed him about the discord his presence was causing. She suggested that his best option would be to move out. Krebs said he would consider it but wanted to wait awhile to see if the unrest would cure itself.

Nine days later, Austin received a call from Sue Peterson. Krebs's landlord told her that she still had no problem with the ex-rapist and that she wanted him to stay.

Six days later, she sang a new tune.

One of Peterson's neighbors, it is not certain who, contacted California's Child Protective Services agency and reported her as a neglectful mother.

"I want him out," Peterson stated emphatically.

Austin called Krebs and informed him it was time to pack up his bags.

The following day, Peterson contacted Austin again. She informed the parole officer that the Child Protective Services case had closed almost as quickly as it had arisen. Krebs could come back if he wanted.

It was too late.

Rex Krebs was already packing.

FORTY

Rex Krebs dialed Greg Vieau's home phone number. He knew that if anyone could help him out of this jam, it would be his boss. Vieau let Krebs know that he would attempt to help the released convict in any way possible. In a matter of days, Vieau found a two-bedroom garage apartment located behind a secluded farmhouse in Davis Canyon, near See Canyon, just twelve miles from downtown San Luis Obispo. The apartment was located near an area called Irish Hills, in between Avila Beach and the Montaña de Oro State Park. The Irish Hills received its name because of the sweeping, majestic hills blanketed with lovely emerald eucalyptus trees. Avila Beach is a quiet, secluded oasis, frequented by locals in search of serenity. Montaña de Oro State Park is one of the most gorgeous public-access coastal parks in the United States. Its sweeping fields of luxurious green are resplendent with white-tailed rabbits, deer, and numerous fine-feathered friends. The park contains numerous hiking trails for the weekend warrior or mountain bike enthusiast and provides breathtaking views of the Pacific Ocean alongside sheer-faced 150-foot-high white cliffs. A visit here makes a trip to Ireland redundant and unnecessary.

Muriel Wright and daughter Debbie owned the blue farmhouse and additional garage apartment. Muriel's son, Larry Wright, knew Krebs from work at 84 Lumber. Krebs worked under Larry, an assistant manager at the lumberyard. Larry heard of Krebs's need from Greg Vieau, so he contacted his

mother to see if the garage apartment was available. Larry
vouched for Krebs. He claimed Rex Krebs was an excellent
employee and would make a great tenant. Muriel had no
problem renting to Krebs, even after she spoke to Debra
Austin about his criminal background. The room went for
$350 a month. The Wrights lived in the main house and Krebs
could move into the smaller apartment in the back.

It was a chore to reach the area from Highway 101, the
main route, but a beautiful drive. If Krebs drove from downtown San Luis Obispo, he would have to drive approximately
seven miles until he exited San Luis Bay Road. At just the
right time in the early-morning hours of dusk, he could spy the
green hills covered in a fog bank that had crept in from Avila
Beach. The combination of mist, green pastures, soaring
mountains, and palm trees brought to mind a hybrid of Ireland
and Southern California. After a mile on San Luis Bay Road,
he would turn right onto smooth, winding See Canyon Road.
Giant weeping willows cascaded across the paved road. Some
of the sights he would take in included the See Canyon apple
farms and the Kelsey See Canyon Vineyards. Krebs could stay
on this road if he wanted to find some of the most majestic
views of the mountains and the ocean of the San Luis Range
and Prefumo Canyon. To get to the Wright residence, however,
he needed to make a cut over onto Davis Canyon Road. It is
here where the comforts of paved roads end. Davis Canyon
Road consists of two worn-down tire tracks. It is rocky and
overgrown with weeds. Low-hanging trees can scratch any vehicles in their path, decorating them with Texas pinstripes.
Houses are few and far between on this road and they are not
in the best of shape. Stray dogs parade around rusted-out
trucks. There are no light posts. Nearly two miles into this
difficult path, Krebs found the Wright house.

Krebs met with Muriel Wright. She showed him the garage
apartment, which she called the "barn apartment," told him
what the rent would be, and mentioned what she expected of
him as far as chores were concerned.

Krebs took a cursory glance around and decided he liked the place. He had no problem helping Muriel out around the property. She had difficulty with her back and needed Krebs to lift anything heavy. She also wanted him to handle the wood supply and to kill any weeds. He had no problem with her requests and agreed to become a tenant.

As he drove away from Muriel Wright's property and a quarter of a mile down the dirt road, he noticed an unusual-looking structure—a beaten-down A-frame house that had seen better days. He would find out later that Muriel had built it back in 1960 on her brother-in-law Sherman Wright's portion of the land. Muriel, her husband, and then their children had lived in the A-frame until 1979 when they built the current home and barn apartment. They abandoned the A-frame and left it in a state of disrepair. Sherman intended to refurbish it. He never did.

Krebs stared at the ominous structure. Dark brown wood, broken windows, and a severely pointed roof. It looked like an evil house of worship.

Krebs grinned as he drove past the A-frame.

Once again he had a new home.

In the beginning Muriel and Debbie Wright enjoyed Rex Krebs's presence. Krebs handled chores around the property and made life simpler for them. Debbie found him especially helpful as most of the heavy chores had landed squarely on her shoulders in the last few years. It was difficult for her because she worked a full-time job. Every morning, as the sun rose above the canyon, Debbie drove seventeen miles into San Luis Obispo to her job as an administrative secretary for the Vineyard Community Church. She appreciated Krebs's physical exertions because it allowed her more time to focus on her job.

Life in the Davis Canyon seemed to work for Rex Krebs. He liked the seclusion, he thought the Wrights were nice women, who did not bother him, and he always had a quiet place to relax after a hard day of work. He wished that he and Roslynn could get back together but had no idea how to get her back.

But then he got bored.

FORTY-ONE

August 1, 1998
Outlaws Bar & Grill, Atascadero, California
Late Evening

Dan Thompson held court behind the maroon mahogany wooden bar inside Outlaws. As he wiped out dusty glasses, he oversaw the patrons of the fine establishment. It was a unique bunch, but they all seemed to have their good qualities. He knew that bikers were unfairly stereotyped. He believed people's ignorance led them to judge the road warriors based solely on their appearance. Once someone took the time to look beyond their rough exteriors, they realized bikers were simply adventurers with a thirst for life.

Others had a thirst for something else. And it came from a robust two-liter glass container that he grabbed from behind his domain. Bikers liked their booze—and plenty of it. Thompson believed another ingredient was necessary for a surefire powder keg in Outlaws. That other ingredient usually consisted of the female persuasion. The combination of flowing liquor and agitated girlfriends was sure to start something.

On this particular night a lethal cocktail brewed. It involved Rex Krebs and Thompson's friend Melissa Copelan.

Melissa and her boyfriend Robert "Gordon" Vesser stopped in for a bite to eat and to say hello to their good friend Thompson. Melissa also happened to be best friends with Dan's girlfriend, Jamie Beth Prisco. Copelan and Vesser walked in, spotted Thompson and exchanged pleasantries with the burly bouncer with a teddy bear's disposition. They informed him that Jamie would meet them there. Thompson rolled his eyes, harrumphed a bit, and muttered something under his breath.

"I'm sorry, Dan, what did you say?" Melissa inquired.

"I said, 'She's right over there.'" Thompson bitterly motioned over his shoulder to the corner of the dimly lit bar. Melissa looked around Dan and noticed Jamie sitting by herself, hunched over a drink. She looked depressed, so Copelan hurried over.

"What's the matter?" she worriedly asked.

"Dan's being an asshole," Prisco replied bitterly.

"About what?"

"You know what."

"No, tell me."

"That stupid bitch. I busted his ass again cuz I know he's screwing around with her, that son of a bitch. She's just a little whore."

Melissa did not know what to say, so she listened to her friend.

"And to make matters worse, the cunt is here."

"Where?" Melissa wanted to know.

"Right over there by the . . ." as she pointed toward the front door, her hand hit Thompson in the stomach. He had stopped by to see what the two young ladies were discussing.

"Watch it asshole," Prisco grumbled.

Thompson hovered over the tiny single mother who had been his live-in lover for the past six months. He could not stand it when she flew into one of her irrational jealous fits. What did she expect? He worked in a bar, ferchrissakes. He was a big guy and all sorts of women would hit on him. Came with the territory. He explained that to her when they first hooked up and told her he did not want any dramatic scenarios to play out because of it. She told him that it was not a problem.

She had lied.

"Why don't you just calm down." Thompson attempted to reason with her.

"Why don't you kiss my ass!" Prisco shouted back. She took a huge swig of her drink and continued her tirade.

"I am so sick of your shit. You're always fucking around behind my back. Always checking out all of the bitches in here. I'm sick of it!" she exploded, slamming her empty glass down on the scratched table, pouncing from her chair, and pushing past Dan. Jamie bolted past the front door and gave her nemesis the evil eye.

Afraid of a catfight inside the bar, Melissa took off after her friend. Jamie, however, did not accost the other woman, but simply strutted past her and out the exit. Copelan continued after her friend and stopped as she came face-to-face with the other woman.

"Lousy slut!" she tossed at her like a rotten potato from a jerry-rigged potato gun.

The accused "slut" stepped back two steps. She backed up into her extremely large boyfriend, known by the patrons of Outlaws simply as "Big Dave." With the alleged home wrecker's jaws agape, Big Dave leaned forward only slightly. The massive man then jerked his head to the left and raised his shoulder. Melissa could see that attached to that beefy shoulder and arm was an incredibly massive hand. Not just a hand—but a fist.

Someone else in the bar noticed that fist also. Rex Krebs.

Big Dave did not rear back and coldcock Melissa Copelan. If he had, she would have been in the hospital. He did begin, however, to scream at her.

"What the hell is your problem, you little cunt!" he screamed.

Melissa, truly scared at this point, ignored Big Dave and took off for the front door.

Rex Krebs, sporting his fancy black cowboy hat, glanced over at Dan Thompson. He made eye contact with his much larger bouncer buddy, which let him know he was about to do some scrapping. He watched as Big Dave stepped through the front door, seemingly to go after both Melissa and Jamie. Krebs strode across the beat-up floor of Outlaws and purposely headed after Big Dave.

Krebs threw open the exit door. He peered around but only saw one person, Melissa Copelan. He walked up to his friend.

"What happened, Melissa?"

"Jamie and Dan had a fight and I need to go get her."

"What about the other guy?" Krebs wanted to know.

"That's the other girl's boyfriend."

"It looked like he was gonna hit you."

"Yeah, I got scared and that's why I ran out here."

"Where is he?"

"I don't know, Rex."

"Here, hold this," Krebs said to Copelan as he handed her his black felt cowboy hat. *This is a chivalrous man,* Melissa thought. *He is here to defend my honor.*

Just then, the front door to Outlaws slammed open. A man ran out of the establishment toward Krebs and Copelan. Thankfully, it was Melissa's boyfriend, Gordon Vesser. Now she had two men to stand up for her.

"Hey guys, what the hell is g—" Vesser interjected, but was interrupted by the sound of bone being crushed. He turned to his left, only to see Krebs grabbing his face and falling to the parking lot. As he slithered downward, the ominous figure of Big Dave loomed overhead. In his hand was a thick steel truck-license-plate holder.

The piercing wails of Rex Krebs cut through the eerie silence. It was his blood on the end of the license plate holder. Krebs clutched his nose as a geyser of blood squirted far enough to make a four-foot-long speckled trail.

Hearing the screams, Dan Thompson bolted out the front door. As he opened it, he witnessed a severe beating taking place. Big Dave and two of his buddies were kicking the hell out of little, scrawny Gordon. He also spotted Krebs flailing on the ground in obvious pain. He also saw rivulets of blood drip off Gordon's face.

Normally, Krebs would be there to back Thompson up when a fight broke out. This time, Krebs lay on the receiving end of a beating. It was apparent that he could not get up. Thompson cleared off the handicap-accessibility ramp of a few stray onlookers. He then realized his friend had gotten his ass kicked. Krebs lay in a heap and started flopping up and down. He went into convulsions and spasmodically bounced on the glass-littered gravel. Dan saw one of Big Dave's boys standing over the hapless ex-convict.

"Yeah, now what are you gonna do?" the thug screamed at Krebs. "Huh, you don't seem all right now, do you, motherfucker?" he stated with glee in his voice.

Krebs turned a different color. His flesh seemed to take on an unhealthy bluish tint. Thompson thought his friend might have started to choke on his own tongue. He got scared.

Oh, my god. Oh, my God, Dan thought as he witnessed the brutality.

Somehow Vesser got up and turned Big Dave around. He cocked back his much smaller fist and knocked Big Dave square in the eye with a full-bodied roundhouse. It was a hell of a punch—so good that it left Big Dave with a permanent scar.

Big Dave was not pleased.

According to Dan Thompson, Big Dave "squared off on him. *Wham!* Busted his nose. It looked just like a cantaloupe. It just exploded."

That's when Thomspon ran toward the melee. Big Dave and his cohorts took off. They knew the law would be there any second. Thompson hightailed it to the scene. He took one look at Krebs.

It wasn't pretty.

Within minutes an ambulance arrived. The paramedics also took one look at Krebs and rushed him to the hospital right away. As they hauled him into the ambulance, one of the emergency medical technicians repeatedly asked him his name. Krebs groggily replied, "Rex Allan Krebs, Rex Allan Krebs." Thompson drove Vesser to the Twin Cities Hospital. He dropped him off at the main entrance, parked his truck, and scurried over to the emergency room to find Rex.

Krebs had already received an examination. He also had his own room. Thompson explained to the nurses that he and Krebs were coworkers and best friends. The nurses, however, would not let him in the room. They said Krebs lay unconscious in his bed and could not be disturbed.

The next morning, Dan returned to pick up Gordon, who seemed no worse for the wear. He also checked in on Krebs, whom he had still not seen since seeing him in the ambulance. One of the nurses informed Dan that Rex Krebs had not stabilized and that he would not be able to see him yet. They also told Dan that Krebs was out cold. He told the nurse that he wanted her to keep him abreast of Krebs's condition. Dan Thompson went home and got some sleep.

The following morning, August 3, Thompson returned to Twin Cities Hospital. Rex Krebs finally woke up.

He did not look good.

His face had swollen to the size of an overripe honeydew melon; his eyes were almost swollen shut and blackened. Krebs felt nauseous. Dan arrived with Jamie's tiny Celica and attempted to place his poor, battered friend into it. Apparently, Jamie's son had finagled with the car so that the driver-side door would not open properly. To get it to shut, Dan had to use the passenger-side headrest to jimmy the door closed. To accomplish this task, he had to get in from the passenger side. Rather dim-wittedly, Thompson let Krebs get in on the passenger side first, where he planted his abused body. Dan crawled over Krebs and unhooked the headrest from the driver's door. At the same moment that 6'5", 290-pound Dan Thompson crawled on top of Rex Krebs, his buddy began to make loud retching noises. Krebs began to convulse as he started to dry heave.

Thompson stared in horror at his pal. "Dude, if you lose it, I'm gone," he warned.

Krebs barely recognized his good friend. He continued to make a sound that reminded Thompson of a dying sheep bleating its last breath.

"I'm serious, dude," he continued, "I'm going right alongside you."

Luckily for Thompson, Krebs controlled his gag reflex and did not throw up in Jamie's car. Thompson fired up the tiny automobile and headed for his and Jamie's small studio apartment.

Krebs moaned as the car lurched forward.

Dan Thompson never realized how small their living quarters were until he brought Rex Krebs home from the hospital. He glanced around the tiny studio apartment and had serious doubts about letting Krebs stay. Not because he did not want to help his friend, but because they were going to be seriously cramped. The apartment belonged to Jamie Prisco and consisted of a master bedroom, which she relinquished to her son. She slept in the living room. When she asked Dan to move in, they shared the living room. Now he needed to find a place for Krebs to stay while they tended to his injuries. There was no doubt in Thompson's mind that he would help his friend, he just wanted to make sure Krebs had everything he needed.

Thompson let Krebs sleep in his and Jamie's bed. He dressed the bed and tucked Krebs in. He noticed bruises all over Krebs's face and a huge cut over his left eye. He could not help but think that Krebs looked like an abused banana.

Thompson also noticed that Krebs continued to dry heave. It almost made him sick, so he insisted that Krebs take something. Krebs finally muttered that the doctor had given him a pain reliever, Compazine, but there was one problem. The pill came in a suppository form. Krebs had no desire to insert the pill into his rectum, not the way he was feeling. Thompson, however, did not care. He was tired of hearing Krebs's dry heaving. Krebs relented and inserted the painkiller. It did the trick. Krebs fell asleep on Thompson's bed.

Krebs spent the next two days recuperating at Dan and Jamie's apartment. At first he seemed somewhat distant to Prisco. He appeared disoriented. He could not shake the cobwebs out of his head. She was not surprised. Getting smacked in the head with a metal license plate holder could do that to a person. Dan also noticed a change in Krebs after the attack. Krebs did not maintain his sunny disposition that he had while working at 84 Lumber. He seemed to withdraw further inside his own shell. He did not appear to be as "flamboyant, fun-loving" or "easygoing," Thompson recalled.

One thing Dan did not notice was the attention Krebs paid to Jamie. He spent a lot of time chatting with her while Dan worked. She found him quite charming. She always noticed that he treated his girlfriend, Roslynn, quite well. She also knew that he had attempted to defend both her and Melissa at Outlaws. She felt flattered by his concern. She decided to tell Dan about how she admired Krebs for what he had done that evening.

"You know, you should take a lesson from Rex," she piped up when Thompson arrived at home from a difficult day's work.

"Huh, what do you mean?" he replied.

"A lesson. You should take a lesson."

"What kind of lesson?"

"On how to be a gentleman."

Thompson's ears perked up, his eyebrows arched, and he cautiously answered her with a question, "How to be a gentleman?"

"Yes, I notice the way Rex treats Roslynn. He is very fond of her and treats her like a lady."

Thompson took a seat at the kitchen table and did not comment.

"You should treat me more like a lady," Jamie continued, "just like Rex does."

The next morning, Dan Thompson calmly asked Rex Krebs to vacate the premises. He did not care that his friend seemed a bit out of it, he wanted him out. There was no need for Krebs's influence over Jamie Prisco. The best way to solve that problem was to send his friend on his way.

Rex Krebs decided to return to the barn apartment in Davis Canyon.

One of Rex's friends from the bar, "J.R.," contacted Roz after he found her phone number on Krebs's pager. He told her about the fight and that Krebs was not in great shape. J.R. also told Roz that it looked like Krebs would need someone to watch over him while he recuperated. Roz did not hesitate and told J.R. that she would be by Krebs's house the next day to take care of him.

When Roz arrived, Rex Krebs apologized for his caddish behavior. She accepted.

Once again the two were an item.

FORTY-TWO

After the brawl at Outlaws, things actually picked up for Rex Krebs. He and Roz got back together. He received a promotion at 84 Lumber to manager trainee. Parole Officer Debra Austin saw Krebs twice at the end of August 1998. Once in her office and the last time on August 25 at his residence in Davis Canyon. She wrote that "everything" is "going very well. No problems." She noted his purchase of a mellow ninety-pound tan pit bull puppy named Buddy. She also jotted down that his work at the lumberyard was fine, as was the work on the Wright property.

Her final words on Rex Krebs were "Subject seems to be doing okay—no problems at present time."

However, something had changed within Rex Krebs. Something that Debra Austin would not see because she had to turn Krebs's file over to his original parole officer, David Zaragoza.

Everything seemed normal to Zaragoza as well. He visited Krebs's new residence for the first time on September 9, 1998. Everything appeared fine to him. He mentioned that Buddy was "very friendly" and that Krebs and Roz saw each other about two to three times a week.

As part of Krebs's parole conditions, he was also required to visit a court-appointed psychiatrist as part of his rehabilitation for sex offenses. Krebs had visited Dr. Randall True, a "three-quarter-time" psychiatrist for the parole division of the California Department of Corrections (CDC), upon his release in September 1997. Dr. True, a graduate of the University of Illinois medical school, entered private practice in 1974. He worked for the CDC in 1987 and moved into the parole division in 1990. At the time of Krebs's release, he headed up the Parole Outpatient Clinic in the San Luis Obispo parole office. He also headed up similar offices for Oxnard, Ventura 1, Ventura 2, and Santa Barbara. He only had one other person working with him and no clerical support staff whatsoever.

Dr. True described his responsibility toward his recent parolees or patients: "Do their intake evaluation and provide whatever kind of treatment from a psychiatric point of view we can do. That would include individual therapy, medications, and referral to other community resources that we might use."

Dr. True's caseload usually consisted of fifty to sixty parolees at one time. This did not afford him much time with each individual.

"I would see people anywhere from once—usually from once a month to once every three months." These meetings were limited in time. "There might be times—and that would be for half-an-hour to an hour," he noted. He did not spend much time with Rex Krebs.

The first time Dr. True met with Rex Krebs occurred on October 2, 1997, one month after Krebs's release from prison. The doctor spoke with Krebs for forty-five minutes. It was the standard "get to know you" meeting with Krebs relating his various histories: criminal, family, drug, etc. Dr. True needed this information so he could place Krebs into the appropriate category for sex offenders. There are different levels of Sexually Violent Predators (SVPs) including high risk, moderate risk, and standard follow-up risk. Dr. True considered Krebs to be a high risk upon his release, but over time that level dropped in his estimation. Dr. True saw Krebs approximately ten times between October 1997 and November 1998. He believed Krebs showed amazing progress and had assimilated into normal society with no difficulty. He noted that Krebs had a good job, a good girlfriend, and that he liked "soaking in the spa." Life looked good for Rex Krebs, according to Dr. True.

Dr. True also headed a sex offender group therapy session for the CDC known as the "290 group." The group gathered paroled sex offenders together and they talked about their crimes and their attempts to readjust outside of prison. Dr. True made recommendations for certain patients to attend the therapy sessions. He did not believe Rex Krebs needed to attend. The reason he later gave was because Krebs worked and the group met during working hours.

Krebs went in to see Dr. True on the morning of November 4, 1998. Dr. True described Krebs in his notes as his "usual talkative self." They spoke about 84 Lumber and his promotion. Krebs mentioned that he and Roz were still together. He claimed he had not used drugs or alcohol. "I'm clean," he told the doctor. He also stated that he was "getting along with people fine," and that he had "no temptations in the sexual area" and that he was "fine with Roz."

The only unusual entry made by Dr. True concerned Buddy, Rex's dog. The doctor seemed slightly worried about the pit bull purchase.

Overall, Dr. True believed Rex was making a fine adjustment back into society. The doctor did note, however, that his propensity to commit another sexual offense was "about average." That is, as long as Rex Krebs stayed sober.

FORTY-THREE

November 12, 1998
Davis Canyon Road, Davis Canyon, California
8:30 P.M.

Rex Krebs grabbed the fifth of Jack Daniel's with his right hand and a shot glass with his left. He carefully poured the dark amber liquid into the glass—no ice—gently positioned the bottle on his kitchen counter, and took a deep breath. He then placed the glass to his lips, separated them slightly, and quickly consumed the alcohol. It was the first of several shots he would drink over the next three hours. After a few more rounds, he decided to drive into town and hit a bar.

Actually, he hit several bars.

Rex Krebs, on parole and forbidden to drink alcoholic beverages, first stepped into Mother's Tavern on Higuera Street. He drank. He then ventured next door to the Library on Higuera Street. He continued to drink. He began to feel less pain.

After a couple of hours of imbibing, Krebs thought about heading home for the night, but he decided to hit one more bar before calling it a night. He piled into his 1993 blue Ford Ranger pickup and drove from Higuera Street over to Bull's Tavern on Chorro Street—one block away from the Jennifer Street Bridge. There he continued to throw back more alcohol.

Krebs looked up at the clock in Bull's Tavern and decided

he definitely needed to go home. He stumbled slightly out of the club, fished around in his pockets for his truck keys, and climbed into his ride. He pulled the truck out of the bar parking lot and headed north on Santa Barbara Street, which then intersected with Osos Street, which he took in a northwest direction. As he headed up Osos Street, something, or rather someone, caught his eye. An attractive young woman staggered alone down the street. Krebs did a double take at the blond woman wearing dark pants and a silky dark blue blouse. Krebs thought she was pretty. He decided to turn around and see where she was heading.

Krebs drove around the block and parked his truck on a side street off Osos Street. He quietly sat in his truck, with the headlights off, and watched as the drunken woman continued walking southeast. Krebs's eyes followed her until she came upon Church Street and Triangle Park.

She's going to the bridge.

Krebs had a premonition that the young woman would walk up to the Jennifer Street Bridge. Once he realized where she was headed, he fired the truck up, shifted into gear, and headed for the bridge. He drove on the right side of the circular driveway toward the bridge. To the left of the driveway lay the Amtrak train station, which serviced the San Luis Obispo County area and would take commuters up north to San Francisco and south down to Santa Barbara, Ventura County, and Southern California. To the right was the Jennifer Street Bridge—a footbridge that provided convenient access for pedestrians and cyclists access into the Jennifer Street neighborhood. Rex Krebs pulled his truck into the first parking spot below the stairs to the bridge.

He waited to see if she would come to him.

The intoxicated woman had two choices to make at this time. She could continue on her way down Osos Street, which would then cut over onto Santa Barbara Street, sending her in the opposite direction from Rex Krebs. On the other hand, she could veer left into the circular driveway, which led to the railroad and the Jennifer Street Bridge.

She veered left toward the bridge.

Rex Krebs smiled as he saw her heading toward the bridge. He reached inside his truck, grabbed something, and headed up the stairs to the top of the bridge. He looked down and saw the woman walking toward the ramp.

She's coming up!

He then took the item in his hand. He stretched it wide with both hands and placed it over his head.

It was a white Halloween skull mask.

He waited.

FORTY-FOUR

Less than two weeks later, David Zaragoza paid Krebs a visit. Yet another routine stop from his parole officer.

Upon arriving, Zaragoza noticed something different about Krebs. He seemed to be growing his hair out. At least what little hair he had on the sides. Zaragoza felt the change in appearance warranted a photograph, so he had Krebs pose for him. The parole officer also noticed a red mark on the left side of Krebs's neck and jaw area. Krebs told Zaragoza that he had a rash and had no idea how it got there. Zaragoza asked Krebs about his job and Roz. Krebs reported that they were both fine.

Thanksgiving and Christmas were rather low-key for Krebs. Things would change, however, in the new year with two unexpected arrivals. The first came from Roz Moore. On January 17, 1999, she found out that she was pregnant with Krebs's child. Surprisingly, the news excited Krebs. They were both shocked, but joyous nonetheless. Unfortunately, the celebration did not last.

Within a matter of days, the excitement left the building. Krebs visited Roz at her house and told her they needed to talk. Krebs, visibly upset, told Roz that he wanted her to get an abortion. He kept saying that this "is not a good idea." When she pressed him for a reason why, he told her because he "did not have a conscience." Moore, who looked forward to having the child, sat in stunned disbelief trying to figure out why he had changed his mind. She could not understand his sudden turnaround. She believed he would make an excellent father. Nevertheless, she stood by her man and told him that she would get rid of the baby.

The second unexpected visit came just weeks later. Krebs's dad, Allan Krebs, showed up at his son's doorstep. Allan wanted to see his son before he headed to the penitentiary for his 1998 drug bust. Rex Krebs had not seen his father in years and had no clue how to react to his tormentor. He decided to welcome him with open arms.

Rex and Allan Krebs spent the next few days enjoying one another's company while fishing and drinking beer. They went out to dinner in downtown San Luis Obispo and brought Roz along with them. She noticed that Rex and his father got along wonderfully. It appeared to her as if they were trying to establish a positive father-son relationship. Krebs even introduced his dad to Greg Vieau, who believed it appeared as if the two men were attempting to reconcile the fractured relationship. As soon as the visit began, however, Allan had to leave.

With the departure of Allan Krebs, one surprise remained out of the picture. The other, their unborn child, however, remained an issue. On February 17, 1999, Moore informed Krebs that she intended to keep the baby.

Two days later, on February 19, 1999, Krebs paid Dr. Randall True another visit. The meeting lasted the usual forty-five minutes and Krebs updated the doctor on his current condition. He reported that he felt fine and told the doctor about Roz's pregnancy. Dr. True denoted that Krebs seemed happy about the new turn of events. The two men spoke about Krebs's impending role as a father and the responsibilities that came with that position. He noted that Krebs seemed rather "ambivalent" about those responsibilities.

They talked about his father's visit and how his dad was on his way to prison very soon. The remainder of their discussion consisted of meaningless chitchat to which Dr. True scribbled in his notepad that Krebs acted "calm, friendly, polite, eurythmic (or normal)." Dr. True also mentioned that he expressed his thoughts coherently. There did not seem to be anything wrong with Rex Krebs.

On March 6, 1999, Muriel Wright dropped by the barn apartment. She told Krebs that she would be leaving the next day for a couple of weeks to Oakley, California. She had offered to house-sit and puppy-sit for her sister. She asked Rex if he would take care of her dog while she was away. He smiled and told her he would be glad to help.

FORTY-FIVE

March 11, 1999
Branch Street, San Luis Obispo, California
2:00 A.M.

Rex Krebs sat in his Ford Ranger pickup truck parked on Branch Street. Even though he knew he had drunk to the point of intoxication, he felt fine. He was a little stressed out about Roz's decision to have the baby, but he felt all right—maybe because he had spent more time drinking at the Gaslight Lounge on Broad Street. On the other hand, maybe because of the attractive young college girl he had been following for the last week.

The average-size dark blond girl caught his eye. She lived on Branch Street and drove a white 1988 Ford Mustang. He had noticed her the week before when he left the Gaslight and drove down Broad Street to go home. She parked her car in the driveway, got out, and headed for the front door of her duplex. Krebs liked how she looked in her white jeans.

He liked her so much he came back three more times.

He usually stayed until the young woman undressed; then he drove home and drank.

On this particular night Krebs decided he wanted an even better view. He slowly drove past her duplex and saw the white Mustang. He noticed all of the lights were off inside the house. He drove around until he eventually came back directly in front of the duplex. He killed the lights, cut the

engine, and exited the truck. He headed straight for her front
door, jiggled the door handle, and realized it was locked. Instead, he snuck up her driveway and made his way to the
sliding glass door. He grabbed the back door handle.

Locked!

He checked the kitchen window next to the sliding glass
door. It too was locked.

Krebs was getting frustrated. He considered leaving when
he looked up and saw an opportunity. He noticed that the tiny
bathroom window appeared to be unlocked. He walked up
and attempted to open it. It scooted up with a bit of noise. He
took a step back, surveyed the area, and reached into his pants
pocket. He pulled out a dark pair of panty hose. He calmly
pulled them over his head and turned his attention back to the
window.

March 12, 1999
Davis Canyon Road, Davis Canyon, California
8:10 A.M.

Debbie Wright climbed into her car for her usual seventeen-
mile jaunt to work. She drove her car up out of the driveway
and onto the two-tire-track dirt road. About halfway between
her residence and the A-frame, she spotted something unusual.

Rex Krebs.

He stood beside his parked truck in a clearing next to the
Wright woodpile. Debbie could not quite make out what he
was doing. She assumed he must be splitting wood with an
ax. As she pulled up alongside his truck, she noticed Krebs
huffing and puffing. He glanced up at her and began to speak.

"I can't do this anymore." He exhaled as he wiped sweat
from his brow.

Debbie thought he meant cutting wood.

"I've gotta quit smoking. It makes this kind of work too
hard," he wistfully stated.

They conducted their small talk for another minute or so when Debbie told Krebs she had to be on her way.

Krebs waved to Debbie as she drove off.

He then hurried back to the barn apartment. He had plenty of time now to do what he wanted to with the girl.

Five days later, David Zaragoza, Rex's parole officer, paid him an unexpected visit.

PART VI

TRIAL

FORTY-SIX

The local media jumped all over the discovery of the bodies of Rachel Newhouse and Aundria Crawford. Word of the arrest of Rex Krebs had the entire county of San Luis Obispo buzzing with fear and relief.

"I'm glad and relieved for the students in the area," Santa Maria resident Sherry Zimmer told the *San Luis Obispo Tribune*. "I know a lot of the students are relieved too."

"This lets all of us know that things like this can happen here," warned Pismo Beach resident Ray Gentry. "But this is good in that we can hopefully get some closure in this case."

Despite Krebs's arrest, some residents still felt fear. "When I first got here, it seemed like a quiet town," said Cuesta College student Natalie Smith. "We could go out to parties and walk home. Now I'm afraid to walk from work to my car at night."

When the residents found out that Krebs was a paroled rapist, they became furious. Krebs's detailed information in Michael Krikorian's article in the *Fresno Bee* extracted strong sentiment from its readers: most agreed with Krebs that he should receive the death penalty.

"I hope he gets what he wants," stated Cal Poly student Tiffinee Brougham. "He's a freak and he's going down. We don't need sex offenders in this county."

Krebs's friends and acquaintances were shocked and confused by the revelation. One woman, who requested anonymity, stated that she befriended Krebs when he lived in Atascadero. She recalled that he would come over to her house and spend the night on the top bunk bed above her child: "If you were to ask me six months ago, I would have said he seemed to be a nice guy, polite. He never really did anything to me. If you were to ask me now, I would say he's an animal."

Krebs's friend Dan Thompson stated, "Rex was a great guy. Is a great guy. But apparently it seems as though he has a demon."

The Newhouse family did not speak to the press after the discovery of their daughter's body. Captain Bart Topham informed the press that "of course they are saddened, we all are, but they are doing good. They are amazing and strong people."

One member of Aundria Crawford's family did speak to the press. Aundria's grandfather, Don Crawford, lashed out at Krebs. "I don't care what he says. He asks, 'Am I a monster?' I say, 'No, you are a piece of slime. Pure, unadulterated slime.'" Don Crawford also expressed his desire for the execution of Krebs. "If it gets down to that, I would tell the jury, 'If you don't fry him, you have no heart.'"

Jason Rerucha, husband of one of Aundria Crawford's best friends, summed up the sentiment best. "Our whole judicial system is screwed up. If he would have never been released in the first place, none of this would have happened. He had better get what he deserves this time."

There were two commemorative events to honor Rachel Newhouse and Aundria Crawford. The first event, a previously scheduled annual "Take Back the Night Rally" to raise awareness for victims of sexual abuse and sexual violence, turned into a candlelight vigil for the two girls. Over five hundred supporters showed up at Cal Poly and vowed to remember Rachel and Aundria. The vigil opened with moving renditions of "You Were Loved" and "Amazing Grace," sung by Cal Poly student Pili Hawes. The tears flowed instantly. Several speakers followed, including San Luis Obispo mayor Allen Settle, to tell the gathered crowd to remember the girls' lives and not their gruesome deaths. After the speakers finished, the marchers lit white candles, cradled them delicately in the palms of their hands, and silently marched up Higuera Street.

"I am so sorry this had to happen to them," said attendant Debbie Semling. "I want to let the families know that their daughters were very special, that they are loved."

The second commemorative event took place on Thursday, April 29, at Cal Poly. Sister Mary Pat White of the Newman Catholic Center and Reverend Donald Smiley of the University Christian Community organized a memorial for Rachel Newhouse. More than 750 people attended, most of whom did not know Rachel.

Biochemistry senior KC Cooper told the Cal Poly *Mustang Daily* newspaper "the whole situation is scary and I think it's not necessarily knowing her, but the fact that it could have happened to anybody. It affects everyone here at school."

The memorial opened with a welcome from the Cal Poly vice president of Student Affairs, Juan Gonzalez. The message he conveyed to the mourners was that the memorial should be the beginning of the healing process.

"This memorial came from the heart. It was an expression of love. I'm speechless," stated the administrator.

Several of Rachel Newhouse's friends attended. They paid tribute to her by lighting a candle and reading a poem entitled "Slow Dance."

Rachel's friends wanted the memorial to celebrate her life—not focus on the tragedy. Irvine High School friend Megan Carter recalled, "She was always real caring and she had this laugh; whenever you heard it, you wanted to laugh too."

Rachel's friends also made sure to include Aundria Crawford, as well as Kristin Smart, during the memorial. Volunteers lit two more candles for each girl, placed them next to a candle for Rachel, and tearfully stated, "Remember, we remember Kristin Smart. Remember, we remember Aundria Crawford." The song "Brown-Eyed Girl" by Van Morrison, which was Rachel's favorite song, played quietly in the background.

The emotional ceremony ended with a prayer offered by Sister Theresa Harpin: "Peace behind us, peace under our feet. Peace within us, peace over us, let all around us be peace." Harpin closed the service with the final line "Neither death nor separation can keep us from their presence."

On Friday, April 30, over six hundred friends and family members gathered in the New Covenant Community Church in Fresno, California, to bury Aundria Crawford. Once again the participants did not come to wallow in pity over her tragic, early end, but rather to celebrate her life. Reverend Jan Van Oosten told the large crowd, "This is a story of tragedy, but also a story of love and immense human kindness."

The crowd then enjoyed a five-minute slide show of Aundria in various states of frolic throughout her short, albeit full, lifetime. There was Aundria swimming with a huge grin on her face, looking elegant while dancing at the Clovis High School senior prom, and playing with a majestic horse. The soothing sounds of Sara McLachlan's "Angel" whispered comfort to the parishioners in the background.

Several of Aundria's closest friends stepped up to the podium to share fond memories of their dearly departed pal. "One word that pinpoints Aundria's personality is loyalty," said Aundria's closest friend in San Luis Obispo, Stephanie Nicolopoulos. "You could open up your heart to her. I am glad I got to be a part of her life. She will always be a part of mine."

Mark Crawford, Aundria's uncle, delivered the eulogy. He recalled his niece's love of horses, ballet, and cars. He spoke of how at the age of sixteen Aundria switched hobbies from ballet to horses. "That was probably the hardest thing she ever had to do. She always begged her grandma to get her a horse."

He concluded by calling Aundria's life an "unfinished work in the beautiful ballet of dreams."

Reverend Van Oosten mentioned that Aundria's internment at the Clovis District Cemetery would be a private ceremony. He then concluded the service with an attempt to console those gathered. "Right now, the grief hurts like the torments of hell. But the person who took Aundria from you must not take your soul too."

That was the only allusion to Rex Krebs.

FORTY-SEVEN

To prevent Rex Krebs from getting "what he deserves," he needed some of the best lawyers in San Luis Obispo County. Krebs's lack of personal finances made hiring a "dream team" unfeasible, so he received court-appointed attorneys from the San Luis Obispo County Public Magistrate's Office. The office, located across the street from the county courthouse on Osos Street, was the business office of two top-notch public defense attorneys, James Maguire III and Patricia Ashbaugh.

If Maguire and Ashbaugh walked out of their office front door and went to the San Luis Obispo City/County Library, they would have witnessed, firsthand, the emotions that the Krebs case had conjured up. A young woman held a sheet of paper that simply stated in bold black letters, FRY HIM.

Thirty-three-year-old Sharron Williamson, the protester, who wore a heavy sweater, dark round glasses, and had her black hair pulled back, understandably wore her emotions on her sleeve. She was a former rape victim. "He should receive the full extent of the law. We live in a society that locks up drug users longer than rapists."

Hastings College of the Law graduate and twenty-nine-year veteran lawyer James Maguire III knew this would be the exact sentiment he would have to battle in representing Rex Krebs. The fifty-five-year-old law firm partner was ready for a fight.

He and his partner, forty-seven-year-old University of California-Davis Law School graduate and twenty-two-year veteran lawyer Patricia Ashbaugh, had renewed their contract in the summer of 1998 as the primary public defender for the County of San Luis Obispo. As per their agreement, their firm provides public-defender services for indigent criminal defendants. According to the official contract, Maguire & Ashbaugh, the law firm, would be the highest paid of three law firms. The firm would receive $2,003,480 for the 1998 to 1999 term, with a 3 percent increase for each of the following two terms. The total amount of the contract: $6,192,556.

The work of the public defender in San Luis Obispo County seldom dealt with death penalty cases. However, these attorneys were more than capable. They would also receive assistance from death penalty expert William McLennan.

Deputy District Attorney John Trice would represent the state of California. Trice received his law degree from Southwestern University School of Law in Los Angeles, California. After law school, he enlisted in the U.S. Air Force as a captain in the JAG Department. He worked for the air force's legal assistance program for retired personnel. After leaving the military he became the San Luis Obispo County deputy district attorney in 1984. He worked on one previous death penalty case in 1988. He successfully helped to convict Dennis Duane Webb, who murdered John and Lori Rainwater of Atascadero.

Trice would be ably assisted by thirty-eight-year-old Deputy District Attorney Timothy Covello, who graduated from the University of Wisconsin Law School.

San Luis Obispo Superior Court judge Barry LaBarbera would oversee the proceedings. He also happened to be the former district attorney for San Luis Obispo County.

For the next two years, Judge LaBarbera mostly oversaw motions filed on behalf of Rex Krebs, first to delay the trial and then to relocate it. The defense argued that due to the intense media coverage of the murders of Rachel Newhouse and Aundria Crawford, there would be a substantial bias against their client. The defense succeeded in their quest for relocation—the trial moved 150 miles north along U.S. Highway 101 to the Superior Court of California in Monterey.

FORTY-EIGHT

March 19, 2001
Superior Court of California, Monterey, California
3:00 P.M.

Finally, after two years of delays, the Rex Krebs murder trial was about to begin. Despite all of the distractions in the courtroom—excessive heat, obnoxious noises emanating from the court reporter's stenotype, and a juror who had a previously booked nonrefundable flight on this day—Deputy District Attorney John Trice was ready to begin the ordeal. The opening argument rested squarely on his thin shoulders, but his appearance was deceiving. He was no lightweight. He needed to outline what the state of California intended to prove. Though he felt a gnawing uneasiness in the pit of his stomach, he displayed a modicum of confidence on the outside. He stood from his black leather chair and casually sauntered over to the jury box.

"I'm John Trice. I'm a deputy district attorney from San Luis Obispo who has been assigned to prosecute this case. With me today is Deputy District Attorney Tim Covello." He also introduced two more members from his team: Larry Hobson, lead investigator, and Gil Rendon, evidence technician.

After the introductions Trice pushed right into the charges against Rex Krebs. "There are two special circumstances that we have to prove in the connection with the murder of Rachel Lindsay Newhouse. The first is that the murder was committed while the defendant was engaged in a kidnapping for sexual purposes. Special circumstance number two is that the murder was committed while the defendant was engaged in a forcible rape.

"There are three special circumstances that pertain to the murder of Aundria Crawford: that the murder was committed while the defendant engaged in a crime of kidnapping for sexual purposes, that the murder was committed while the defendant was involved in the crime of forcible rape, and that the murder was committed while the defendant was involved in a crime of forcible sodomy."

Trice also listed all of the charges against Krebs. In addition to murder, there were charges for multiple rapes, multiple kidnappings, sodomy, and burglary.

After he listed the charges, Trice painted a picture of the town of San Luis Obispo for the Monterey courtroom jury. He described the beautiful beaches of Avila, the peaceful stretch of Highway 1 from Morro Bay to San Simeon. He described Cal Poly and Cuesta College. He even quoted a 1994 issue of *National Geographic* that said of the Central Coast of California: "'North of Los Angeles, south of San Francisco and east of Eden lies a once in a future land called the Middle Kingdom. A tucked away preserve of the good life where California has been lovingly resurrected.' San Luis Obispo, for those of us who live there, is a little corner of paradise."

In a more somber tone, he mentioned Tortilla Flats and the Jennifer Street Bridge. He spoke of the homes where Rachel Newhouse and Aundria Crawford lived.

"I don't know if any of you were fortunate to go to college down there," he addressed the jury personally, "but what an experience it must be to go to such schools and live in such a small-town atmosphere. That's what our two young women must have thought.

"Rachel Lindsay Newhouse from Irvine, California, born on June 16, 1978. She was twenty years old when the defendant killed her. And Aundria Lynn Crawford from Clovis,

California, in the valley near Fresno, born July 10, 1978. She was twenty years old when the defendant killed her," he stated as he looked at Krebs.

"Two beautiful young women who came to our little corner of paradise in San Luis Obispo County to begin their adult lives and get a great education. To just enjoy being young.

"As far as we know, they didn't know each other. And yet their two names, Rachel Newhouse and Aundria Crawford, will be forever linked in time in what must be considered one of the more horrific chapters in the history of San Luis Obispo." Trice paused, then stridently looked back at Krebs. "Because of him," he spat out. "Rex Allan Krebs is the person who caused this."

Trice looked back at the jurors. He had their rapt attention. "The evidence will show that that man is evil personified. Rex Allan Krebs brutally kidnapped these two twenty-year-old girls. He brutally raped them. He strangled them to death, and then he dumped them in a dirt hole and buried them like garbage. And that's what we will prove to you in the next few weeks."

Trice proceeded to lay out a skeletal outline of the days that Rachel and Aundria went missing. He discussed Parole Officer David Zaragoza's intuition that Krebs was somehow involved in Aundria's disappearance. He turned around behind his desk and pointed at Detective Larry Hobson. "This man sat down over a period of weeks with Rex Krebs and he began to talk to him about the disappearances of Rachel and Aundria. At the beginning he denied he knew anything about this. He wanted to help the police find the real killer. He wanted to be a detective. He denied any involvement whatsoever."

Trice turned his attention back toward Krebs. "But then, only after being confronted with undeniable physical evidence did he begin to tell investigator Hobson what he had done to these girls. And what Rex Allan Krebs told investigator Hobson about what he did to these girls will stagger you and make you question your basic belief in humanity."

Trice ended his opening statement. The courtroom was completely silent. Judge LaBarbera looked at his watch, 3:00 P.M. He ordered a twenty-minute break. Defense attorney James Maguire III would be next.

After the break the professorial Maguire took his place in front of the jury.

"Thank you, Your Honor. Counsel, ladies and gentlemen, I'd like to begin by reading a quote to you: 'As there is much beast and some devil in man, so there is some angel and some good in him. The beast and the devil may be conquered, but in this life never wholly destroyed.' This is a quote written by Samuel Taylor Coleridge from 'Rime of the Ancient Mariner.'

"That statement is about the struggle in all of us between good and evil. It talks about what goes on inside us.

"What I'd like to talk about for a few minutes is what goes on inside this case. You've heard a presentation by Mr. Trice from the prosecution. You've heard their story. I'd like to ask you as you listen to this trial, that you listen for the story inside the story."

Maguire patiently strode closer to the jury box. "There's going to be two questions that you're going to need to deal with in this trial. First question is 'what happened?' You're also going to have to concern yourself with the 'why' part. Why did these things happen ultimately?"

Maguire forged onward. "There are a couple of things you need to know as part of this story within a story. The first and most important thing is that Rex Krebs confessed. He confessed totally, completely, and in great detail." Maguire laid out how Krebs confessed to the murders of Rachel Newhouse and Aundria Crawford.

"He told investigator Hobson in detail what he did and how he did it. He confessed to his girlfriend. He confessed to his boss. He confessed to a newspaper reporter. He told the reporter, 'I'm a monster.' In these same discussions there is the story within the story that I've been referring to. There's information that when he was a very small boy, his parents separated. She married a man who was cruel to him. He was sent to live with his father, who beat him with his fists, with his feet.

"You'll hear he developed a tremendous amount of anger. What's surprising is that the anger was not focused on his father, but on his mother, because she had abandoned him, because she would not protect him. And still at a very young age, thirteen or fourteen, he starts having sexual fantasies and not just about sexual pleasure, but sexual pleasure, plus dominance, rape. And, again, what's surprising is the victim in this fantasy is his mother.

"These same fantasies never left. They never went away. They dominated his life."

Maguire talked about Krebs's "Jekyll and Hyde" personality. "Rex Krebs is actually two people. He's a good person and he's a bad person. He's a good person and he's a devil." Maguire blamed the transformation on the old wicked moonshine. "For Rex Krebs that lethal chemical combination was alcohol. He started drinking again while he was on parole. Because of the drinking, the fantasies returned and they were worse."

Maguire wrapped up his opening argument with a plea for the jurors to dig deeper into this case. "The number one witness in the prosecution's case is Rex Allan Krebs. They're going to be asking you to believe what he says when he tells you that he did these things.

"I'm also going to be asking you to believe Rex Krebs when he says the other things, the story within the story. When he talks about what happened to him when he was growing up. You'll see a man in misery telling his story.

"The important job that I ask of you is to look in the corners, look behind, look around what's being handed to you during this first phase of the trial. Listen for the other information. Listen for the story within the story. Listen to what Rex Krebs tells you and what other people may tell you eventually about what happened in his life that has resulted in him sitting in this courtroom in front of you, accused of these crimes. Thank you."

Opening arguments had ceased.

The first witness would testify the following morning.

Her name? Shelly Crosby.

The prosecution laid out their case beginning with Krebs's first 1987 rape. From there, they painted a picture of the disappearance of Rachel Newhouse. Andrea West testified to the fight that she and Rachel had in the Flats. Witness Theresa Audino described the blood she saw on the Jennifer Street Bridge. Police officers at the scene of Aundria Crawford's residence testified to what they saw there. Muriel and Debbie Wright spoke of Krebs and his tenancy on their property. Parole Officer David Zaragoza detailed his suspicions of Krebs after reading the paper. FBI Agent David Kice and other crime scene investigators spoke of the discovery of the bodies in Davis Canyon.

After three-and-a-half days of laying the groundwork for the two murders, the prosecution was ready to play its trump card.

FORTY-NINE

On the afternoon of March 26, 2001, Prosecutor John Trice knew he had the ace in the hole with his next witness, lead investigator for the district attorney's office, Detective Larry Hobson. It became apparent to everyone in the courtroom why he was the star witness for the prosecution.

Detective Hobson confidently strolled up to the witness stand, his physical appearance reminiscent of an ex-pro football offensive lineman. He was a little on the heavy side, but in an intimidating way. Hefty, yet nimble. Fierce, yet polished. His overall neat demeanor did not betray a hint of the intensity inside this man.

After swearing in Hobson, Trice asked for his credentials. "It's Assistant Chief Investigator Hobson, is that correct, sir?"

"Yes, sir," he replied in a quiet manner.

"By whom are you currently employed?"

"The District Attorney's Office, County of San Luis Obispo."

"And the assistant chief investigator, what does that person do?"

"Well, I'm assigned to the major crimes unit. It's a supervisory position where we carry a caseload. And I also supervise eight other deputy DA investigators."

Trice proceeded to inquire about Hobson's background. Hobson informed the court that he had been in law enforcement in one capacity or another for more than thirty years. He graduated from Cal Poly in the late 1960s, where he garnered a bachelor of arts degree in criminal justice. After graduation he worked the patrol division for two-and-a-half years in San Luis Obispo County. He received a promotion to narcotics and worked in numerous surrounding counties, including Kern, Fresno, Santa Barbara, and Monterey, as an undercover agent. He then received a promotion to the detective division, where he worked crimes against persons (CAP). This division oversaw crimes such as sexual assault, robbery, kidnapping, and homicides. While working in the CAP department, Hobson wanted to broaden his experiences and sought out additional education in the realm of interrogation and interviewing. In 1984 he enrolled himself, on his own nickel, in Baxter's School of Lie Detection in San Diego. The intense eight-week course covered all of the necessary polygraph techniques, including physiology, psychology, and interviewing strategies.

In September 1984 he received a job offer from the district attorney's office to be an investigator. He conducted polygraph examinations on the side.

In 1989 he attended a six-week polygraph course at the FBI National Academy in Quantico, Virginia. He traveled to several states to learn about polygraph and interrogation techniques over the years. He was so well versed in interrogation methods that he became a favorite on the lecture circuit, even traveling to Beijing, China, in 1996 to lecture their local police academy. Furthermore, he also taught interviews and interrogations at the Allan Hancock College for the Police Academy.

In 1994 Detective Hobson received another promotion: assistant chief investigator for the district attorney's office.

After laying out Hobson's credentials, Trice brought him around to the matter at hand. "You were the lead investigator for the district attorney's office in the investigation of the disappearance of Rachel and Aundria, is that correct?"

"Yes, sir."

"And you've worked on many, many homicides during your career?"

"More than one hundred."

"Would it be safe to say one of the major contributions you made to the investigations was a series of interviews you conducted with the defendant between March 21, 1999, and May 6, 1999?"

"Yes."

"What significant event took place on March 21, 1999?"

"I worked on Sunday, just like any other day since November 13, 1998. Went out and interviewed people during the day, followed up leads. We came back for a briefing at four o'clock at the police department, and Detective Jerome Tushbant, the primary investigator for the disappearance of Aundria Crawford, briefed us on two people that had been arrested over the weekend. And I was assigned to interview one of those two people."

"And one of those two people was whom?"

"Rex Allan Krebs."

"And did you interview him that day?"

"Yes, I did."

"Where was this interview conducted?"

"It took place at the San Luis Obispo Police Department. We had to have Rex transported from the county jail."

"How long did that interview take?"

"Approximately forty-five minutes to an hour."

"What was the first thing you covered with him?"

"I asked him if he had any idea as to why we wanted to talk to him. He said he assumed it was over the disappearance of the two girls, since he was on parole for rape and had a prior sex offense."

"How did you end this first interview you had with him?"

"I asked him if he would be willing to assist us with the investigation, since he had prior experience with sex offenses. Rex Krebs told me that he couldn't even remember the crimes he committed before because he put that all behind him. He said he couldn't help me. He said he would be willing to do anything he can to prove to us that he's not responsible for the abduction of these two women."

Hobson continued to testify that he contacted Krebs's girlfriend, Roslynn Moore, and asked for her help. He wanted to
tap her home phone and record a conversation with Krebs
concerning the disappearances of Rachel and Aundria.
Moore, stunned, agreed to do so, but only because she believed Krebs to be innocent and incapable of such malice.
Hobson testified that on March 24 he set up the recording de-
vice on her phone. Moore received a call from Krebs at 11:00
A.M., which Hobson taped along with two more calls.

"And are there any admissions by the defendant on any of
those tapes?" asked Trice.

"No, there's not," replied Detective Hobson.

"Is there anything that he said that you attached any evi-
dentiary significance to?"

"What struck me as significant were the things he didn't
say, such as denying that he was responsible for the crimes to
Roslynn Moore. And also, he wanted to know through her
what we were doing, as far as the investigation."

"You had another interview with the defendant on April 1,
1999, is that correct?" inquired Trice.

"Yes, sir."

"How long did this interview take?"

"Forty-five minutes or less."

"Did you tell him that as a result of your investigation you
were going to have to be displaying pictures of him and his
vehicles in public?"

"Yes, I did. He was cooperative."

"He told you he was confident he would be cleared, didn't
he?"

"Yes, he did."

"And on this interview on the first of April, did you go over
the details again of March tenth and eleventh?"

"Yes."

"And were there some differences this time?"

"Just one. One difference in the story that he told me the
first time. The second time on the morning of March

eleventh, after he got up and made coffee, instead of walking down to the woodpile to cut wood, he drove his truck down to the woodpile and cut wood."

"And he told you he had never been on Branch Street." Trice wanted to know if Krebs had ever traveled on Aundria Crawford's street.

"That's correct."

"What did he tell you this time?"

"I asked him if there was any reason why someone would identify either his truck or him when we show the pictures in the neighborhood around Branch Street, anywhere near Aundria Crawford's house."

"What did he say to that?"

"After thinking about it, he said there probably was. For the first time he told me that he had driven down that street two or three times when he left the Gaslight to go see his friend that lived at the end of Branch Street."

"Did you go over the story again about the eight ball and prison?"

"Yes. I told him we had had the opportunity to do some testing on the eight ball that he said he found on the yard at Soledad in about 1996. I said based on the testing, we found out that the eight ball that we took from his house had not been manufactured until 1998. I asked him how it was possible he had possession of it then. His response was a period of silence as he scratched his chin and said, 'That's strange.' "

"The next time you interviewed the defendant was on April 21, 1999?"

"Yes."

"That would have been right after results were received concerning blood on the jump seat?"

"Actually, the same morning we received it."

"Why did you interview him then on the twenty-first?"

"Because at that time, for the first time in five months, we had our first viable suspect in the disappearance of Rachel Newhouse and Aundria Crawford."

"How long did this interview take place?"

"It lasted approximately two hours."

"You offered him a hypothetical question, is that right?"

"I asked him to think about it—if he decided to stalk and kidnap somebody, how would he go about doing it?"

"And what did he tell you?"

"He says, 'I'm not even going to think like that, Larry. Thinking like that is dangerous.'"

"Did you talk to him about whether he had fantasized about abducting these two girls?"

"Yes. He admitted that he fantasized during the first part of his sentence at Soledad. He said he couldn't deny that he had fantasies about that, but that he also worked those fantasies out a little bit at a time."

"Did he tell you whether he had an opinion about whether people made him do those things"—referring to his earlier sexual offenses—"or if he made himself do those things?"

"Yes, he did. He told me it was because he hated women."

"Which women?"

"He said, 'All women. I have no respect for them.'"

"And you said, 'Why couldn't you be the person that took these two girls,' right?"

"Right."

"And his response?"

"'Cause it's not in my makeup.'"

Trice was ready to move in for the kill. The jurors sat at attention as Hobson detailed his interviews with Krebs. "Eventually you got around to talking about the jump seat?"

"I told Rex when we went through his truck, we noticed something very significant. It was missing one of the jump seats."

"And then you told him about the blood?"

"That's correct. I told him when we found it, we found signs that someone had cleaned it, but there were still traces of blood underneath in the railing. I also told him that we sent that jump seat off to the lab in Fresno to have it analyzed as far as DNA evidence to link him to one of our two victims."

"And what did he say to that?"

"He said he understood. I then told him that the blood that was found on that jump seat belonged to Rachel Newhouse. Then he went silent for a long period of time.

"I asked him to take me to the location where we could find the girls."

"And did he say he would do that?" asked Trice.

"He asked me if I could give him a cigarette and a half an hour to think about it?"

"Did you ask him what he was thinking about?"

"Yes."

"What did he say?"

" 'Dying.' "

"Eventually you took him back to the jail?" continued Trice. Hobson responded, "Yes, I did."

"How long of a drive?"

"Probably twenty minutes."

"And he was in the backseat smoking?"

"Yes."

"Did he say anything to you while you're driving?"

"Not at first. At first I could hear him back there crying. I asked him what he was thinking about and he said, 'A dead man walking.' "

"Did you ask him any questions as you got back to the jail?"

"I turned to him and asked if he was ready to take me where I could find Rachel and Aundria."

Krebs rejected Hobson's request. Hobson took Krebs back to jail and told him he would stop by tomorrow to continue their conversation.

The next morning, at 9:45, Hobson escorted Krebs into the employee break room at the San Luis Obispo County Jail. The two men sat down and Krebs looked up at the detective.

"What do you want me to tell you?" the haggard thirty-three-year-old asked.

"I told him I wanted him to tell me the truth. He says, 'I'll talk to you, but let's go someplace else.'"

Hobson removed Krebs from the jail, placed him in his car, and drove back over to the San Luis Obispo Police Department.

Trice continued to draw the information out of Hobson. "And before doing that, did you do anything in relation to him?"

"I wanted to make sure that Rex Krebs knew exactly where we were going and why we were going there." Hobson then recounted how he read Krebs his Miranda rights and then asked the pivotal question.

"I asked him if he was responsible for the disappearance of Rachel Newhouse and Aundria Crawford. He said, 'Yes.' I asked him if he was responsible for their deaths. He said, 'Yes.'"

Hobson testified how he needed to get the details on videotape, how he brought Krebs into the tiny interrogation room in the police department at 10:40 A.M. Waiting for answers—answers that no one outside of the lawyers' offices and courtroom chambers could hear for the past two years. Answers that would finally be forthcoming.

Nevertheless, they would have to wait one more day.

FIFTY

The following morning, Larry Hobson popped a videotape dated April 22, 1999, into the VCR. The television screen beamed a dull glow with the black-and-white video of the detective and Rex Krebs.

In the video Hobson walked up to Krebs with a slight hesitation and then gently placed his large hand on Krebs's shoulder. "Stand up, we'll get this stuff off you." He motioned toward Krebs's handcuffed wrists. He unlocked the suspect and motioned to the chair behind the wooden table. Hobson took his chair opposite Krebs and began the Miranda warning process.

Upon completion, Hobson jumped right into the key information.

"Are you responsible for the disappearance of the two girls?" Hobson asked Krebs point-blank.

Rex Krebs looked at the officer and then down at his lap. He looked up once again and slowly began to nod his head.

"Are we going to find either girl alive?" Hobson queried.

"No," came the unemotional reply from Krebs.

"Where do you want to start talking? I know this isn't easy. Like I said, the Rex Krebs that I spent a month getting to know by reading your stuff and searching your house, searching your trucks, isn't the same Rex Krebs that I'm dealing with right now as far as what happened to these two girls. But I need to have you tell me what did happen, so we can put it in the proper perspective," the officer calmly asked of Krebs.

"There is no perspective," was his response.

"The issue isn't whether it happened, it's why it happened," Hobson impatiently shot back. "Had you seen Rachel before November twelfth?"

"No."

"What were the circumstances where you first saw her that night?"

"Walking down the street drunk," Krebs replied in reference to Rachel Newhouse's inebriated state five months earlier.

"Whereabouts did you see her?"

"Santa Barbara Street, I believe it is. I saw her walking up toward the railroad station."

"How do you know she was drunk?"

"Staggering."

"She was staggering?" Hobson asked. The officer reached into his shirt pocket and pulled out a pack of cigarettes. He effortlessly flicked the packet forward at a forty-five-degree tilt with his wrist. A cigarette slid halfway out of the pack. He directed the offering to Krebs, who accepted. Instead of asking for a light, however, Krebs began to chew on the tobacco. Hobson continued the query. He was only just beginning. "What were you doing?"

"Drinking," Krebs replied rather nonchalantly.

"Where had you been drinking that night?"

"I think I'd been into Mother's, Library, Bull's."

"About what time of night did you see her?"

"I don't know. It was late. Midnight."

"When you saw her, what did you do?"

"Drove by her. I was driving up toward Santa Barbara Street."

"Then what'd you do?"

"Stalked her," Krebs stated.

Hobson was getting the information he wanted, but he felt as if the conversation was moving too rapidly. He needed more specifics as to what happened that night. He attempted to get Krebs to speak in a more detailed fashion. "When you say you stalked her, what are you talking about?" he asked in hopes of eliciting more detailed information.

It did not work.

Krebs's response was simple: "Drove around the block."

Hobson returned to a chronological structure. "Then what'd you do?"

"I watched her."

"Did you pull over and stop?"

"I stopped on one of the side streets."

"Then what'd you do?"

"Watched where she was walking."

"Did she continue staggering down Osos Street toward Santa Barbara Street?"

"Uh-huh."

"And eventually did she turn on this little side street that led to the bridge?"

Krebs paused for a moment and then glared up at Hobson. "I had a—oh, what do you call it?—premonition . . . where she was going."

Hobson, once again, look nonplussed as he replied, "A premonition, OK. And where did you think she was going?"

"Up on the bridge."

"And so what did you do after the premonition?"

"Drove in, parked my truck, went up on the bridge."

"So as she's staggering, you had a premonition that she was going to the bridge."

"Uh-huh."

"Did you know for sure she was going there?"

"No."

"What would happen if she continued on Santa Barbara?"

"She'd be safe." Krebs made it sound as if Rachel Newhouse had a choice as to her fate that night. And, unfortunately for her, she had made the wrong decision.

Hobson shook his head and continued the interrogation. "Then what'd she do?"

"She went up on the bridge. She walked up the ramp."

"And you were already up there?"

"Yeah."

"What was your intent to do then? What was going through your head?"

"There really wasn't anything going through my head."

"What was going to happen?"

"Don't know."

"OK, now Rachel comes up the ramp, you're standing to the side. Does she see you?"

"Uh-huh."

"Do you talk to her?"

"No."

"Does she talk to you?"

"No, she walks, like she's going to walk around me."

"Then where does she go?"

"Walks behind me like she's going to go down the bridge."

"What happens next?"

"I attacked her."

"When you say you attacked her, what do you mean?"

"I turned around and hit her."

"What'd you hit her with?"

"My hand."

Hobson looked up impassively at Krebs and asked, "Just a fist?" Krebs nodded his head in the affirmative. "Where did you hit her?"

"Across the jaw, I believe," Krebs answered calmly.

"And when you hit her, did she go down?"

"She staggered over against the rail."

"Then what happened?" Hobson prodded.

"She screamed; I grabbed her, picked her up, and threw her down. Picked her up and I threw her on the platform."

"Just threw her down headfirst, feetfirst, backfirst?"

"Uh, flat."

"Flat? On her stomach, face, back?"

"I think on her back."

"What happened when you threw her down?"

"Dazed her."

"Then what?"

"Then I hit her again and knocked her out."

"So while she's on the ground you hit her and she's unconscious now? What happens?"

"I grabbed her and drug her down to my truck."

"You didn't carry her down?"

"No."

"How'd you drag her?"

"By her hair. I grabbed her hair and I pulled her down the stairs."

"Where was she bleeding at this point?"

"I think from the back of her head, where I smashed her on the platform."

"Was she bleeding about the mouth or anywhere you hit her?"

"I believe so, yeah."

Hobson paused for a brief moment and resumed his questions about the attack on the bridge the previous November. "You drug her down to your truck?" he continued.

"Uh-huh."

"What'd you do when you got down there?"

"Put her in the back of the truck behind the seats."

"Did you have to lay her down while you opened up your truck?"

"Yeah."

"Where did you lay her down at?"

"Right next to the truck on the passenger side." Krebs had placed the unconscious Newhouse on the asphalt next to his truck as he opened the passenger door. Apparently, no one was in the area, despite the close proximity to several stores, restaurants, and a train station.

"Were you afraid somebody was going to come by?" Hobson wondered aloud.

"Very," Krebs replied, along with a vigorous nodding of his head.

"Once you got your door open, where did you put her in the truck?"

"Behind the seats."

"OK, so you folded your seat forward?"

"Uh-huh."

"And you lifted her up and put her in—"

"Right," Krebs interrupted.

"—where the jumps seats are?" Hobson finished.

"Uh-huh. I stuck her head and shoulders in and then I lifted her, uh, legs up and flopped them over."

"So she's in the passenger rear part of your truck in the cab area on that little jump seat."

"The jump seats were closed."

"She's still unconscious?"

Krebs nodded affirmatively.

"What'd you do then?" Hobson posited.

"Took some rope out of the back of the truck that I had in there for tying stuff in and I tied her up." Krebs seemed very methodical in his descriptions at this point—as if tying Rachel Newhouse up with rope were something he would do on any normal day.

"The rope was in the bed of the truck?" Hobson asked.

"Uh-huh."

"Where were you standing when you tie her up?"

"Leaning in from the passenger side."

"Did anybody drive by while you were standing there?"

Krebs shook his head. No one had driven by as he placed his victim's unconscious body into his blue Ford Ranger pickup truck.

"Did anybody walk by?"

Again Krebs shook his head in the negative.

"How did you tie her up?"

"On her stomach with her hands behind her back."

"So she's laying facedown on her stomach and you tied her hands behind her back. Did you tie her feet or anything?"

"No."

"Did you gag her or anything so she couldn't scream?"

"No."

"Did you use any duct tape?"

"No."

"Just the rope?"

"Uh-huh."

"Then what'd you do?" Hobson continued the probing.

"Got in the truck and then I drove down the railroad tracks. Away from population. There's a flat spot down there I drove down to. It's pretty big and open. Down past Pacific Home Improvement Center."

"And what'd you do there?"

"Then I stopped and I tied her legs."

"OK. Is she still unconscious?"

"Uh-huh."

"And you tied her legs. Same rope?"

"Uh-huh."

"Then what'd you do?"

Krebs sat erect in his chair as he answered, "I gagged her with her panties."

"How'd you get her panties?"

"Ripped them off."

"How'd you get her pants off? Not her panties but her pants?" Hobson wanted to know.

"Didn't take her pants off."

"Did you pull them down?"

"No."

"Well, how did you get her panties? What's she wearing?" Hobson asked, exasperated.

"She was wearing a pair of pants."

"Okay. But you said you ripped her panties off."

"I reached down the back of her pants and I ripped her panties off."

"And you stuffed her panties in her mouth?"

"Uh-huh."

"Then what?"

"There's still some rope left over, so I tied it through her mouth."

"To tie the panties in?"

"Uh-huh."

"Then what?"

"I left town."

Hobson paused to collect his thoughts. Krebs was giving him everything he wanted, but he needed to know more. Truth be told, the two men were just getting started.

"You said you'd been drinking earlier. What had you been drinking?" Hobson wanted to know.

"Jack Daniel's."

"How much Jack Daniel's? What time did you start drinking?"

"About eight-thirty, nine (P.M.)."

"How many Jack Daniel's do you think you consumed? Do you mix it with anything or Jack Daniel's on the rocks?"

"Jack Daniel's straight."

"Between eight-thirty, nine, and the time you first saw Rachel, how many Jack Daniel's did you have?"

"A few."

"What's a few?"

"Probably six or seven shots."

"On a scale of one to ten, ten being passed out and one being sober, where were you?"

"About eight."

Hobson refocused the discussion to Krebs's abduction of Rachel Newhouse. "So you drove up to your house. When you got to the house, what did you do?"

Krebs looked up at the officer. He paused. "Raped her."

Hobson realized Krebs was taking him down the path that everyone wanted to know about. He was going to spill the beans. Hobson needed more information, so he led Krebs systematically.

"Did you take her out of the car?"

"Yeah."

"Did you park your car or truck where you usually park it?"

"No, I went down to the, uh . . . I stopped at the cabin."

"The abandoned cabin?"

"Uh-huh."

"Where did you take Rachel then?"

"Into the cabin."

"You had to carry her?"

"Yeah."

"How'd you carry her?"

"Over my shoulder."

"Is she conscious now?"

"Yeah."

Hobson had Krebs and Rachel placed in the abandoned A-frame structure deep in Davis Canyon. He continued to dig for more details. "You get her inside the abandoned cabin, it's still dark, and what happens in there?"

"I raped her," Krebs repeated for the second time in less than three minutes.

"She's tied up. Do you untie her?" Hobson forged onward

"Her legs."

"What happens to her pants?"

"I pulled them off."

"Did you have a knife, where you cut them off?"

"No, I pulled them off."

"Did you untie the panties from her mouth?"

"Yeah."

Despite the grim nature of the confession, Hobson continued to ply details from the paroled convict. "Did you talk to her?"

"No."

"Did she talk to you?"

"Yeah. She was cussing me. 'Fuck you, you piece of shit.' "

"Was she sober, intoxicated?"

"She was drunk," Krebs spat out, almost convinced that this was justification for his actions.

"Did she say anything else to you?"

" 'Get out of me.' "

"When she called you, said, 'Fuck you, you're a piece of shit,' how'd that make you feel?"

"About the way I feel right now," Krebs replied as he shifted uncomfortably in the tiny wooden chair.

"Then what did you do to her?"

"After raping her, I retied her."

"When you say you raped her, what do you mean by raped her? What did you do? Did you put your penis in her vagina?"

"Yes."

"Did you sodomize her?"

"Huh-uh," he stated emphatically, denying the accusation.

"Did you ejaculate?"

"Yeah."

"Was she fighting during this process?"

"Yeah," he stated yet again.

"Did you go down on her?"

"No."

"Did you make her go down on you?"

"No."

"So it was strictly vaginal intercourse. Then what'd you do?"

"Turned her over on her stomach, retied her legs."

"Like they were before?"

"Yeah." Krebs acknowledged the hog-tied position.

"Now when you say you tied her legs, are her legs attached to any part of her body or her hands?"

"Her hands."

"So she's hog-tied then . . . Her legs are pulled up in a *L* shape?"

"Yeah."

"Tied to her hands?"

Krebs again nodded his head.

"So she's clothed on the top half, but she's naked from the bottom half, right?" Hobson continued.

"Right."

"Then what happened?"

"I run the loop above, rope around her neck to keep her, uh, make her keep her legs up."

"Her feet were tied to her hands and then looped around her neck?"

"Uh-huh," Krebs grunted.

"Then what happened?"

"I went home."

"And you just left her there?"

Krebs nodded yes again. "So then you got in your truck and drove up to your house. What'd you do when you got home?" Hobson continued.

Krebs looked up pensively at the detective. He sighed and finally told him, "Can't remember what the hell I was doing."

"Did you have something to drink?"

"I think I did have a shot of whiskey."

"And did you sit down and think what the hell was I doing?"

Krebs, staring off into space, nodded. "Sat down and thought what the hell was I doing."

"When you left her"—Hobson kept the conversation going—"was she gagged?"

"Yeah."

"How'd you gag her again?"

"Stuffed her panties back in her mouth."

"So she's left there; she's alive, but she's gagged so she can't scream."

"Right."

"Then what'd you do?"

"I went back down."

"How much later? The next morning?"

"No, about ten or fifteen minutes."

Hobson adjusted himself in his seat and hunkered down to nail the specifics of what happened next. "So you drove up to the house, had a shot of whiskey, thought about it, and drove back down." Krebs nodded again and Hobson asked what happened next.

Krebs responded, "When I went in, she was dead."

Hobson finally found out what everyone in San Luis Obispo had waited for five months to know. Rachel Newhouse was dead and Rex Krebs was involved. "She was dead?" he asked incredulously. "What killed her?"

"The rope around her neck."

"When you tied the rope around her neck, Rex, was it in such a position that she couldn't breathe?"

"No."

"She could breathe when you left?"

Once again Krebs nodded his head.

"So what you're telling me, then, is her struggling caused her to strangle herself?"

"That or her legs relaxed or something. I don't know," Krebs responded with a straight face.

"How do you know she was dead?"

"'Cause she wasn't breathing when I untied her."

"Then what'd you do?"

"Panicked."

"It's understandable," Hobson reassured. "When you panicked, what'd you do?"

"I walked around in circles. Carried her out of the cabin."

"Where did you take her?"

"Behind the cabin."

"Then what'd you do?"

"Went home."

"When did you come back?"

"The next morning."

"Would this have been after Debbie left for work?"

"Yeah," Krebs responded.

"She leaves for work at what time?"

"Around eight (A.M.) or so, I guess."

"Is Muriel home?"

"I don't know."

Hobson returned the conversation to what happened after Krebs found Rachel Newhouse's dead body. "So you got back in your truck and you drove back to the cabin. Then what'd you do?"

"Actually, I didn't drive back to the cabin," Krebs recalled. "I drove down the road farther, where I'd been cutting wood."

"To the woodpile?"

"Farther down than that. Where I was putting the wood in."

"And then where did you go on foot?"

"Up to where I was cutting wood. I took a shovel with me. Dug a grave and I buried her."

"She's still at the cabin, though, right?"

"Uh-huh."

"So you parked your truck where you were cutting wood, went up the hill?"

"Uh-huh," Krebs proffered yet again.

"And dug a grave. And then how did you get her?"

"Waited till that night."

"All right. What time do you think?"

"Late."

"This would be on Friday the thirteenth then, right?"

"I guess."

"And when you say late, what are we talking about?"

"Eleven-thirty (P.M.), twelve (P.M.)."

"What did you do during the day after you dug the grave? You're off work, right? What'd you do during the day? Did you stay home or did you go someplace?"

"Stayed home."

"Didn't go anywhere that day?"

"No."

"What'd you do then?"

"Went and got her. Put her in the back of the truck. Drove down to where I dug the grave, picked her up."

"And you lifted her out of the back, put her over your shoulder?"

Krebs nodded.

"How far off of the road is the grave?" Hobson continued.

"Twenty yards."

"Is it up a hill or flat?"

"Up a hill."

"By trees?"

"Kind of in a flat spot."

"And then after that, what'd you do?"

"Went back home."

"Did you see Roslynn that weekend?"

"I think I did, yeah."

"And did she come out and stay at your place?"

"Yeah."

"At any time, did you have Rachel inside your house?"

"No."

"When did you notice the blood in the back of your truck?"

"When I took her out of the truck. At the cabin."

"You realized she bled quite a bit in the back of your truck?" Krebs again nodded. "When did you clean up that blood?" Hobson queried.

"Sometime during the day . . . same day that I buried her."

"So after you dug the grave, you went back and cleaned your truck before you put her in the grave?"

Krebs again shook his head yes.

"What did you do to clean that truck?" Hobson wanted to know.

"Took the seat out of it."

"Was there blood on the seat?"

"Yeah."

"Was there blood on your carpet?"

"Uh-huh."

"Did you cut any carpets out?"

"Cut the carpet out."

"Okay. What'd you do with the carpet?"

"Threw it away."

"What'd you clean the jump seat with?"

"Some kind of a carpet cleaner."

"But it didn't work? So then you cut it out?"

"There was too much."

"What'd you cut it out with?"

"Utility knife."

"Where'd you put it? Well, when you cleaned it, you thought it was clean, right?"

"No, if it was clean, I would have put it back in the truck," Krebs responded somewhat sarcastically.

"Where did you put that jump seat then after you did your best?" Hobson tried again.

"Where you found it."

"Which was where?"

"In the downstairs at the cabin. In the barn."

"Where in the room did you put it?"

" 'Bout halfway back on the right-hand side."

"Did you do anything else to your truck that you had to clean up?"

"There was some blood on the seat belt, so I cut it out. The passenger seat belt."

"So she bled up to that point also? Was there any other blood in your truck?"

"Not that I can think of."

"When you put her in the grave site, was she still tied?"

Krebs paused before he answered. "No, I think I cut the rope."

Hobson countered, "But her hands and her feet were tied, you just cut the rope from the hog-tied position?"

"I believe so."

"Had you ever seen Rachel before that night?"

"No."

"That was the first time you saw her?" Krebs nodded his head in the affirmative. "When you saw Rachel, did you have any plan as to what you were going to do or did it just kind of spiral on you?" Again Krebs nodded yes. "One thing progressed to the next? Did you intend to kill her, Rex?"

"No," Krebs stated quietly.

"What were you going to do with her?" Hobson asked.

"I hadn't really thought about that."

"She could identify you, though, right?"

"Possibly. She was pretty drunk; I hit her pretty fast."

"So you don't think she'd be able to identify you."

"No."

"What were you going to do with her the next day when you went down there and she was tied up, had she been alive?"

"I was going to take her back into town and let her go."

"Did you think you would be contacted about Rachel?"

"Yeah."

"What'd you think when you weren't contacted?"

"Ask David Zaragoza," Krebs said, referring to his parole agent.

"What does that mean?"

"Ask David Zaragoza" Krebs pointedly repeated.

"Why, he knows?"

"He knows exactly what I was thinking."

"What'd you tell him?"

"I told him I was pissed."

"That nobody contacted you?" Krebs nodded his head yes. "Suppose somebody had contacted you, what would you say?"

"Of course, I would have lied."

Larry Hobson had elicited the confession he wanted. He got Rex Krebs to admit that he had assaulted, kidnapped, raped, and possibly murdered Rachel Newhouse. Now he also knew exactly where her body would be located.

But Larry Hobson was not done with Krebs just yet.

He wanted to find out what happened to Aundria Crawford.

FIFTY-ONE

The videotaped confession continued. Larry Hobson extracted information from Rex Krebs like he was squeezing tangy juice from a lemon. He was on a roll and not ready for the release to stop. He egged the convict on.

"This is Aundria now." He steered the conversation toward the second missing person that Krebs was the prime suspect in a possible murder.

"First time I seen Aundria . . . first time I seen Aundria . . . driving past her house, leaving the, uh, Gaslight," Krebs recalled.

"It was nighttime or daytime?" Hobson prompted.

"At night. Getting out of her car, going in her house."

"Where was her car parked?"

"Next to her house."

"What kind of car was it?"

"White car."

"How could you see her?" Hobson wanted to know.

"She was wearing white pants."

"How many times did you go back and watch her at her house?" Hobson inquired. He was aware that Krebs had been stalking Crawford for some time and wanted to know exactly how long he had done so.

"That night would have been the first night," Krebs recollected.

"And what'd you do after you saw her and parked?"

"Drove up on the next block. Walked back."

"Did you go around to the back of the house?"

"Uh-huh," Krebs grunted.

"What's at the back of the house that you remember?"

"There's a deck and a fence, and I looked through the back window."

"Window? Were there curtains or something covering them?"

"Yeah, there's a little gap at the bottom," Krebs clearly recalled.

"OK. Could you see her at all?"

"Little bit."

Krebs's short replies were mildly annoying to Detective Hobson; however, he remained calm and focused. "How long did you stay there?" he continued.

"Three or four minutes."

"Did you do anything while you were there?"

"No."

"And when did you come back?" Hobson wanted Krebs to detail each of his stalking experiences with Crawford.

"About a week later."

"You never drove the Dodge Colt over there?" Hobson alluded to Krebs's other car that he owned.

"No."

"Never?"

"Never," he abruptly responded.

"You never parked that Dodge Colt anywhere on her block?" Hobson persisted.

"Larry," an annoyed Krebs stated.

"No, I—I hear what you're saying. I'm just—I want to make sure I hear it," Hobson sputtered out rather unconvincingly.

"Larry. Your eyewitnesses are bullshit."

"OK."

"That car was never on the street."

Hobson quickly dropped that line of questioning and attempted to extract more meaningful information from his number one suspect.

"OK, the second time was a week after the first time," Hobson resumed the discussion of Krebs's penchant for stalking Aundria Crawford. "Had you been drinking?"

Krebs nodded and said, "Every time I went over there, I'd been drinking."

"Remember the day of the week it was?"

"Middle of the week."

"What'd you do that time?"

"Looked at the place."

"From out front?"

"Uh-huh. Walked around the block."

"What were you thinking about?"

Krebs looked down at his lap and slowly raised his head toward Hobson. He took a deep breath and calmly replied, "Taking her."

"What did you do that night, the second night?"

"Looked."

"Did you ever get up on her roof?"

"No."

"Did you get on the roof behind her house? There's a roof back there, a flat roof. Did you get on that roof?"

"Yeah."

"There's a pile of leaves up there. Did you sit on those leaves?"

"Pushed them to the side."

"Then from that location, you could look in and see her loft up there?"

"Uh-huh."

"Is she the type of person that went to bed early at night or is—"

"Seemed like late," Krebs threw out before Hobson could finish his question.

"From this location, could you watch her get ready to go to bed?" Hobson continued without missing a beat.

"Uh-huh."

"Did you see her take her clothes off?"

"One time."

"How many times were you actually here on the roof?"

"Actually there on the roof?" Krebs repeated. He thought about it for a split second and quickly answered "Twice."

"About how long do you think you sat up there and watched?"

"Ten or fifteen minutes."

"That's all? Did you masturbate?"

"No."

"And what'd you do then?"

"Went and got more drunk."

"You went where to get drunk?"

"My truck."

"You had some booze in your truck?" Krebs nodded his head in the affirmative. "Did you come back after you drank?"

"No, I went home."

"How many days passed before you went back?"

"Four, five, something like that."

"This is the third time you went back. What did you do this time?"

"Went through a, uh, driveway on the back side. Went over a fence, in this house's yard, went over the fence."

"Did you get up on the roof again?"

"Yeah."

"How'd you get up on the roof? Off of the fence?"

"Tree."

"Was she up in the loft?" Hobson referred to Crawford.

"Uh-huh."

"And what time of night is it?"

"Late."

"What's she doing?"

"Moving around back and forth in her house."

"When she wasn't up in her loft, you couldn't see her—could you—from here?"

"Just through the . . . uh—"

"The blinds?" Hobson interrupted.

Again, slightly annoyed at the intrusion, Krebs responded with an edge, "The door."

"How long did you watch her?" Hobson calmly asked, trying to get back in good graces with Krebs.

"Probably about the same. Ten or fifteen minutes," Krebs replied as he shook his head no, then switched directions and nodded yes.

"Then what'd you do?"

"Went. Left."

"Had you been drinking that night?"

"Yeah."

"Had you been drinking the second night?"

Krebs shook his head yes.

"You were drinking the first night," Hobson continued as Krebs nodded. "How many days did you wait before you went back again?"

"Would have been the night I took her."

"Were you only there four times, Rex?"

"Yeah."

"That was it? No more? Did you ever get up on top of her roof?"

"No."

"The fourth time you went, where did you park?"

"The fourth time. Right in front of her house."

Hobson had zeroed in on the night of Aundria Crawford's abduction. "What time of night is this now?"

"Late night, early morning."

"So it's after midnight?"

"Yeah."

"Where do you go when you park in front?" Hobson asked while pointing toward the diagram of Aundria's Branch Street duplex apartment.

"Check the doors."

"Is her door locked?"

Krebs nodded yes.

"How do you know she's home?" Hobson wanted to know.

"Her car is there," Krebs muttered as he laid his head down onto the table.

"You go around in the back?"

"Check the sliding glass door, it's locked."

"Did you start to go in the house through the sliding glass door and she saw you and you ran?"

"No," he replied, and looked up quizzically at Hobson.

"No? Because she had a prowler there, end of February, sometime about two weeks prior. That wasn't you?"

"That wasn't me."

"So the door is locked back there," Hobson stated as he pointed at the diagram yet again. "Can you see her in there?"

"No. It's dark."

"Are all her lights off?"

"The house is dark."

"Where had you been drinking that night?" Hobson switched gears.

"Home," came the monosyllabic reply.

"Could it be as late as two or three in the morning?"

"Yeah."

"And on this day that you went there, you worked until six-thirty that night?"

"Yeah."

"What did you do after you got off work?"

"Went home."

"And what'd you do at home?"

"Made dinner and drank."

"What'd you drink?"

"Jack Daniel's."

"Is it Jack Daniel's or Yukon Jack?"

"Jack Daniel's."

"How much did you drink?"

"Probably about half a fifth."

"After drinking, you decided that would be the time to go back in there and take her?"

"Sure." He shrugged nonchalantly.

"What do you do next?" Hobson continued.

"Check the windows. One back by the sliding glass door."

"Is it locked?"

"Uh-huh. Kitchen window. It's locked. See the little bathroom window's open."

"Where's the bathroom window located?"

"Left of the door."

"Which door?"

"Front door."

"How big is that window?" Hobson asked, and tilted his head down toward Krebs's feet.

"Tiny."

"Show me with your hands." Krebs placed his right hand above his left to indicate a height of ten to twelve inches. "How wide?" He placed his hands this time side by side, but eighteen to twenty-four inches apart. "OK. And it was not latched? Was there a screen on there?"

"Yeah."

"What'd you do with the screen?"

"I folded it and threw it away."

"How did you reach up to that window? It's up pretty high."

"Stood on the, uh, rail by the steps."

"What do you do?"

"Crawled in."

"How do you go in? Headfirst, feetfirst?"

"Feetfirst."

Hobson seemed surprised. "Feetfirst? OK. And when you go in that window, where does it come out to?"

"Shower stall."

"Are you making quite a bit of noise when you go in there?"

"Yeah."

"How do you lower yourself down?"

"Arch my back."

"Where do you put your feet?"

"On, uh, I think it's a soap—"

"Soap dish?" Hobson cut in.

"Soap, right," Krebs responded. "It's like it's a little tiny bathroom," he stated as he rubbed his weary eyes. He then gently lowered his head into his hands as if saying a silent prayer.

"Does she wake up?"

"I hear a little bit of noise on the other side of the door."

"Where do you hear noise at?"

"It's like a bathroom area with a toilet and a door. Then there's the sink area. And there's another door. When I get in here," he stated as he again pointed toward Hobson's diagram, just outside the interior of Aundria Crawford's bathroom, "I hear noise in here."

"OK. What's that noise?"

Krebs looked up at Hobson and said, "Turns out it was her cat." He then lowered his head back into his hands and slumped over in his chair. He looked defeated. He continued, though. "I wait until the noise stops."

"Do you see the cat?"

"No, not directly. When the noise stops, I wait a few minutes; my heart's beating. Thinking all I want to do now is get out." Krebs paused to recollect the nightmare. "Afraid I woke her up. Scared. I want to leave. But I know I can't go back out that window without making a bunch more noise."

"So what do you do?"

"I wait. And I open the door and find out it's just a cat. Cat goes by me into, uh, shower area. Close the door behind it. I'm getting ready to go out the bathroom door. The only thing I'm thinking of is leaving right then"—Krebs paused and looked directly at Hobson—"when she opens the door."

"What happens?" Hobson prodded.

"I hit her."

"You punched her?"

"Yeah."

"Where?"

"In the mouth."

"What's she wearing?"

"A T-shirt and a pair of underwear."

"When you punched her, what happened to her?"

"It knocks her back against the wall and I keep punching her."

"How many times did you punch her?"

"Three or four times."

"And what happens to her?"

"Goes unconscious," Krebs recalled without a hint of remorse or regret.

"Where is she laying?"

"In the entranceway, right in front of the door."

"Then what do you do?"

"Tie her up," Krebs coolly replied.

"OK, where did you get the rope?"

"Brought it with me."

"Is it the same rope you used on Rachel?"

"Yeah."

"You didn't leave the rope on Rachel?"

"Same type of rope. White nylon."

"How'd you tie her up?"

"Hog-tie, same as before."

"When you say hog-tie, explain it to me." Hobson wanted to hear it directly from Krebs's mouth.

"Hands behind the back, feet tied together, bunched up to the hands," Krebs unemotionally replied as he dropped his head down and rested his hands placidly in his lap.

"Is there a rope around her neck?"

"No."

"Do you gag her?"

"Yeah."

"How do you gag her?"

"I brought duct tape with me."

"So you put duct tape across her mouth?"

"Uh-huh."

"Do you ever go upstairs?"

"Yeah."

"What do you go upstairs for?"

"Pillowcases."

"What do you do with the pillowcases?"

"One pillowcase, put it over her head and tie it on."

"Why did you do that?"

"So she couldn't identify me."

"Was she bleeding?"

"Yeah."

"Were you wearing a mask?"

Krebs paused interminably before he responded. His voice was quiet, only slightly above a whisper. "Panty hose over my head."

"And you had gloves on?"

"Yeah. Brown gloves. Brown cloth gloves."

"Where did you get the panty hose from?"

Krebs shrugged his shoulders and lifted his hands up. "Uh, I don't know. I think they were at the ranch."

"Anything else you take from upstairs?"

After a ten-second pause, he finally answered, "Some CDs, I think."

"What kind of CDs were they?"

"All kinds of CDs. Rock, country, easy listening, I guess you'd call it."

"Do you put them in a pillowcase or do you just carry them?"

"Put them in a pillowcase."

"Anything else you took from upstairs?" Hobson inquired one more time.

"I think I stuffed some clothes in there."

"Some of her clothes?"

"Some sweats, yeah."

"Why'd you take the sweats?"

"To keep her warm. Took the stuff out of my truck."

"What else did you take from the house?"

"VCR."

"Why'd you take the VCR?"

"I don't know."

"What'd you do with the VCR?"

"Threw it away."

"Did you take anything else from downstairs?"

"Videotapes for the VCR."

"Where'd you throw the VCR away at?"

"Dumpster."

"What Dumpster?"

"No, not a Dumpster," Krebs corrected himself as he rolled his head around to pop his neck.

"Hmmm?" Hobson did not quite hear him.

"I said, 'No, not a Dumpster.'" Then, rather curiously, Krebs said to Hobson, "I haven't been lying so far, there's no sense of starting now."

"That's true. I appreciate that. Did you take anything home with you from her house?"

"Just the clothes and the CDs."

"OK, and all that got dumped out here?"

"No. Some of the clothes are in the closet at home."

"Your closet?" Krebs nodded yes. "Which closet, the one in your bedroom?"

"Yeah."

"What are the clothes that are in there?"

"Some sweats."

"What color?"

"Black, I think."

"Black sweats. Just one pair?"

Krebs waited several seconds before he responded. "I don't know, Larry."

"Why'd you keep the sweats?"

"Stupid."

"All right. What do you do then?"

"Looked around, seen nobody was around, went back into the house, got her."

"She's still unconscious?"

"No."

"She's conscious now?"

"Yeah."

"Is she struggling at all or . . ."

"Yeah," Krebs quickly responded.

"OK. What do you do with her?"

"Take her out and put her in the truck."

"Yeah."

"Where do you put her?"

"Behind the seats."

"Same location?" Krebs silently nodded his head in the affirmative. "OK. The pillowcase is over her head now, right, so she can't see you?"

"No."

"What do you do to the house?"

"Go back in, try and wipe up the blood."

"How'd you wipe it up with?"

"The towel that was there."

"A towel or a rug?"

"A towel."

"Did you do anything to the cat?"

"No."

"Did you leave him some food or something?"

"No."

"Cat's still wandering around?"

"Uh, cat I locked in the bathroom, I believe."

"Then what'd you do?"

"Went home."

"Where was her purse at? Did you ever see it?" Krebs shook his head no. "What about the eight ball?"

"That was on her keys."

"Where did you get that at?"

"Off the coffee table."

"Why did you take her keys with the eight ball?"

"Don't have a clue."

"Does (the number) eight have some significance to you?"

"Subconsciously, yeah, maybe."

"What'd you do with the key ring and the stuff that was on there?"

"It's out by the ranch."

"Where?"

"Throw'd off, up in the bushes."

"When did you do that? Was that the day you knew you were going to be searched?" Hobson continued the questioning.

"No, it's before then."

"Before. The day that you knew they were going to search your house and you got home earlier?"

"Uh-huh."

"Did you hide or destroy anything?"

"No."

"Everything was already gone?" Krebs silently nodded his head yes. "But you forgot about the eight ball?"

"Didn't even think about the eight ball."

"And where did you put it after you got home?"

"In the wooden box."

"You took the keys on the eight ball with you when you walked out? Did you lock the door?"

"I believe so."

"So you carry her out, put her in your truck, how about a belt buckle? Did you take a belt buckle?"

"No."

"Like the ones you design?" Hobson mentioned this in reference to Krebs's prison hobby of making oversize belt buckles with an infinity logo. "No belt buckle was taken?" Krebs shook his head no again.

"Then where did you go?"

"Home."

"So you're driving down the freeway, she's in the back, tied up, conscious now, but she's got duct tape on her mouth, right? She can't scream, yell? OK, and then you get off the freeway where?"

"Same place, San Luis Bay Drive."

"Then where do you go?"

"See Canyon Road. Davis Canyon Road. Go to my house this time."

"Where do you park the truck?"

"I take that back. I put her at the cabin," Krebs replied, referring to the A-frame cabin, where he murdered Rachel Newhouse less than four months earlier.

"You went to the cabin first?"

"Uh-huh."

"Same one?"

"Uh-huh."

"Pull in that little driveway?" Krebs nodded his head yes. "Carry her up to the cabin?" Again he nodded his head. "Then what do you do?"

"Leave her on the couch."

"Then where do you go?"

"Home."

"Then what do you do?" Hobson asked, attempting to keep Krebs focused.

Krebs stopped for a moment, placing his hands behind his head and clasping them together; then he spread his chained legs.

"Drink some more," he finally replied after a seemingly endless wait.

"OK, you drink some Yukon Jack or . . ."

"Jack Daniel's."

"Is the sun coming up yet?"

"It's starting to get light. That's why I put her at the cabin instead of bringing her to the house."

"Then what do you do?"

Krebs shifted in his chair uncomfortably. "Real close to what I told you before."

"Do you go down to the woodpile?"

"Yeah."

"How do you get there?"

"Truck."

"So you drive your truck down there. Why do you drive down to the woodpile?"

"'Cause I know Debbie's gonna be going to work soon." Krebs was referring to Debbie Wright.

"OK, and you want Debbie to see you?"

"Yeah."

"And does Debbie come by and see you?"

"Yeah."

"What are you doing when she comes by?"

"I split some wood. Talked to her for a minute. She goes off to work."

"What do you do?"

"Go down and get Aundria."

"Where do you put her?"

"Bring her up to the house."

"You put her in the truck?"

"Yeah."

"In the front or the back?"

"Back."

"And she's conscious?"

"Yes."

"Then you take her up to the house, and what happens?"

"Raped her a couple of times through the day."

Hobson wanted Krebs to slow down and backtrack on the details now. "You get her up to the house between eight and eight-thirty? She's still wearing panties and a T-shirt?"

"Yeah."

"Where do you put her at the house?"

"On the bed."

"In your bedroom? OK, and you cut the ropes off?"

"Freed her hands and her feet. Her hands are still tied, her feet are still tied, but they're not tied together."

"Is this when you raped her the first time?"

"Yeah," he replied unemotionally.

"Did you rip her panties off, take them off?"

"Pulled them off."

"Were they torn? It's gonna be a little—"

"I believe so," Krebs interjected.

"It's gonna be a little hard to get them over her feet if they aren't torn," Hobson continued.

"Yeah," Krebs muttered as he shifted position in his tiny chair and crossed his muscular arms across his chest.

"When you said you raped her, what did you do to her?"

"Uh, vaginal and sodomize."

"Did you untie her feet at that point?"

"Yeah."

"So her feet are not tied. OK. You had vaginal intercourse and sodomy. Did you go down on her, have her go down on you? Did you do anything else to her?"

"No."

"Did you ejaculate?"

"Yeah."

"Then what did you do?"

"Left her in the bed."

"Did you tie her feet back up?"

"Yeah."

"Did you ever take the pillowcase or the duct tape off?"

"Later."

"So you left her in bed—then what did you do?"

"Went in the kitchen. Drank some Yukon Jack with some coffee."

"Now there was nobody home at Muriel's, right? Muriel was out of town?" Krebs nodded his head yes. "Did you know she was out of town?"

"Yeah."

"She tell you she was leaving?"

"Yeah."

"And Debbie doesn't come home until when?"

"Late evening."

"What'd you do after you drank the Yukon and coffee or the Jack Daniel's and coffee?"

"Passed out."

"Where'd you pass out at?"

"Couch."

"And she's on your bed? What time'd you wake up?"

"Maybe an hour or so later."

"Then what'd you do?"

"Raped her again."

"And did you take the ropes off?"

"Yeah."

"Was she still wearing the T-shirt?"

"No, I cut the T-shirt off of her with a pair of scissors. The first time."

"So when you raped her the first time, she's totally nude except for the ropes and the pillowcase. And you used a pair of scissors? And when you went back in again after you took a nap and you raped her?" Krebs slowly nodded his head up and down. "You cut the ropes off her feet?"

"Actually, I untied them."

"And did you have vaginal intercourse?" Again Krebs nodded yes. "Sodomy, no? Go down on her? She go down on you? You just had vaginal intercourse? Did you take the tape off her mouth?"

"Yeah."

"When you took the tape off her mouth, what'd she say?"

Krebs looked up at Hobson and spoke in a quiet voice: " 'Why are you doing this?' "

"And what'd you say?"

"I didn't."

"Did you talk to her at all?"

"No."

"What else did she say to you? Did she ask you to stop or plead for you to let her go?"

"Yeah."

"Was she crying?"

"Yeah."

"Can you remember what she said to you?"

"No."

"That she was pleading with you to let her go?"

"Yeah, but not real vehemently."

"After you had vaginal intercourse the second time, what did you do?"

"I had taken her out of the bed, still blindfolded."

"By blindfolded, you mean the pillowcase?"

"With the pillowcase. Had her kneel by the coffee table. Took the, uh, pillowcase off her head. Put a bandana blindfold on her."

"OK, she's tied at the feet and the hands at this time (that) she's kneeling at the coffee table?"

"Just her hands."

"Her feet aren't tied?"

"No."

"Does she get up and try to run away?"

"No."

"Does she see you when you take the pillowcase off?"

"No, I got her back to me."

"So you take the pillowcase off and put a blindfold across her eyes?" Krebs nodded yes. "Is her mouth still free?"

"That's when I freed her mouth."

"Then what?"

"I told her, 'Don't try and look at me.'"

"Did she?"

"Later."

"She did look at you?" Krebs again nodded his head forward. "So after you put the blindfold on her, what did you do?"

"That's when I raped her the second time."

"That was the second time. That was when she was bent over the coffee table?" Krebs once again nodded. "Did you sodomize her?"

"Not that time, no."

"Just had vaginal intercourse from behind? So the first one occurred on the bed. The second one, while she was kneeling over the coffee table?" Krebs nodded. "Then what'd you do?"

"Put her back in the bedroom after I let her put a pair of sweats on."

"Was it her own sweats?"

"Yeah."

"So she had black sweats and a black sweatshirt that you brought with you?"

"Uh-huh."

"So you dressed her. Is she still—"

"I pulled it over her head," Krebs tossed in.

"OK, so it's not going through her arms because her arms are tied, right?"

"Right, right."

"Now she's back on the bed. Is she tied up, hands and feet?"

"Just her hands."

"Does she stay on the bed?" Krebs bowed his head in agreement. "Then what happens?"

"I go to sleep on the couch again. I hear a noise; I wake up. She's coming out of the bedroom. Got her blindfold off."

"She's still tied behind her back, her hands?"

"Uh-huh."

"What's she saying?"

"She was saying nothing."

"What do you do?"

"Strangle her."

"How did you strangle her?" Hobson asked nonplussed.

"Piece of rope."

"The same one you'd used to tie her feet?" Krebs nodded his head yes. "How did you strangle her?"

"From behind," Krebs stated quietly.

"Did you put her on the ground or was she standing up?"

"On the ground."

"Was she on her back, her stomach?"

"Stomach."

"And then you put the rope around her neck?" Krebs nodded yes. "And you pulled it tight?" Again yes. "And what happened?"

"She died." Simple as that.

"I'm sorry, Rex, I couldn't hear you."

"She died, Larry."

"Then what'd you do?"

Krebs did not answer Hobson's question immediately. After several seconds he responded, "Got really drunk. Put her on the floor of the bathroom so I wouldn't have to look at what I'd done."

"Then what'd you do?"

"Went out and dug a grave for her in the yard."

"Where in your yard, Rex?"

"Just the other side of the fence toward the right-hand side if you're looking at the creek."

Hobson began to draw a diagram of where Rex claimed Aundria Crawford's body was located.

"She'd be over here," Krebs proclaimed as he pointed to the diagram.

"I guess the fence goes like this?" Hobson asked Krebs as he referred to the schematic. "Your woodpile is down here." Krebs drew on the diagram. "The embankment, that's the wire fence?"

"That's the wire fence," Krebs answered. "Creek's down here. Should be right there."

"How deep are these graves, Rex? How far down do you think you dug?"

"Three-and-a-half, four feet."

"Did you bury the ropes and things with her?"

"Yes."

"OK, when you buried her, she didn't have anything on top?"

"She's got a black sweatshirt on."

"And then at some point you went into 84 Lumber, is that

right?" Krebs nodded yes. "You never fell in the woodpile? Hurt your ribs. Is that true?"

"I screwed up my ribs going through the window."

"So this was the morning you were supposed to meet Roslynn at the doctor's office?" Krebs shook his head up and down again. "But you couldn't meet her—"

"I completely forgot about it."

"What time do you think it was when you buried her?"

"Early afternoon."

"Does Roslynn know anything about this one?"

"Nobody knows anything about them."

"Just you and I."

"Just you and me."

Hobson stopped for a moment. He took a deep breath and then continued: "Rex, we've talked about Aundria and Rachel. . . ."

"There aren't any more, Larry," Krebs responded without hesitation.

"That's it?"

"Just those two."

"No others?"

"No."

"Nothing happened before Rachel?"

"No."

"Did you do any prowling or anything before Rachel?"

"No."

"No? So for thirteen months you didn't do anything? After you got released?"

"Not a thing."

"What do you think brought this on again with Rachel? The first time."

"I don't know, Larry. I wish I did."

"When you went out that night with Rachel, when you found Rachel and the night you decided to take Aundria, had you thought about it ahead of time?"

"Rachel, no."

"But when you drove to Aundria's, you knew; you knew you were going to take her?"

"That's right."

"Rachel, that was just somebody that was walking along and you saw her, huh?" Krebs nodded his head yes.

Krebs's head remained down as he placed his right hand to his forehead. Hobson was almost done.

"We probably won't have any trouble finding Aundria here, but I need to have you take me out there and show me, so we don't spend a lot of time just digging up dirt. Is that OK?"

Krebs did not answer for fifteen seconds. Finally "Yeah." Then, after shifting in his seat with his head still bowed down, he commented that "everybody's gonna know like wildfire."

Hobson stood up, took out his pack of cigarettes, thumped one out, and offered it to Krebs, who gladly accepted.

"Question," Krebs said to Hobson.

"Yeah?"

"It won't make any difference, anyway?"

"Go ahead and ask."

"If you go out there today and dig them up . . ."

"Uh-huh."

"I'm not gonna have a chance to tell Roz or Greg or anybody else. Because everybody's gonna know."

"Maybe I can arrange for you to sit down and talk to Roz this afternoon."

"Roz has got to have somebody here for her. What's today?"

"Today's Thursday."

"Is there any way you can put it off until Saturday, Larry?"

"Let me go talk to my boss. See what he says."

Hobson stood up and left the interrogation room. Krebs sat in his chair with his head down. He began to pick at his fingers. He then rubbed his eye, crossed his legs, but never lifted his head up.

He placed the cigarette in his jail-issue-shirt breast pocket.

That was the end of the April 22, 1999, videotaped confession. There was, however, a problem with one of the jurors.

Juror five, a female juror, began to cry during the confession when Krebs spoke of strangling Aundria Crawford. Judge LaBarbera addressed the matter with the attorneys. He noted that the juror filled out the initial questionnaire and mentioned that she cried easily. He brought the juror before the court, out of the presence of the other jurors, and questioned her ability to continue in a fair and unprejudiced manner against the defendant. The juror complained of tightness in her chest but stated that she felt better. She also stated that she got emotional over some of the things Krebs confessed to and that she found them "disturbing." She then apologized for her behavior and assured the court that she could carry out her duty without bias. The judge informed both parties that no infraction had taken place and asked the prosecution to show the next piece of evidence.

Detective Hobson resumed his familiar position on the witness stand. By this time the entire gallery's attention was focused directly on the veteran detective. They wanted to be sure not to miss a single word he uttered. Deputy District Attorney John Trice next steered the detective to the "drive-through tape." After Rex Krebs confessed to the murders of Rachel Newhouse and Aundria Crawford, Hobson asked him to go for a ride out to Davis Canyon. He wanted Krebs to show him where the girls' bodies were located.

"We put Rex Krebs in my car," Hobson recalled. "I rode in the back with Rex. Bill Hanley, one of the investigators that works for me, drove. We were followed by two officers from the San Luis Obispo Police Department, Keith Storton and Russ Griffith, who videotaped the process of going out to the canyon."

"And can you explain to the jury, so we won't have to stop and start this tape," continued Trice, "as you head out See Canyon toward Davis Canyon, you stop at some point. Is that correct?"

"Yes."

"Where did you first stop?"

"We make one stop, where you see Bill Hanley get out of the car. That's just for logistics. That's nothing.

"The second stop that we stopped, and you actually see Rex Krebs get out of the car, is the site where he buried Rachel Newhouse. We then drive past the A-frame and we didn't videotape the A-frame, but you'll see a mailbox on the left-hand side, where it goes down the driveway to the abandoned A-frame.

"The next stop was made at Rex Krebs's house, where he points out the grave site of Aundria Crawford, and then he takes us inside of the house to point some things out to us."

Trice approached Hobson and said, "Let me show you a tape. It's marked as 153 for identification. Ask you if you recognize this exhibit?"

"Yes," replied Hobson.

"What's that?"

"This is the videotape that was made of the trip to Davis Canyon with Rex Krebs."

"And that was on April 22, 1999?"

"Yes, it was. Around twelve-thirty, one o'clock in the afternoon."

The jurors attentively watched as the "drive-through" tape started.

FIFTY-TWO

Detective Larry Hobson was not done yet. He spoke of his duties from April 22, 1999, until two days later. The most significant events during that time for Hobson were the exhumation of the bodies and the subsequent autopsies. After observing the bodies, he noticed a few discrepancies between Rex Krebs's confession and the evidence on the corpses. The most significant one was the use of flex ties on Aundria Crawford's wrists. He knew he needed to go back and clarify several issues with Krebs. He wanted the best information possible to secure the charges against him.

In the courtroom all eyes returned to the state's star witness. They would soon turn their attention to yet another videotape.

Hobson popped in the cassette. The familiar black-and-white image of Hobson and Krebs appeared on the screen.

On April 24, 1999, Hobson pressed Krebs for even more specifics as to the murders and subsequent burial of the bodies. Hobson began his probe with the murder of Rachel Newhouse in the A-frame.

"All right, when you laid her down on the couch, what happened?" asked Hobson.

"I sat her up," Krebs replied in a monotone voice. "She's still pretty drunk. I cut through the back of her collar with the utility knife. Back of her shirt collar."

"That's the first time I've heard about the utility knife."

"I took it out of my back pocket."

"Why did you take the utility knife with you?"

"To cut her clothes off. After I cut through the collar, I ripped the blouse down the back."

"What was she wearing under the blouse?"

"A bra."

"A bra. Did you cut it off?"

"No."

"What did you do with the shirt you ripped off?"

"Left it on her."

"It's just kind of hanging there?"

"Yeah."

"Do you remember what color it was?"

"A light color. Light blue, I think." Rachel's blouse was actually a dark blue.

"You'd already ripped her panties off and stuffed them in her mouth, and when did you take the panties and duct tape off her mouth?"

"She spit the, uh, panties out in the truck on the way up."

"So she was cussing you then, coming up in the truck then?"

"Yeah."

"Before you got to the canyon?"

"No, after I started up the canyon."

"Now what do you do with the pants?"

"I pulled them off."

"Is she still talking to you at this time?"

"Yeah."

"And she's still cussing you?" Krebs nodded his head up and down. "What were some of the other things she was telling you?"

"I don't know."

"Did she ask you to let her go?"

"Yeah."

"And what did you tell her when she asked to be let go?"

"No."

"So you pull her pants off now; then what happens?"

"I unbutton her blouse."

"Did you unbutton it all the way down?"

"Yeah. Pulled it down onto her arms. I start touching her."

"You're touching . . . you're touching her breasts?"

"Yeah."

"Then what happens?"

Krebs sat silent for a moment. "I raped her."

"How did you rape her, what position?" Hobson wanted to know.

"Laying down on her back."

"Did you take all your clothes off or just your pants?"

"Just my pants."

"What were you wearing?"

"Pair of Levi's. Long-sleeved blue T-shirt."

"Where is that clothing now?"

"I got rid of it at the same time I got rid of her pants. In the Dumpster behind Texaco on Los Osos Valley Road."

"The one toward the freeway?"

"Yeah."

Krebs continued with the details of the sexual assault of Rachel Newhouse.

"When I was getting on her, after I started, um, raping her, she's fighting me a lot."

"How's she fighting you—with her feet? Legs?"

"Moving around a lot. Jumping, trying to keep me from raping her."

"When you say rape, you're talking about your penis going in her vagina, right?"

"Yes, sir."

"And your penis did go in her vagina, right?"

"Yes."

"And you ejaculated in her vagina?"

"Yes."

"And then after that, what did you do?"

"Rolled her over and retied her legs. A trucker's hitch."

"Did you want to go rape her again?"

"No. I had to go, let her go."

"You were going to let her go? And how were you going to do that?"

"Thought I'd take her back downtown somewhere and let her go."

Hobson still had difficulty with Krebs's assertion that he would free Rachel after he raped her. "Your intent when you went back down there was to take her back into San Luis and just let her go. Even though there was a possibility she could identify you and/or your truck?"

"Yes, sir."

"Where were you going to take her?"

"I figured I'd let her go down by the railroad tracks."

"What happened when you got back there?"

"She was dead."

"What do you think caused her to die?"

"I tied the rope too tight."

"When you found her dead, what did you do then?"

"I untied her and I took her out behind the barn. There's some blood on one of the cushions."

"What did you do with the blood on the cushion and on the floor?"

"I turned the cushion upside down."

"What about the blood on the floor?"

"I think I smeared it around."

"How'd you smear it?"

"With dirt."

"Then you took Rachel with no ropes at all on her and where did you take her?"

"Across a little bridge, up past the outhouse. There's the outhouse; then there's a little bridge behind the outhouse to a flat spot."

"That goes away from the A-frame?"

"Yeah."

"Did you hide her there?"

"Yeah. I covered her up with leaves."

"How much longer was it until the sun came up when you finally covered her up with leaves?"

"I don't know."

"Hour estimate. One, two, three, four, five?"

Krebs appeared annoyed. "I don't know, Larry."

"Did you go back to the house and—"

"Drank," replied Krebs immediately. He then paused for several more seconds before resuming: "Tried cleaning the blood out of the back of my truck."

"How did you do that again?"

"Carpet cleaner." That did not work. "So I cut the carpet out."

"How big was that piece? 'Bout three foot square?"

"'Bout that, 'bout that wide, the length the back of the truck."

"Why didn't you take the jump seat out and clean it and put it back in?"

"'Cause I was stupid."

"And where did the carpet go?"

"To the Dumpster."

"What'd you do when you got back to the ranch?"

"Started drinking again."

"Have you ever had a period of time where you've drank so much you blacked out?"

"Yeah."

"Have you had any blackouts?"

"Twice."

"And when were those?"

"One time was at Outlaws when I went to the hospital."

"When was the other time you had a blackout?"

"Around Christmastime. I was out at the bars."

Hobson began to speak about Rachel's makeshift grave. "Why did you pick that particular spot?" he asked, referring to the embankment where Krebs buried the twenty-year-old.

"Actually, I started digging a hole before it got dark."

"So it was familiar to you?"

"Yeah."

"Why not leave her where she was at the A-frame?"

"Don't know. Probably 'cause I'd look out of place if anybody drove by and seen me there."

"Why bury her at all?"

Krebs paused. "I don't know."

"Were you afraid to put her in the car and transport her to another location?"

"Makes sense."

"And is there some reason, though, you chose to dig a hole rather than just dump her?"

"If she's buried, then it's over. There isn't anything to point to where she is."

"When you buried her, you assumed nobody would ever find her?"

"Yeah."

"What did you think about each day you drove by that location, knowing that you had buried her up there?"

"I thought about it every day."

"When was the first time you heard about the news on Rachel Newhouse?"

"Roslynn bought a newspaper."

"Did you read the article?"

"No."

"Did you know if the police had any suspects?" Krebs shook his head no. "Did you expect to be contacted by your parole officer?"

"Yeah."

"Were you contacted?"

"No."

"At what point, timewise, did you feel safe about what you had done? That you weren't going to get caught?"

"Probably about two weeks after my monthly visit from Zaragoza."

"So he came to visit you when?"

"I think it was like the following week."

"The following week after the thirteenth, Friday the thirteenth of November?"

"Yeah."

"Did he talk to you about anything to do with the missing person?"

"I brought it up."

"What did you say?"

"I don't remember exactly."

"When did you first start thinking about doing it again?"

"A couple of nights after I drove by and saw Aundria [looking] in the trunk of her car."

"Is there something about Aundria and Rachel that was attractive to you?"

"I don't think so."

"What was it about Aundria that caught your eye?"

"I don't know."

"Why did she stand out more than some other lady down the street that you would have passed?"

"I don't know, Larry."

"Was it her age?" Hobson continued to press on.

"I don't know."

"So maybe it has something to do with her age, her youth?" Krebs compliantly nodded yes as though all he wanted was for Hobson to end this particular line of questioning.

"When you began thinking about raping Aundria"—Hobson decided to get back on with the specifics of the Aundria Crawford abduction, rape, murder, and burial—"those thoughts went on for how long a period of time?"

"Maybe a week."

"You went back there, how many times to look at her?"

"Three, four."

"The fourth time was the time you took her. Did you tie her up the same way that you tied Rachel up or did you bring some other types of devices to tie her up?"

"No, I tied her up the same way. With rope."

"You didn't use any of those plastic flex cuffs?"

"I used those when I got to the ranch."

"Did she have the rope around her neck and then around her feet?"

"No."

"You get up toward the ranch now and it's getting to be close to daylight, so you decided to do what?"

"Put her at the cabin."

"So you left her there for a period of what, three or four hours?" Krebs again nodded his head in the affirmative. "So it's probably some time, five-thirty, six in the morning. Maybe a little earlier?"

"It's around five."

"OK, and you just wait then for eight o'clock to come? You don't go to sleep?"

"I made coffee. Make it look like normal." Krebs then went on to speak of his purposeful encounter with Debbie Wright.

"Then what did you do?"

"Went down and got Aundria."

"Was she conscious when you left her in the A-frame?"

"Yes."

"Did you talk to her or was she still duct-taped?"

"She's still duct-taped."

"Did you say anything to her, even though she couldn't talk?"

"Told her to be quiet."

"What was she wearing?"

"Black sweatpants. Black sweatshirt pulled over."

"What was she wearing when you caught her at her house?"

"Panties and a T-shirt."

"So you walk her into the house. And what do you do when you get her in the house?"

"Put her in the bedroom in the bed. Went and got a pair of scissors. Cut her T-shirt off."

"What happened to that T-shirt?"

"I burned it. Fireplace."

"Was she wearing a bra?"

"No."

"And what'd you do with the panties?"

"Burned them too."

"So at this point, she's tied only with the wrists behind her back; her legs aren't tied. She's laying on the bed, and over her head, she has what?"

"A, uh, pillowcase."

"And what was the reason for the pillowcase?"

"So she couldn't see me."

"Was she bleeding at all?"

"A little bit on her mouth."

"How are you keeping the pillowcase on?"

"It's tied in a knot behind her head."

"Now what do you do?"

"I rape her."

"Do you ejaculate when you're on top of her?" Krebs nodded yes. "Then what did you do?"

"Turned her over and sodomized her."

"And when you talk about sodomy, we're talking about your penis in her anus, right?" Krebs again nodded his head. "Do you ejaculate again?"

"No."

"Did you have an erection when you sodomized her?"

"Yes."

"Then what did you do?"

"Put her sweatpants on her. To keep her warm."

Krebs continued to tell Hobson how he tied the girl back up after he raped her. The real horror for Aundria Crawford had only just begun.

"Then what'd you do?" prodded Detective Hobson.

"Went out, drank some coffee. Drank some Jack Daniel's. Screwed around the house, laid down on the couch. Passed out."

"How long did you sleep?"

"I don't know."

"What happened next?"

"I woke up with the door opening. The bedroom door. That's when I put the blindfold on her."

Hobson needed Krebs to backtrack a bit. "So after you wake up, what happens next?"

"When I wake up, she's standing in the doorway."

"Is she still tied?"

"No. She's got everything untied."

"She's completely untied? Her hands, everything? Got the pillowcase off her head? Duct tape off her mouth?"

"Uh-huh."

"You hear the door to your bedroom open?"

"Yeah."

"Does it make a noise when it opens?"

"Yeah. It closes real hard. You've got to lift it up."

"Because of the weather it swells up?"

"Yeah."

"So she's fully dressed now?" Krebs again nodded yes. "Now what do you do at this point?"

"Attack her." Plain and simple. No beating around the bush for Krebs.

"When you say 'attack her,' do you tackle her? What do you do to her?"

"Yeah. I tackle her back into the bedroom and retie her. I retied her with the ropes; then I went and got the zip ties."

"How did you tie her this time?"

"Just with her hands behind her back. Run the rope around her feet a couple of times."

"In the hog-tied position?"

"Yeah."

"Then what?"

"Then I go and get the zip ties."

"How many zip ties did you use?"

"Three, I think."

"So while her hands are behind her back, you put one zip tie on one hand, one zip tie on the other. Around the wrist?"

"Right."

"Now what do you do about her eyes?"

"Put a black bandana over them."

"Then where do you put her?"

"Bend her over the coffee table and I rape her again."

"So you bend her over the coffee table facedown?" Krebs again nodded yes. "Did you rape her or sodomize her?"

"I raped her."

"Then do you ejaculate again?"

"Yeah."

"Is she cussing you out? Is she calling you names?"

"No."

"What is she saying?"

"She's not saying anything."

"What did she say when you caught her trying to get out of the bedroom?"

"She screamed."

"How'd you stop her from screaming?"

"Put my hand over her mouth, told her to be quiet."

"Did she say anything else to you?"

"Yeah. I told her she saw me; she said, 'I didn't see you.' I says, 'You saw me.'"

"What did you feel at the point where she had seen you?"

"I was scared."

"Did her seeing you tell you something else that was going to have to happen?"

"Yeah."

"Which was what?"

Krebs waited a few seconds before he answered: "I was going to have to kill her."

"So after you had sex with her from behind, where did you put her?"

"Put her back in the bedroom."

"Did that have something to do with wanting to keep her with you for a period of time?"

"Maybe, I don't know."

"Had you ever read or heard about somebody else keeping somebody with them for a period of time?"

"Yeah, I think so."

"And who was that?"

"It was one of the—what do you call those, like me—one of those high-profile cases. On the news or something."

"Did you ever hear anything on the news about that Ng guy up in Sacramento?" Charles Ng and Leonard Lake built a wilderness encampment in Wilseyville, California, in 1985, where they hid their kidnap victims and used them as sex slaves. The duo tortured the women and caught it all on videotape. When they were finished with their victims, they murdered them. Lake committed suicide after his capture and Ng went on the lam to Canada until he was extradited to the United States and convicted in 1999.

"No," replied Krebs.

Hobson decided to let Krebs get back on track with Aundria.

"She's hog-tied again," Krebs continued. "No, I'm sorry, she's not hog-tied; she's leashed to the bed frame."

"How did you leash her to the bed frame?"

"Tied both of her feet together and then run the rope underneath the bed and tied it to the frame. Went in the kitchen and started drinking real heavy."

"Were you upset over the fact that she had seen you?"

"Yeah."

"What did you do after you finished drinking?"

"Went and killed her."

The courtroom remained silent. All eyes focused on the television set.

"At some point you decided you had to kill her?"

"Yeah."

"Then what did you do?"

"I strangled her."

"Did you have sex with her again?"

"No."

"How did you kill her?"

Miraculously, at this point the interrogation videotape abruptly ended. Some portions of this crucial part of the confession were not recorded. The prosecution, however, did not lose momentum. Hobson inserted the next tape and the damning confession continued.

Hobson's back appeared on-screen again as he asked Krebs, "How did you strangle her with the rope?"

"Wrapped it around her neck," a nonremorseful Krebs replied. "I pushed her over onto her stomach. I guess you'd say I kneeled on her."

"Where was your leg? Your knee?"

"On her back. I left her there and I went and dug the hole for her."

"Was there any doubt in your mind she wasn't dead?"

"I don't know."

"The time of day, is it before noon, afternoon, early?"

"Probably right around noon."

"Then what'd you do?"

"Went down and dug her grave."

"For some reason you decided to dig this one right in your backyard. Why not go back to the same spot where Rachel was? What were you thinking that you decided to do it right there?"

"I don't think I was thinking."

"Where's that shovel now?"

"Out at the ranch. Probably in the shed."

"Where's the shed?"

"Underneath my bedroom."

Referring to Aundria's grave, Hobson asked, "You dug it about how deep?"

" 'Bout three, four feet."

"When you had dug it, what'd you do?"

"Went up and got Aundria and put her in it."

"How did you get down that tiny, narrow staircase?"

"It wasn't easy."

"How did you put her into the grave?"

"I think she was faceup."

"What did you cover the dirt up with?"

"Leaves and garbage that was out there."

"Why the wire and the rocks? What was the significance of that?"

"Keep animals from digging."

"Where did the two pillowcases go and her T-shirt and panties?"

"I burned them. In the fireplace."

"Inside that fireplace, Rex, we found some little, small animal bones."

"Chicken bones."

"Again I'm having a little trouble understanding why you would want to put her so close to your house."

"What's there to understand about any of it, Larry?"

"What'd you think every time you stepped outside to leave and go to work?"

"I was kind of sick."

"What would have happened if we'd come and talked to you like that after Rachel? Do you think you would have taken Aundria?"

"No."

"What would have stopped you if we talked to you? I mean, we didn't know anything. What if we just came and talked to you as part of the investigation?"

"I would have been scared. Reality might have set in."

"You were arrested nine days after you took Aundria from her house. During that nine-day period, were you thinking about doing it again?"

"No."

"What was it that caused you not to think about it?"

"When I had to kill her with my hands."

"Kill her with your hands. I thought you used a rope?"

"It's the same thing. It wasn't an accident. I honestly had to do it. And I did it."

"What if she hadn't seen you, Rex?"

"I think I would have washed her and turned her loose. Back into town somewhere."

Hobson moved the conversation up to the day when Krebs

was arrested. "Did you think we would find anything at your house?"

"Yeah. The jump seat."

"Did you think we'd find the eight ball?"

"I didn't even think about it."

"The significance of the eight ball wasn't the fact that it belonged to Aundria, it was what the number eight means to you?"

"I don't know."

"And the number eight, based on what we're reading, stands for the eight letters of 'I love you'?"

"And the Egyptian symbol for infinity."

"Do you ever talk about eights or use eights with Roslynn?"

"No. It's just a symbol. A design for my grandfather when he died."

"You did an eight symbol for your grandfather, an Egyptian eight? For infinity for your grandfather?"

"It's on a weight belt and on my belt buckle."

Hobson again steered the discussion back to Aundria Crawford's burial. "Why not just load her up and take her to Santa Maria, for instance, and dump her in the riverbed?"

"I just didn't think about it."

"Is there any significance to how you put Aundria and Rachel in the grave sites or was it just a matter of getting them there? Nothing significant about it?"

"No."

"What about the shoes you were wearing when you went in Aundria's house?"

"Threw those away at the Texaco. They're white Reeboks."

"The reason you threw your tennis shoes away was . . . ?"

"They had little spots of blood on them."

"After you buried Aundria, that's the same night that you brought Roslynn up to the cabin, right?"

"Yeah. Finally realized how much I needed her."

"What was it that separated Roslynn from someone like Rachel or Aundria?"

"I don't know."

"Were they like two different lifestyles? Roslynn never saw the Rex that was around Rachel or Aundria?"

"She didn't."

"Is there anything from your first offense that got you caught that you learned, you knew, you couldn't do in this one and you had to do something different?"

"Fingerprints."

"So that's the reason for the gloves, right? But you didn't use gloves with Rachel, right?"

"No."

"Your fingerprints could have been left on that bridge railing, right? Were you worried about that?"

"Never thought about it until right now."

"How about identity? Is that why you used the nylons over your head with Aundria and the pillowcases?"

"Yeah."

"Anything in your relationship with Roslynn ever go sour as far as your sexual relationship? Did you ever scare her in any way?"

"I don't think so."

"Did you ever tie her up?"

"No."

"Did you ever sodomize her?"

"We tried a couple of times. It hurt too much."

"It was a voluntary type of thing?"

"Yeah."

"Someone told me that Roslynn was possibly bisexual."

"Where the hell'd you get that?"

"I don't know."

"No."

Hobson was ready to close up shop for the day. "Hang loose for just a second here. Let me see if I haven't forgot everything."

"I'm not in a real big hurry to run back and get locked up again"—Krebs calmly spoke to Hobson—"so if you want to come up and ask some more questions, that's all right too."

Hobson decided he did indeed want to ask Krebs a few more questions. He pulled up his chair and sat down next to Krebs. "This is a tough question, but try to answer it truthfully. If we hadn't come or your parole officer hadn't come and violated you—"

"Would this have happened again . . . ?" Krebs interrupted knowing where Hobson was going with this line of questioning. "No."

"Now think about it before you say that, because that's what you said after Rachel. But then you went and you started drinking a little bit."

"No," Krebs emphatically repeated.

"It's probably a good possibility it could happen again if you kept drinking, right?"

"Nah. I never killed anybody with my hands before, Larry."

"The things you did this time with Aundria, were those something that you had a fantasy about in prison?"

"Yeah."

"Is that to punish her because she's a woman?"

"Maybe."

"Did your fantasy ever involve killing her?"

"No."

"You must have had more than one fantasy, right?"

"I think they all died."

Hobson was about ready to wrap it up for real this time. "I try to put myself in your spot, as to what I would do, but I'm having a hard time."

"How can you do that? You're sane."

"Well, you're sane."

"Now maybe."

"You've always been sane; you just have fantasies that got out of control. Fantasies that became realities."

Detective Hobson was done with Rex Krebs. The convict looked up at the authority figure and asked him, "I'm being a big help to you, ain't I?"

FIFTY-THREE

Detective Hobson was still not free to go. Rex Krebs's lead defense attorney, James Maguire III, stepped up to the witness stand to cross-examine him. His questioning was short and succinct.

"Isn't it true, that after you had confronted him with that information," Maguire inquired, referring to the bloody jump seat, "he basically became silent and stopped talking to you?"

"Yes, sir," Hobson responded politely.

"In fact, he was silent for a period of about fifteen or sixteen minutes while you talked to him and asked him to continue with the interview. Is that right?"

"That's correct."

"During that same period of time, you told him that you knew that this was a situation that he had something in him that was beyond his control that caused him to do these things. You told him that, didn't you?"

"That's what I told him, yes."

"Do you recall that when Roslynn Moore came into the room where Rex Krebs was located, he said, 'The Rex Krebs that did this is not the Rex Krebs that you know.' Remember that statement?"

"Yes."

"And she became very upset at this disclosure, is that true?"

"She did."

"In fact, paramedics had to be called?"

"Yes, they did."

"You then get into a discussion with Mr. Krebs about the feelings that he has," Maguire continued. "Eventually you identified them as fantasies. Do you remember that part of the conversation?"

"Yes, I do." Hobson nodded as he replied.

"You said that these thoughts or fantasies obviously have never disappeared and reappear when you're drinking, is that right, and he says 'Right.' Do you remember that question and answer?"

"Yes."

"I assume that you asked about fantasies for a reason. You asked Mr. Krebs about fantasies for a reason?"

"That's correct."

"And that's because you knew that people involved in sex offenses are often responding to fantasies that they have about things that they end up doing, crimes that they end up committing, is that right?"

"That's correct."

"And finally Mr. Krebs says, 'You don't always think real good when you're drunk, obviously.' Remember that comment?"

"Yes."

Maguire, however, had not finished. After a quick recess he had more questions for the detective. "He told you that he blamed his mother because she knew what his dad was doing but she didn't stop it or take him back. He told you that also, didn't he?"

"That's what Rex Krebs told me, yes."

"Do you remember saying to him, 'I need to know what happened. I need to know where I can find Aundria and Rachel. Can you help me find them? I know you care. There were tears. I'm not wrong about this, Rex. Where there's tears, that tells me somebody cares. People don't fake tears. If you didn't give a shit, there wouldn't have been tears. So the tears tell me a lot.

" 'It doesn't make it right, but it tells me what ever happened has bothered you a great deal, and it shows me that you care. You're not a cold-blooded killer.' Do you remember telling him that?"

"Yes, that's what I told him."

Maguire was finished. For now.

Trice, however, was not.

Hobson remained seated in the witness chair. Trice wanted to clear up a few things in the redirect examination. "You brought up the fact that Mr. Maguire's client is a person of honesty and integrity. You don't believe that, do you?"

"No."

"Mr. Maguire brought up the fact that you told him that you thought the defendant is a person who cares. You don't believe that, do you?"

"No."

"Why were you saying such things to him?"

"Unfortunately, crimes this heinous, you have to say some things that you don't really believe or mean. To get someone to sit down and talk to you about something this terrible, you have to have some rapport. And before that person's going to talk to you, they have to respect you; they have to like you; they have to trust you. And, unfortunately, to get to that point, you have to say some things that you don't believe or mean."

"Even when he talked about all the intimate details of how he killed these girls, did he ever cry then?"

"Rex Krebs did not cry."

Prosecutor Trice had no more questions.

Now Maguire had some serious salvaging to undertake: "You didn't say, 'By the way, Rex, this is an investigation technique I'm using. I don't really believe this myself,' did you?"

"No, I did not."

"You wanted him to believe you, right?"

"That's what I was talking about, the rapport building that you need to have."

"But in order for you to have some credibility with him,

you have to be saying things that have some basis in fact, don't you think so?"

"No," Hobson bluntly replied.

There was nothing else James Maguire III could do. He had no more questions for the witness. Detective Hobson finally stepped down.

John Trice and Tim Covello knew the case was closed.

"People rest their case."

Judge Barry LaBarbera responded, "OK. Mr. Maguire?"

"Your Honor, we have no testimony to offer at this time. Defense rests also."

FIFTY-FOUR

Prosecutor John Trice felt confident, yet somewhat insecure. Whenever it came time to give a closing argument, his nerves would get to him—especially in such an important case as the Rex Krebs double-murder trial. Still, he felt confident after Larry Hobson's testimony. He believed that once the jury had seen Krebs's confession, the case ended. Now he had to make it official.

Trice opened up his presentation on a light note. He mentioned to the twelve assembled jury members that he seemed to be suffering from allergies. This seemed to lessen the enormity of the conclusion that he was about to give.

"On behalf of the people of San Luis Obispo County, I'd like to thank you for your attention the last few weeks. It's been a long process that began with the abductions and the investigation, the eventual arrest and the charging decisions that finally led to this trial."

Trice discussed the various roles performed by the legal representatives for both sides as well as the judge's responsibility. He then read, one more time, all of the charges placed on Rex Krebs's head. Every count for his crimes against Rachel Newhouse. Every count for his crimes against Aundria Crawford. He then moved in for the kill.

"In this case the proof and analysis of people versus Rex Allan Krebs is not complex. First, because of the confession obtained after the defendant was confronted after he lied and lied and lied, after he was confronted with the blood evidence that was gathered by the investigators in this case, and once he was confronted by the property taken from Aundria's home, the property he stole, as he stole her.

"And secondly, this case is not very complex because of the legal doctrine called the felony murder rule." He jumped right into the definition of first-degree murder under the felony murder rule.

"I want to talk to you and show how simply it fits this case. 'The unlawful killing of a human being, whether intentional, unintentional, or accidental, which occurs during the commission of the crime of kidnapping, rape, or sodomy, is murder of the first degree when the perpetrator had the specific intent to commit that crime.'

"So, as it goes with this case, if the defendant had the specific intent to commit kidnapping, rape, or sodomy, and during the course of any of those crimes somebody dies, even if it's an accident, he's guilty of murder in the first degree. Very simple.

"And so, as in our case, once this defendant kidnaps Rachel, once this defendant kidnaps Aundria, and they die, he is guilty of murder in the first degree since their deaths occur during the commission of kidnapping. That's how simple it is.

"So even if you want to believe this cock-and-bull story that Rachel Newhouse killed herself, you want to believe that, go right ahead. Even if you want to believe that, he is still guilty of first-degree murder under the felony murder rule. That's how simple that is."

Trice made his point, clear and simple. He concluded by hinting at Rex Krebs's possible future. "There will come a time, weeks from now at the end of the penalty phase, when I will have a lot more to say about what Rex Allan Krebs, this animal, did to Rachel and Aundria. And we will talk then about the price he's going to pay for all this mayhem.

"But for now, Mr. Covello and I have proved this case beyond a reasonable doubt, as I said we would, and now I ask you to do your duty to return verdicts of guilt on all of those charges and each of those special circumstances.

"Thank you."

Judge LaBarbera turned toward the defense counsel table. "Ms. Ashbaugh."

"Yes, Your Honor," the immaculate defense attorney acknowledged the judge, then focused on the twelve jury members. "Good morning, ladies and gentlemen of the jury."

Ashbaugh zeroed in on Larry Hobson's interrogation of Rex Krebs. She spoke of how Hobson mentioned that Krebs was someone who cares, that he had seen Rex cry and he wanted to help the police find the bodies of the two young women.

Ashbaugh then reminded the jurors of the various witnesses they heard testimony from during the trial. "You've also heard from the most important witness—that's Rex Krebs himself, the person who told what happened.

"But as each witness has testified, there has been the story within the story that we told you about. There has been the story of the small boy, neglected and abandoned by his mother, the child abused by his father, a boy so psychologically broken that he fantasized about women since the age of fourteen. A man so driven that he destroys his opportunity to marry, to raise a child, and fulfill a promising career at 84 Lumber.

"You've seen the two sides of Rex Krebs. You've seen that struggle between good and evil.

"This information has not been given to you to provide an excuse. No. We will not and will never ask you to excuse this conduct. We're here to ask you to consider the why. Why could this happen in the beautiful college town of San Luis Obispo? And why could it happen to these two women?"

Ashbaugh had definitely grabbed the jurors' attention.

"The why is just as important as the what."

Ashbaugh acknowledged that Krebs willingly confessed to Larry Hobson. Her strategy, however, would be to force the jurors to determine if the prosecution had actually proven Krebs's guilt beyond a reasonable doubt.

Her weapon of choice?

"First I'm going to talk about what I call the 'corpus delicti' rule. Mr. Trice referenced it. He didn't use that fancy Latin name. I use it. I took Latin. I figure I should try to incorporate that in a little bit.

"It's a basic foundational requirement that a person should not be found guilty of a crime based exclusively on his statements. As a result, the law requires that before you can consider the statements of a defendant in establishing his guilt of a crime, you first must determine that there is some evidence, independent of his statements, that supports a finding that a crime occurred."

Ashbaugh moved on to the next topic. "The second legal issue is whether there was an intent to kill and whether there was a deliberate, premeditated murder of both Aundria Crawford and Rachel Newhouse.

"With respect to murder, the courts and the rules of the law say that you need to have malice. It can be express or implied.

"Under the facts before you, you cannot find beyond a reasonable doubt that Rex Krebs had an intent to kill Rachel Newhouse and that there was a willful, deliberate, and premeditated murder of Ms. Newhouse."

Ashbaugh clearly laid out her points of argument and vigorously defended her client. "Let's look at the information that you have. From the moment Ms. Andrea West parted ways with Ms. Newhouse at the bar, Tortilla Flats, in November of 1998, until the time of the exhumation of her body, the only information as to what happened comes from Rex Krebs himself.

"The prosecutor has argued and suggested to you he's a liar with his 'cock-and-bull' story. He's the personification of evil. He shouldn't be believed. How very convenient.

"Let me digress and tell you a little story. When I was a little girl, my grandfather used to come over and visit with my sister and I. And he liked to spend time with us. And sometimes my mom was making dinner or something, he would call me in and say, 'Tish'—that's my nickname—'want to play a little game?'

"And he'd pull out of his pocket a little quarter like this. And he'd say, 'OK, this is the game. I toss this and you call it, but heads I win and tails you lose.'

"Well, he'd do that over and over. I thought my grandfather was the luckiest person around because—remember the rule—heads I win, tails you lose.

"Well, one day my mother sauntered through that room. She stopped. She looked at what he was doing and she said, 'Dad, that's just not fair.'

"Now, why do I tell you this story? I tell you this story because it reminds me of what the prosecutor wants you to do. He wants you to take all those pieces of information that helps him prove and build his case and say believe it, he's telling the truth about all those things. But then when there are pieces of information that he doesn't like or he thinks doesn't really support the theory that he wants to advance, he says you just disregard that. Mr. Krebs is a liar.

"Well, that's just not fair. Remember, there is no physical evidence on that bridge that links Rex Krebs to the abduction of Rachel Newhouse. They didn't find his blood. They don't have his hair. They never did find a fingerprint. They don't have a footprint. They don't have a tire print. They don't present any evidence that would show anything that would link Mr. Krebs to that crime scene."

Ashbaugh next focused on Parole Officer David Zaragoza's discovery of Aundria Crawford's eight ball key chain, the key piece of evidence that led to Krebs's arrest and subsequent charges of murder. She claimed it was a generic key chain, that anyone could buy it at a convenience store. "There's nothing that you specifically can use to say that's Aundria's. I'd suggest to you that with only that piece of information, they could not have brought a prosecution of Mr. Krebs.

"The second piece we have is the jump seat. We know that the laboratory didn't really start comparison analysis until April nineteenth." Ashbaugh was referring to the tests run on the Jennifer Street Bridge blood by the DOJ lab. "The report was not generated until September of 1999. I'd suggest there's probably no conclusive proof on April twenty-second that they had a match.

"So why am I discussing this with you? It's because the police did not have sufficient evidence to arrest Rex Krebs prior to confessing on April twenty-second.

"One of the most telling questions asked by Mr. Hobson was one of the first ones on the twenty-second. 'Rex, will we find them alive?' They didn't know. They only have suspicions. They could not locate those bodies.

"On the morning of the 22nd, everything changes. Rex Krebs made a choice. He chose to tell them the story and lead them to the bodies. But it was he alone who brought closure to these families and this case. He did not receive any favors or promises from Mr. Hobson. No deals for leniency were made. He just told them.

"Remember Mr. Hobson said, 'Rex, everyone says that you have honesty, integrity, and truth. Rex, help us. Rex, give closure to these families.'

"And Rex did. And when asked by Mr. Hobson why he finally decided to confess, what was the one word he used? 'Conscience.' "

Ashbaugh had reached the conclusion of her closing argument.

"I know the past two weeks, and especially this week, has been difficult for all of you. It's not easy to be here. It's not easy to listen to this information regarding the deaths of Rachel Newhouse and Aundria Crawford. Each and every person in this courtroom has been deeply affected.

"We thank you for your attention and your efforts. We now turn this case over to you to assess the extent and the level of Rex Allan Krebs's responsibility with regard to each and every charge and allegation made against him.

"Thank you."

Since the burden of proof rests with the state, they have the final say. John Trice approached the jury box. He stopped, looked over his shoulder at the defendant, and slowly shook his head. He looked back at the jury.

"Rex Krebs. What a gracious thing he has done for the members of the community in San Luis Obispo. What a great helper he has been. One of the more outrageous things I've heard in twenty-something years in this business." The disgust in his voice was obvious.

Trice took the jury back to the felony murder rule. "We don't have to talk about premeditation and deliberation on Rachel Newhouse because this defendant is guilty of both these murders under a simple analysis under the felony murder rule. Once he kidnapped them and they die, he's done. Murder in the first degree."

Trice steamed through his rebuttal. "And you know who she didn't talk about?" referring to Ashbaugh. "She didn't talk about Shelly Crosby. And I wonder why she didn't? She stands up here and basically is saying because her slick client, this gem of our community, who's so gracious in helping us solve this horrible crime and bringing closure to those families, this nice fellow—because he was so successful in lying to the police and evading apprehension for so long, that the bodies of these girls rotted in the ground and whatever evidence we may have had went with them."

Trice moved in one more time for what he assumed would be the final nail in Krebs's coffin. "You know what Rex Allan Krebs does to a woman when he cuts her clothes off. You know what Rex Allan Krebs does when he crawls in a woman's window in the middle of the night with rope and a knife. He goes in to tie them up, to control them, to rape and sodomize them. Ask Shelly Crosby."

Trice turned to the judge and, with a note of disgust in his voice, stated, "That's all I have."

After a lunch break Judge LaBarbera read the concluding instructions for deliberation to the jury. Standard protocol: pick a foreperson; if there were any questions about evidence, ask and they would get to see the information in question, etc. One key issue he stressed is that if they found the defendant not guilty of murder in the first degree, they then had to go back and determine whether he was guilty in the second degree.

No one on either side of the counsel table knew how long the jury would take. Would it be a slam dunk and over before the day ended? Could it take longer than the actual presentation of the evidence itself? No one could be sure.

At 4:30 P.M., on March 29, 2001, Judge LaBarbera brought the court to order. He received a request from the jury to hear David Zaragoza's testimony in its entirety. The judge sent the court reporter to read the testimony to the jurors. No one heard from them again that day.

On Friday, March 30, the jury asked for a few clarifications on the instructions. Otherwise, not a word. Everyone would head into the weekend not knowing the fate of Rex Allan Krebs.

On Monday, April 2, 2001, the jurors sent in another request. They wanted to rewatch a portion of the Davis Canyon drive-through videotape when Rex Krebs pointed out the grave site locations to investigator Larry Hobson. Judge LaBarbera made sure they received the tape. He then broke for lunch.

Upon their return to court for the afternoon session, Judge LaBarbera informed the attorneys that the jury had reached a verdict. After discussing a few dates and details for a possible penalty phase, he asked the bailiff to bring the jurors into the courtroom. The nine women and three men that comprised the jury quietly walked to their seats in the jury box. None of them looked Rex Krebs in the eye.

The time was 3:49 P.M.

"The ladies and gentlemen of the jury are present." Judge LaBarbera took control of the situation.

"Good afternoon.

"I understand, Madam Foreperson, that you've reached verdicts."

"Yes, we have," she replied.

"Could you hand those to the bailiff, please? Thank you."

The bailiff took the sheet of paper and walked toward the judge's bench. He handed the paper to the judge, who glanced over it, handed it back to the bailiff, who then handed it to the clerk.

"If the defendant would please stand, and the clerk will read the verdicts." Krebs, dressed in a dark blue suit, with a dark blue striped tie, slowly stood up from behind the defense counsel's table. Once everyone stood up, the clerk began to read the verdicts.

"Superior Court of California, County of San Luis Obispo. *The People of the State of California, Plaintiff,* versus *Rex Allan Krebs, Defendant, number F283378,* verdict of jury.

"Count one, murder in the first degree; victim, Rachel Lindsay Newhouse. We, the jury, find the defendant, Rex Allan Krebs, guilty of the crime of murder in the first degree in violation of Section 187 of the Penal Code of the State of California. Dated April 2, 2001, number 265, foreperson."

Rex Krebs showed no emotion. He continued to look straight at the clerk. The audience seemed to let out a collective sigh of relief. An enormous amount of pressure instantly drained out of the courtroom.

The clerk continued to read the verdicts: "Count two, murder in the first degree; victim, Aundria Lynn Crawford. We, the jury, find the defendant, Rex Allan Krebs, guilty of the crime of murder in the first degree in violation of Section 187 of the Penal Code of the State of California. Dated April 2, 2001, number 265, foreperson."

All remaining pressure vanished from the courthouse—at least on the victims' side.

The clerk continued down the litany of charges against Krebs. He was found guilty of all special circumstances including the kidnapping and rape of Rachel Newhouse and the kidnapping, rape, and sodomizing of Aundria Crawford. The jury also found Krebs guilty of multiple convictions of murder, kidnapping with the intent to rape and sodomize, rape and sodomize by force, and burglary.

The proceedings returned to Judge LaBarbera. He polled the jurors for their individual verdicts. Each one voted guilty on all eleven charges.

"Ladies and gentlemen," the judge addressed the jury, "as I mentioned to you regarding the penalty trial, we will begin evidence on April seventeenth at nine o'clock, which is the Tuesday after Easter."

The district attorney's office had stated from the outset that they wanted to send Krebs to San Quentin to face his own death by lethal injection. The defense had two weeks to prepare. They did not have much time.

FIFTY-FIVE

The defense put up a good fight. They summonsed anyone and everyone from Rex Krebs's past. Family members, school officials from North Idaho Children's Home, and a nationally renowned specialist in sexual disorders testified on behalf of Krebs. The cumulative testimonials were an attempt to paint a disturbing picture of a young man who could not control his destiny from the beginning. From the early days of abuse at his father's hands to the latter-day sexual compulsion from which he suffered, the defense attempted to unveil a sympathetic portrait of a tormented man who could truly be a decent human being.

In total, the defense called upon forty-eight witnesses to testify on Krebs's behalf. The testimony stretched over a period of eight workdays.

The prosecution called on seven people. It only took one afternoon session.

Deputy District Attorney John Trice knew he needed to end the penalty phase with a powerful message to the jury. He called a few of the women who were closest to Rachel and Aundria during their all-too-brief lives. The first witness to testify was Patricia Turner, Rachel's aunt and Montel Newhouse's sister.

"Could you tell the jury about your relationship with Rachel?" Trice gently inquired.

"My daughter was six weeks old when Rachel was born, so we raised our daughters together. I knew every aspect of her," Turner tearfully replied. "Rachel was my niece and she was a dream child. She was a straight A student and an athlete. Montel always was concerned that possibly she was too much of a perfectionist, that she wouldn't enjoy her happiness until everything was perfect. The last summer I saw her, she had accomplished that. She had found her balance. She was balanced and perfect."

"And that would have been the summer of '98?"

"Correct."

"Have you personally seen how the loss of Rachel has affected their family?"

"I saw Montel's world change completely. Everything that happened after that is different, in that Montel lived in the same house that Rachel was born and she works in the school that Rachel attended, and all of those things that she does every day will never be the same. Instead of celebrating a good job of raising Rachel, she is torn between that and sadness. So her life will never be the same again.

"I've seen Phil have a daily battle with trying to balance celebrating her life with the nightmare that did not define her in any way. I've watched him struggle to celebrate every day and keep a positive attitude. He's done that. He's been able to do that and he's done an excellent job.

"The Newhouse family has struggled every day to celebrate Rachel and not to grieve or think anything but positive thoughts."

After Turner, Trice next called Rachel's mother, Montel Newhouse, to the witness stand. They quickly discussed her marriage of twenty-seven years to Phil Newhouse, her three children, including Rachel, and that they lived in Irvine, California, for the last twenty-three years.

Trice then asked Mrs. Newhouse about her daughter. "What type of student was Rachel Newhouse?"

"She was very conscientious. She kind of had that perfectionist thing going that was sometimes difficult. She wasn't brilliant, but she set her sights very high and she worked really hard. She had a good work ethic and she did very well. She graduated from high school with a 4.0 grade point average."

Mrs. Newhouse spoke about Rachel's numerous interests as she grew up. Camping, hiking, running, her friends and family. She then spoke of Rachel's activities in San Luis Obispo. A full class load every semester combined with different jobs from baby-sitter to restaurant hostess.

"Did you ever talk to her when she was at Cal Poly about her personal goals, marriage or children?"

"I think that was in her plans. I know she would have been a good mom. She was always telling me stories from her baby-sitting experiences. She enjoyed the kids a lot and I think that was a long-term goal."

"In November of 1998, did things seem to be going well for your daughter?"

"Yeah, I had visited her in October. Her grandmother and I came for a visit and we had a great time and things were going well. I talked to her last on Wednesday night, the eleventh. We had a long conversation and she was upbeat; things were going well."

"How did you hear that your daughter Rachel was missing?"

"It was on Friday, November thirteenth. Phil and I were watching a movie and Nichole called and said that no one had seen her since the previous night. At the time we were just kind of in shock, disbelief. We ended up coming up the following morning. We met at a rescue center that they had going and we met Detective Cindy Dunn."

"What were the next three or four months like then?"

"I don't know a way to describe it. It's a fear, a magnitude that I've never experienced and an anxiety that I don't think you can measure."

"How did you find out that Rachel had finally been found?"

"We got a phone call from Cindy Dunn that was a little more urgent than some of the other contacts we had. We came up on Thursday and we stayed up here and finally heard definitively on Saturday afternoon."

"Is it possible to explain how her death has affected you and your family?"

"I hesitate because I feel like it isn't fair to compare our pain with maybe what her pain and suffering was. There's another part that we've been able to cope by basically remaining kind of private. I think that's where we get our strength. I think when you describe the pain that you've been through, it takes away from the joy that Rachel brought to us. There aren't words to express that kind of loss."

Next up were the two most important women in Aundria Crawford's life: her grandmother Jody Crawford and her mother and best friend, Gail Crawford Eberhart.

Jody Crawford testified to how she had helped her daughter Gail raise Aundria after the divorce. She also spoke of how close she had become to her granddaughter. She talked about Aundria's interests in ballet, horses, and cars. She also talked about helping Aundria get settled into San Luis Obispo for college.

"Did you ever go with Aundria to Cuesta College?" prodded Trice.

"Oh yes. I helped her get registered. I bought her books. I was over there a lot."

"Do you know what her long-term plans were?"

"She really did want to get married and have children, but she wanted to own her own horse ranch in Wyoming."

"How long did she live in San Luis Obispo before she died?"

"From May of '98 to March of '99."

"By March of 1999, how were things going for your granddaughter? Things going well?"

"Yes, I think so."

"When was the last time you spoke to her?"

"I spoke to her on Tuesday, which would have been the ninth."

"How did it come about that you heard that she was missing?"

"Gail came by that night and I asked her if she'd heard

from Aundria and she said no. She went home around nine-thirty. About one in the morning, she called and she said she had not had any response from Aundria and she had called the police and asked them to check the apartment. About seven-thirty she called me back. They found that she was not there. We drove to San Luis Obispo as fast as we could."

"What did you do?"

"We started looking for her ourselves. We went all over San Luis Obispo County. We looked under bridges. We looked in trash dumps. We saw things we don't ever want to look at again. We did that for six weeks."

"How did you find out that your granddaughter had been found?"

"The police called us into the office on April twenty-second."

"After six weeks, were you still holding out hope that your granddaughter might still be alive?"

"We always held out hope, but we were discouraged. But we didn't give up hope."

"You worked every single day for six weeks trying to find her?"

"Every day. Gail said she would not leave until she found her daughter."

"Is it possible to explain to the jury how this has affected you?"

"It has affected our entire family to some degree. Everybody in the family has trouble with it."

"How about Gail?"

"She's changed a lot. She hasn't gone to work for two years."

"How has your life changed?"

"I am separated. Gail and I had both moved out of state. We felt like we needed to move away from Fresno. It's a total change of life for me. Well, Gail too. But for me, since I lived in the house for forty years in Fresno, it's a big change."

"Thank you. That's all I have, Your Honor."

Trice then called Gail to the stand. "Can you tell the jury

as she was growing up, how close you were with your daughter, Aundria?"

Gail immediately broke into tears. Judge LaBarbera halted the proceeding. "Do you want to take a few minutes?" the judge asked. Gail Crawford shook her head no. "Take your time."

"She was a real open child," the mother tearfully responded. "We were best friends. I knew all of her secrets. She would come home and tell me. Just a real open, loving . . ." She trailed off without finishing her thought.

Trice again talked about Aundria's hobbies as a child. Crawford mentioned her daughter's love of ballet, then horses.

"What type of student was she?"

"She was a good student. She was honor roll until she was about fifteen, sixteen. When the ballet problem came up, she got real frustrated, so her senior year she struggled, but she graduated."

Trice asked Crawford about Aundria's life in San Luis Obispo.

"She was homesick, but she was happy here."

"And her plans for the future?"

"Oh, she had a lot of plans. She wanted to get married. She wanted to have children. She wanted to be an interior designer—architect. She wanted to run her own business. She wanted to move to Wyoming to have a horse ranch. She wanted all of it. She wanted everything."

"Do you remember the last time you saw her or spoke with her?"

"I spoke with her Tuesday afternoon. That would have been the ninth. She was calling about a drafting board she needed to purchase. We had expected to hear from her by Thursday, because she called a lot. And that's when I started calling her. We hadn't heard from her in two days. It was unusual."

"When you came over to San Luis, what did you do there?"

"When we first arrived, we went to her apartment and it was taped off. If her car was there, there was something wrong, because she took that car everywhere. She would take it on dates. She would drive, because if she ever got in a situation she couldn't get out of, or didn't like, she could take herself home."

"Is it possible to explain how your life has changed as a result of losing your daughter?"

"She was my life. Because we were so close, we talked almost every day. It's a huge void. She was my family. I've lost my whole family."

The courtroom was silent.

John Trice had no more questions for Gail Crawford. The defense declined to ask her any questions.

FIFTY-SIX

Perhaps the most interesting portion of the penalty phase was the testimony of two psychiatric expert witnesses: Dr. Fred Berlin and renowned forensic psychiatrist Dr. Park Dietz.

Dr. Berlin testified on behalf of Rex Krebs beginning on April 30, 2001. He graduated with a Ph.D. in psychology and has a medical degree. He is chief resident in psychiatry at Johns Hopkins Hospital in Baltimore, Maryland. He is a board-certified psychiatrist as well as a certified forensic psychiatrist. He is also an associate professor and an attending physician at Johns Hopkins. He is the founder of the Johns Hopkins Sexual Disorders Clinic and the director of the National Institute for the Study, Prevention, and Treatment of Sexual Trauma. He then described his three main responsibilities: clinical care, teaching, and research.

"My primary area of interest is the area of sexual disorders," Dr. Berlin informed the court.

The doctor spoke about his numerous publications for such prestigious journals as the *New England Journal of Medicine* and the *American Journal of Psychiatry*. His articles ranged from chemical causation of sexual offenses, to recidivism rates of sexual offenders, to genetic causation for sexual disorders. He also published articles on sexual sadism. Specifically, the case of Connecticut sexual serial killer Michael Ross, a Cornell University graduate with a 122 IQ, who raped and murdered eight women in Connecticut, and possibly New York, in 1985.

Dr. Berlin also testified on behalf of one of the country's most infamous murderers: Milwaukee serial killer and cannibal Jeffrey Dahmer.

"Have you evaluated Rex Krebs clinically?" defense attorney William McLennan asked Dr. Berlin.

"Yes. I did see Mr. Krebs on two occasions. March of last year. Then I saw him in January of this year. The amount of total time I spent with him is about twelve-and-a-half hours."

When asked what the purpose for examining Krebs was, Berlin replied, "Trying to make a determination whether or not he had a psychiatric disorder."

Berlin continued, saying that "I don't want to be a psychiatrist who is excusing by labeling it psychopathology and get somebody off the hook who is of sound mind."

"When you are doing an evaluation of a prior rapist," continued McLennan, "are there guidelines and principles involved?"

"I'm going to look at it from three perspectives. The behavior itself. The consequences of the behavior. Then I'm going to try to appreciate the mental state of the individual out of which this behavior emerged." He was then asked to give a couple of examples of the different types of rapists.

"One who rapes might be a self-centered person, an opportunistic person. Someone who is antisocial. He comes upon a woman who is vulnerable.

"A second example of rape—and it's rare, but it does happen—are people who have psychotic illnesses. These are conditions in which people are delusional. They are completely out of touch with reality. They may believe if they rape, for example, they will conceive the Messiah.

"Let me give one more that is pertinent to this case. That's where people commit a rape because they have some sort of a sexual disorder. They are driven by abnormal sexual cravings to repeatedly engage in this kind of criminal behavior."

Dr. Berlin laid out the examples to show that he needed to

know what he was getting into before he could make an evaluation. He moved to the actual interviews with Krebs.

"There seemed to be a very ritualistic nature to what he had done. In the (1987) case where he raped the woman, he cut off her clothing in a particular fashion. In the two incidents that we are talking about here, Rachel and Aundria, there was evidence that he had bound these women up in a particular fashion. He had hog-tied them. He had seemed to want to be dominating them. If you looked at the description in the way Aundria Crawford was tied up, it was in a very ritualistic way.

"This is someone who is motivated to rape out of a very specific pathology. This is likely a sexually disordered person who is enacting some sort of fantasy in a ritualistic way, but not somebody who is of sound mind and antisocial."

Dr. Berlin sped through his testimony. He spoke so rapidly that the court reporter had to ask the judge for him to slow down.

"I'm trying to concentrate on slowing down," Dr. Berlin apologized.

"Dr. Berlin, in the case of Rex Krebs, were you able to make more than one diagnosis in the case?"

"I made two diagnoses with conviction. The first diagnosis is of sexual sadism, which is one of the sexual disorders. The second diagnosis I made was of alcoholism. And the third one, which I considered and debated pretty closely in my mind, was antisocial personality disorder."

"You said you diagnosed sexual sadism. Can you tell us what a sexual disorder is?"

"There is a tremendous spectrum of differences amongst human beings in their sexual makeup. There's really two ways in which people differ from one another sexually.

"The first way is regarding the kind of partner that he or she is or isn't attracted to. An example of sexual disorder based upon that would be pedophilia, which is a condition in which some individuals are attracted to prepubescent children.

"A second way is regarding the kinds of sexual behaviors

that either do or don't excite them or arouse them erotically. One example of a sexual disorder based on that is transvestitic fetishism. In everyday English that refers to a condition in which a person is very aroused, usually a man, by dressing in the clothing of the opposite gender. Now, you couldn't pay the average man enough money to do that, and yet clinically I have seen men who are aroused by dressing in that way that they have to struggle if they stop doing it."

Dr. Berlin gave one more example of a sexual disorder. "Sexual masochism. That's a condition in which a person is extremely aroused by their own suffering, degradation, humiliation. It's one of the few sexual disorders that occurs as often in women as it does in men.

"Now most of us haven't the slightest sense (of) being aroused by having someone denigrate us, humiliate, and injure us. And yet I have clinically seen cases of people who are aroused by behaving in this way, aroused sexually.

"Now this case, sexual sadism is kind of the opposite end of the coin from sexual masochism. The degradation, the humiliation, in some cases, the suffering or injury of another person is what is arousing to the individual. And again clinically I have seen cases where people are much more aroused sexually by engaging in coercive and sadistic sexual acts than they are by consenting acts. They will leave the availability of a consenting partner because the urge to engage in coercive or sadistic activities is so much more powerful. That's not normal. That's a sexually disordered person when you see something like that."

McLennan asked for Dr. Berlin to recite the definition of "sexual sadism."

Dr. Berlin read from the *Diagnostic and Statistic Manual of Mental Disorders*. "If you read the definition, it would indicate the individual with a sexual disorder experiences intense, recurrent, erotically amusing fantasies about something there.

"If it were pedophilia, that something would be about having sex with a little child. In sexual sadism, that would be about having fantasies about having sex in a coercive and sadistic fashion rather than in a consenting fashion."

"In the case of Rex Krebs, what does he specifically experience at these reoccurring urges?"

"The urge is to enact the fantasy. In Mr. Krebs's case, there is a theme of domination, of wanting to be in control and dominating a woman. There's very much a preoccupation about tying women up and tying them up in a particular fashion. There also seems to be an aspect of this about cutting off the clothing of women in a particular way.

"The specific fantasies he has can vary, but the common theme in all of them is he has a woman who is at his mercy. He is dominating this woman. He has her tied up and he's cut off her clothing.

"I apologize. I know this is pretty gruesome."

"What is it about this behavior that is sexually arousing for him?" prodded McLennan.

"Again it is the enactment of the fantasy. Having sex in the conventional way is not what's arousing for him. He had the availability of a consenting partner."

"Does the *Diagnostic and Statistic Manual* divide sadism into any types of subtypes?"

"The one major subtype is whether it's present in an exclusive or nonexclusive form. In the exclusive form the only way in which a person could become sexually aroused is by engaging in these abnormal kinds of sexual behavior.

"In the exclusive form of sexual sadism, the only way a person could be aroused sexually is by engaging in sadistic behavior. That's why it's exclusive. They can't be aroused by consenting behavior.

"In the nonexclusive form, the person is capable of being aroused by conventional sexual activity, and that is the case with Mr. Krebs."

"Dr. Berlin, is this diagnosis of sexual sadism based on behavior alone?"

"No. I think an important point to appreciate about sexual

sadism is that we are talking about an abnormality in the mental makeup of the individual. In their sexual makeup."

"Is it ordinarily difficult for a person such as Rex Krebs to resist acting on these urges?"

"Obviously, from what I said, it is. I don't think it takes a mental-health expert to appreciate what a problematic and, in this case, dangerous situation that can be."

"Do you have an opinion if the sexual sadism of Rex Krebs impaired his ability to be in full control of himself?"

"Yes, I do have an opinion that his ability to be in full control of himself was impaired."

"Is there a specific treatment for sexual sadism that demonstrates that impairment of volitional capabilities?"

"I think there is. One of the kinds of treatment is medicine to lower the intensity of their sexual drives. People have heard of this so-called chemical castration, which I think is misleading. Essentially, it is medicine that lowers testosterone, which is the hormone that fuels sexual drive in males.

"The medication has conferred upon them a capacity of self-control that they didn't have before the medication came aboard."

"Dr. Berlin, if the evidence showed that Rex Krebs had premeditated and planned these crimes, and then he took efforts to cover up the acts that he's done, is that proof that he could control himself?"

"No."

"Could Rex Krebs have gained control of his sexual sadism through masturbation?"

"No. When most people masturbate, it doesn't make them no longer want to have sex. Mr. Krebs said he was masturbating as often as three or four times a day. I don't mean to be cynical here, but if it was that simple, we would take everyone with a sexual disorder and have them come into a back room of a doctor's office and have them masturbate three times a day and the problem is solved."

On that note Judge LaBarbera requested a lunch break.

* * *

"In a secure prison setting," McLennan resumed his questioning of Dr. Berlin in the afternoon session, "is this something that might cause Rex Krebs to be in some way a danger?"

"My opinion is no. To help explain why I'm saying no, I want to talk about a very simple concept that talks about internal controls and external controls. Internal control means the ability for a person himself, the control is within him to be in control in a given situation. External controls are those things that control the situation outside of the individual.

"Now, to give an example of how they interact and to answer it with respect to Mr. Krebs, if a man were standing next to a very attractive woman and his wife is standing next to him, he's going to be far less tempted to approach that attractive woman in a sexual way because his wife is, in effect, an external control that's affecting the situation.

"The real test for the man is his wife's not there—the external control is removed—then the temptation can be much stronger. And if this happens to be a man with a sexual disorder who's impaired in his internal controls, that's where the real test is going to come.

"So in a prison setting where there are all sorts of external controls present, men with sexual sadism tend to be model prisoners."

"What's the impact of alcoholism on sexual sadism?"

"The impact on sexual sadism is like pouring a fuel on the fire. If I have a condition where I'm already having difficulty inhibiting my impulses, and now I'm intoxicated and being intoxicated impairs my judgment, it disinhibits me in my ability to be in control of myself. It's certainly going to make it much worse."

"Were you able to look at the materials that were available and determine if there was a personality disorder here?"

"Yes. The third issue I looked at carefully but didn't come down in terms of actually making a diagnosis was antisocial personality disorder. What that means is a person who just tends to be, in a pervasive way, irresponsible and nonproductive, self-centered, things of that nature."

Dr. Berlin listed some of Krebs's antisocial behaviors that he exhibited throughout his life. He then stated that as part of his testing of Krebs, he wanted to know if he was "just an antisocial person, but then I have to balance that against a lot of other things. He was described as being very kind and caring. I began to get a sense that this is a complicated person.

"But I just felt it didn't do justice to him to diagnose him an antisocial personality disorder as though that were pervasive in the totality of who he is as a person. So I didn't. But it was a close call."

"Dr. Berlin, what are the causes of sexual sadism?"

"I'll make three points. The first is the most important one, and that's what it's not due to. And that is, it's not due to a voluntary decision. None of us decide, none of us think about it, make choices as little children about the nature of our own sexual makeup.

"In Mr. Krebs's case he has discovered—not decided, discovered—that he's afflicted with an incredibly awful sexual disorder. I wouldn't wish it on my worst enemy.

"What are the factors that seem to play a contributory role in terms of the medical and psychiatric literature?" Dr. Berlin continued. "Nurture means the effect of early life experiences. One of the factors that contribute to the development of this pathological sexual makeup is early childhood abuse.

"The other thing is nature. That's what the role of biology might be as opposed to early life experiences. There may be some abnormality in the brain in sexual sadism. I think it's less compelling than the evidence about the influence of having been an abused child.

"But, to close, what I think is most important here is simply to appreciate that he didn't choose this as an alternative state of mind.

"Because you wish you could sort of teach someone to get

rid of it, there have been dramatic examples of how that can't be done. One example, a number of years ago here in Atascadero Hospital, a man named Theodore Frank, who was a known sadist and pedophile, and they tried to do some conditioning, some behavior therapy to get him to masturbate to different fantasies, to not think about his sadism. They thought they had cured him.

"They released him into the community, and horribly, he sadistically raped and killed a young child. So it isn't something where you can unlearn it by practicing a different kind of fantasy and masturbating."

McLennan honed in on his client's condition. "Was Rex Krebs under the influence of extreme mental or emotional disturbance?"

"Yes. I would consider the sexual sadism to be extreme emotional disturbance. I mean, something is horribly wrong when a person is walking around preoccupied in this way.

"If he just didn't have a real strong desire to do this, why, when so much was going well in his life, would he have acted this way?

"I think there's something terribly wrong with this man in his mental makeup. I don't think he was so impaired cognitively that he didn't know right from wrong because I think he did.

"But I do think he was impaired in his ability to be in full control of himself.

"I'm not defending him or excusing anything, but in terms of trying to explain an answer, but for the presence of the sexual sadism, which he has, I do not believe that he would have been a threat to these women or particularly to any other women."

"Thank you, Dr. Berlin"—McLennan closed with this witness—"I have nothing further."

Deputy District Attorney John Trice seemed to be licking his chops. He had kept quiet during the majority of Dr. Berlin's testimony, but now he was ready to pounce.

"So you're not trying to excuse the conduct that this jury has found him guilty of, are you?"

"Oh, my goodness," the offended Berlin responded. "I mean, he is either going to be put to death or spend the rest of his life in prison. Nobody is here to excuse it. What he did was horrible. The issue here is whether he has a mental disorder."

"So that's a 'no'?"

"If you want me to be—yes, sir. I'm sorry."

"You can give me a 'yes' or 'no' every now and then. It will make this go a little faster."

"All right."

"Sometimes you go around the country testifying in 'not guilty by reason of insanity' cases, isn't that right?"

"There's probably a handful of those. But the answer is yes."

"So when you testified in Jeffrey Dahmer, that was 'not guilty by reason of insanity,' is that correct?"

"Yes, that's correct."

"The case you testified in Connecticut, the first Michael Ross case, one of the reasons you went there and testified before the jury was to convince the jury that Michael Ross was insane, is that correct?"

"No, sir. It's not my job to convince the jury of anything. It's my job to provide them with information that hopefully enables them to make a more enlightened decision."

"So your job was to go there. And the information you provided to the jury was that your opinion was he was insane under the laws of the state of Connecticut?"

"I don't remember if Connecticut used that word. I did feel in the case of Michael Ross that he lacked substantial capacity to control his behavior."

"In Connecticut they call that NMR, isn't that correct? 'Not mentally responsible.'"

"If you tell me that, I have no reason to disbelieve it. But I don't recall."

Trice decided to switch tactics. He began to cast some

doubt on Dr. Berlin's credentials. "The last time you went to the White House as a presenter was 1983, is that accurate?"

"That's correct."

"When's the last time you talked to colleges of judges?"

"It's been several years."

"And the Senate subcommittee, that was several years ago?"

"Yes, sir."

Trice switched gears back to Berlin's earlier testimony in other high-profile cases. "When you testified in the Jeffrey Dahmer case, did you testify for the prosecution in that case?"

"No, I was asked in by the defense."

"And in that case you expressed in the opinion in Wisconsin that Jeffrey Dahmer was insane, is that correct?"

"I don't mean to be facetious. I really don't want to be taken this way because this is a real serious matter. But I don't know how many people someone would have to try to eat before somebody was going to say they had a mental disorder. Because this man is disturbed as anyone I've seen.

"So I respect the jury's decision, but it wasn't difficult for me to conclude that this man had a mental disorder."

"OK." An annoyed Trice attempted to steer the conversation back. "I think that question was, you went out to Wisconsin and expressed an opinion that he was insane. Is that 'yes'?"

"Well, again, I don't think they used the term 'insane.' I think it was whether he had a mental disorder.

"But I don't want to beg the question with you. I was testifying in a way where I felt that he had a mental illness whereby his responsibility, criminally, was diminished."

Trice brought the cross-examination back to the Krebs case. "You believe everything that Mr. Krebs told you, don't you?"

"Not necessarily," responded Dr. Berlin.

"What don't you believe?"

"Oh, that's a broad question."

"Let me ask you this: you believe Rachel Newhouse strangled herself to death like he told you?"

"He didn't tell me she strangled herself to death. He said that he had left the ropes on her in a particular way without intending to kill her, and then she was strangled as a result of the way in which he tied them and, presumably, her movements."

"Do you believe when he told investigator Hobson that he was going to wash up these girls and douche them and take them back to San Luis Obispo and set them free?"

Defense attorney William McLennan jumped in: "I'm going to object, Your Honor, as irrelevant—"

Trice interrupted and continued to pound on Berlin: "Do you believe that?"

Judge LaBarbera barely got in, "Objection is overruled."

An uncomfortable Dr. Berlin shifted in his chair. "I don't know. I'm not a mind reader. I have no idea."

Trice continued to drive it on home. "One of the problems you have in the diagnosis is, for instance, Aundria Crawford; the sex acts are over with, he thinks she can identify him, and he makes a conscious decision—does he not?—to put that rope around her neck and strangle her to death. What has that got to do with sexual sadism?"

McLennan objected again. Judge LaBarbera overruled him again.

"First of all," Dr. Berlin answered, "he does not claim with respect to Aundria Crawford that the killing was as a result of the sexual sadism. He says he panicked because she saw him and he ended up killing her. I haven't disagreed with that."

"You said, 'First of all.' Is there a second of all?"

"Well, I'm sorry," stated the flustered doctor. "I guess you asked me about Rachel Newhouse."

"No, I didn't ask you about her."

"I thought you asked both. But if you didn't, that's fine."

"I asked you if you believed that she strangled herself to death, and you said you did."

"I didn't say that. You're mischaracterizing. I said I don't know. It is hard to take a human life. And prior to Rachel Newhouse, he'd never taken one. So I don't know that perhaps he wasn't struggling with the idea that he wouldn't go that far, and that maybe the first death was one which hadn't been intended. It's certainly a possibility."

Trice needed to nail down the definition of sexual sadism in regard to Krebs's case. "When he approached Rachel at the Jennifer Street Bridge, you're saying he was suffering from sexual sadism at the time?"

"I'm saying that he had sexual sadism at that time, yes."

"When he knocked her down and drug her down the steps, he was doing that for sexual pleasure?"

"No. I think it was a means to an end."

"When would you think the sexual pleasure began for him?"

"Obviously sexual gratification would come at the time of the sexual act."

"Are you able to focus on any specific moment in time, when you think, when the sexual pleasure would have begun for him?"

"Let me answer it this way: that the end of the sexual act is the pleasure that's tied to it. But until one can have the act, it can be sort of a frustration or sexual tensions that are pushing the individual. I think he was being pushed by these discomforting tensions and at the same time aroused and ultimately gained gratification at the time of the sex acts themselves."

"Your opinion is, he wasn't experiencing any sexual pleasure while he had her tied up and she was screaming at him?"

"Yeah. I don't think it's the same sexual pleasure that he would have at the moment that he was doing this. It's kind of like the distinction between foreplay and ultimately being involved sexually. This is kind of the foreplay of this disturbed disorder. There's a certain excitement in anticipating what's about to happen."

"I'm trying to figure out when the sexual pleasure starts for Mr. Krebs over there." Trice tossed another disgusted look toward the defendant. "All the things we've been talking about sound like just violent things of a mean individual."

"The drive, I think, is with him the whole way. The pleasure comes at the time that he, to be blunt about it, ejaculates."

"So when he took this knife and cut her shirt off the back, he wasn't getting any sexual pleasure from that?"

"I'm not completely satisfied with the term 'foreplay,' but I think that may convey it. I think that was part of the turn-on for him, part of the sadistic drive that was pushing him."

Trice approached closer to the doctor. "So when he lifted her up over his head and slammed her down on the concrete, that's what you could loosely call foreplay? When he drug her down the stairs by her hair, is that what you would call foreplay for sexual sadists?"

"As I said, I'm struggling with the term. I do think it was part of the actual way in which he does it."

"You say he has the ability to defer these urges?"

"Yes, but not to stop himself completely over the long haul."

"Well, he stopped himself for ten years at Soledad, right?"

"No, sir. . . ."

"He didn't?"

"He was stopped for ten years at Soledad."

"Did he have those sexual urges for ten years at Soledad and Corcoran?"

"He had them initially. He worked very hard in those early years and was able to get them down and thought they were gone. I would say that they were latent rather than they were entirely missing."

Trice was almost done with the witness. "I'm sure you asked him what steps he took after he got out of prison to try to resist the urges. Did you ask him that?"

"I don't remember that specifically, but if you'll allow me to say more than 'yes' or 'no,' I can tell you what I did ask him.

"He said that after these urges had come back, and he dates

it to the incident in which he was in the bar fight, that after fighting so hard for so many years to resist it, he kind of became demoralized and gave up and kind of stopped fighting as hard as he had previously."

John Trice had heard enough. "That's all I have. Thank you." He turned his back to Dr. Berlin and walked back to the prosecution table.

John Trice, however, changed his mind. He was not done with Dr. Berlin. He wanted to address Dr. Berlin's notes that he took during the two interviews with Rex Krebs.

"You wrote, 'Roz tried to tell that he had trouble as a kid, that it wasn't his fault,' and he said, 'Bullshit.' Is that the word he used?"

"Yes. That's correct," responded Dr. Berlin.

"Said, 'It's my fault no matter what I go through as a kid.'"

"That's right."

"He admits responsibility. 'Think and do what's right. I didn't think and do what's right.' Is that what he told you?"

"Yes, sir."

"He told you when he got out in 1997 if he had a doctor to talk with, maybe it would have made a difference, he would be less likely to act out, is that correct?"

"That's correct."

"He told you he didn't trust that doctor with parole?"

"That's correct, and then he says, 'I realize I should have.'"

"Later in there he told you that the word 'fantasy,' he never thought about that. His word may have been 'daydream,' correct?"

"Yes. He said that the police officer had used the word 'fantasy.'"

"He says he got this 'fantasy' word from Larry?"

"Yes, meaning Mr. Hobson."

"And then you went on and you were talking to him. 'How do you go from fantasy to action?' Is that correct?"

"Yes. He said, 'I don't know. Try to resist. Also at times just go with them. Little bit of both. No, don't want fantasies to be part of my life. I'd like to get rid of them. Get rid of hard. Hard while they're there. While in prison thought I had it beat, guess I kidded myself.' "

"You actually asked him, 'Why didn't you seek help?' Right?"

"Yes, I did. He said, 'It's not something you tell even your closest friend. I couldn't bring myself to do that.' "

"There was another reason, right?"

"His last statement there is, I apologize for the language, 'Doctors are pretty fucking expensive.' "

"He told you the only doctor that doesn't cost too much is the doctor he had from the parole department, right?"

"Yes, and he said he didn't trust him."

"Well, he said, he'd stick his—excuse my language—his ass back in prison."

"That's correct."

Trice moved on to ask how Krebs felt after he murdered Rachel Newhouse. "You asked him a question, and then he said, 'When Rachel died, although not my intention for her to die, knew she was dead, and not shit I could do to bring her back.' Is that what he said?"

"That's correct."

"He went on to say nothing in the world changed, right?"

"Well, 'Nothing in the world changed. Took and buried her, told self to never do that again.' "

"Then you wrote, 'Killing Aundria'—excuse my language—'not fuck with him a bit,' is that correct?"

"He said that act at the time had not bothered him, and he tied it into having an awful experience as a child. But he said as soon as he realized what he had done, 'it just disgusted me.' "

"You asked him why there was so much violence on the bridge, apparently. Did you ask him that?"

"Yes, I did. (He said) 'That's what I lived with from nine to seventeen.' "

Trice asked Dr. Berlin about Krebs's thoughts on the attempted rape of Anishka Constantine. "He told you that one was easier because he had done that once before, is that correct?"

"Yes. He basically said once you've crossed the line, it's easier to do it a second time."

"He told you how much he started to drink again. If he had to point the finger at one thing, it would probably be the alcohol?"

"Yes. Then he went on to explain that alcohol, in his words, 'uninhibits my judgment.'"

"You would point to the fantasies as the driving force, not the alcohol, right?"

"Yes. As I said, alcohol is like pouring fuel on the fire."

"It was his understanding, if he wanted to, he could have requested a placement at a state hospital?"

"Absolutely."

"He never did that, did he?"

"He just explained why he had deceived himself into thinking it wasn't necessary."

"He told you that three times he sat in his living room waiting for his father to come home, and he planned to kill him but he couldn't bring himself to do it.

"Wouldn't a plan to shoot somebody be an indication of an antisocial personality disorder?"

"I think it was an indication," Dr. Berlin responded, "of how badly abused he was as a child. He couldn't take it anymore. He had thoughts of killing his father, and if anything, he had a conscience that wouldn't let him do it."

Trice returned to Krebs's killing of Rachel and Aundria. "You asked him, 'Why were you so brutal?'"

"Yes. And he says, 'The only time [I use] any brutality is to gain control.'"

"Then you said, 'Do you care?' And he said, 'At the time, no.'"

"Yeah. Well, he said, 'At the time, no. Now I care that I caused them grief I've caused them.'

"I thought it was a very candid and not self-serving statement," Dr. Berlin continued.

"Wait a minute"—Trice leaped through the open door—"On the next page right after that, you said to him, 'Why don't you just say I'm just so sorry?' Right?"

"Yes, sir."

"And he said—excuse my language—'Because sorry means fuck.' Isn't that what he said?"

"The answer is yes."

"And then he went on to say, 'It doesn't change anything, solve anything, or even help my conscience. It doesn't help them, and it doesn't salve my conscience.' Isn't that what he said?"

"That's correct."

Trice then turned the cross-examination over to the topics of blame. "You said, 'Say, if my father had spent a little more time with his son rather than work, drink, sex, perhaps I turned out fine.' Right?"

"Yes. And then he said he's not blaming his father but can't help wondering if it would have been different."

"So he didn't blame his father?"

"No. He did not."

Concerning the two 1987 cases, Trice asked Dr. Berlin: "He thought alcohol was a contributory factor, is that correct?"

"It is."

"At one point he was talking about methamphetamine; he said that was just an excuse, something to hide behind. It's not the meth that caused the problems; it's the fantasies. Is that what he told you?"

"Yes."

"He told you he was beginning to have problems with fantasies when Roslynn was in one room and he was in the other room masturbating to a rape fantasy, is that correct?"

"That's correct."

"Did he give you a time frame on that?"

"That period after the bar fight."

"At the bottom of thirty-seven, you said, 'If you could do it over again, what could have stopped you?' "

"He says, 'What could I have done to stop myself?' He kind of repeats my question."

"And he said, 'Only what I never could have done, ask somebody for help,' " Trice added.

"Yes."

"And he went on to say that he went into prison wanting help, that he didn't get any, but he didn't blame the prison system. Is that what he told you?"

"Yes. His exact words. He didn't get help.

"He doesn't blame them, but what he learned when he went in, everybody in prison looks down on his crime, so he hid in the woodwork and didn't ask for help," Berlin added.

"Then he goes on to say, 'Reach a point—' "

Berlin interrupted: "Yes, 'Reach a point of not want kill anyone but stop care about self and stop fight urge to rape or more. Try to stop think about it like it would just go away. Not actually fight like did before.'

"And then I asked him," Berlin continued, "if his resolve was weakened—and I don't know if you want me to continue?"

"No," Trice stated succinctly. "My question was when he said not actually fight like he did before, what period of time are we talking about there?"

"That's a fair question. I think he's talking about after he killed Rachel and before Aundria, that at some point he just gives up to the illness, if I can put it that way."

"No further questions." Trice walked back to his chair.

FIFTY-SEVEN

The prosecution brought in their own expert witness in violence and sexual sadism to combat the testimony of Dr. Berlin. Dr. Park Dietz, renowned forensic psychiatrist, had sat in the courtroom since Monday, April 30, 2001. The court allowed him to hear the testimony of Dr. Berlin. He did not take the witness stand until late Thursday morning, May 3, 2001.

At $500 an hour, most attorneys would not have an expert witness merely sit and listen for three days.

The prosecution, however, believed he would be worth every penny.

The reason why could be found in Dr. Dietz's curriculum vitae, or résumé. The doctor owns two companies: Park Dietz and Associates, a firm that provides consultations for attorneys in both criminal and civil matters of litigation, and Threat Assessment Group, a violence prevention firm that works for large corporations, government agencies, and celebrities to insure the safety of their clients. His businesses are located in the South Bay, about fifty minutes southwest of Los Angeles, specifically in Newport Beach, California.

Dr. Dietz graduated from Cornell University in 1970. He received his medical degree from Johns Hopkins University School of Medicine, the same school that Dr. Berlin received his medical degree from as well, in 1975. He earned his master's degree in public health from Johns Hopkins that same year. He later received his Ph.D. in sociology from the same university.

Dr. Dietz and Dr. Berlin were both residents at Johns Hopkins Hospital from 1975 to 1977. Dr. Dietz transferred to the University of Pennsylvania, where he completed his residency.

Dr. Dietz's first job out of school was as an assistant professor of psychiatry at the Harvard Medical School from 1978 to 1982. His initial position was the director of forensic psychiatry at Harvard's private hospital, McLean Hospital. He also oversaw a program at the notorious Bridgewater State Hospital, a maximum-security prison for the criminally insane, where he worked for two years.

In 1984 Dr. Dietz's world changed instantly. He received a request from the United States Attorney's Office in Washington, D.C., to oversee the evaluation of John Hinckley Jr., better known as the young man who attempted to assassinate then-President Ronald Reagan in 1981 to prove his love for actress Jodie Foster. He worked on the case for the next year.

Dr. Dietz returned to Boston, where he conducted research for a year on the relationship between mental disorder and criminal behavior. He then took a job as the medical director of the Institute of Law Psychiatry and Public Policy at the University of Virginia. He received a promotion to professor of law and professor of behavioral medicine and psychiatry. He continued his research, which took him around the country, including the FBI's Behavioral Science Unit at Quantico, Virginia, now known as the Profiling and Behavioral Assessment Unit. The BSU has become famous for launching the "profiling" careers of Robert Ressler and John Douglas, the inspiration for the Jack Crawford character played by Scott Glenn in the multiple Academy Award–winning film *The Silence of the Lambs*, which starred Anthony Hopkins as serial killer Hannibal Lecter and, ironically enough, Jodie Foster as FBI Agent Clarice Starling. Dr. Dietz has been the forensic psychiatry consultant for the BSU since 1981.

By the late 1980s Dr. Dietz made an important decision. He no longer wanted to be a full-time academic. Subsequently he packed his bags and headed West to open his two businesses, where he still resides and works.

Due to Dr. Dietz's expertise on violence and the criminal mind, he has testified in hundreds of murder trials. Trice asked the doctor to list some of the more notorious cases.

"You were involved in the Jeffrey Dahmer case?"

"Yes," replied Dr. Dietz. "I was the government's expert on the case, and I spent three days interviewing Mr. Dahmer."

"Susan Smith case?"

"Yes. I was a consultant to the DA's office. That's the woman who drowned her two children but pretended that they had been kidnapped by someone else."

"William Bonin, the 'Freeway Killer'?"

"Yes."

"Richard Allen Davis, the Polly Klaas case?"

"I was an expert in that case and testified at the sentencing of Mr. Davis."

"Robert Bardo—he killed Rebecca Schaeffer, the actress—is that correct?"

"I was a defense witness in that case."

"The Ng case in Orange County?"

"Charles Ng and Leonard Lake were two serial killers from Calaveras County who had sadistically tortured their victims, and I consulted to the attorney general's office."

"Joel Rifkin, the New York sexual sadist?"

"He killed seventeen prostitutes, and I testified at his trial after I examined him."

"Arthur Shawcross, New York serial killer?"

"Yes. He too strangled, I think, seventeen prostitutes, and I examined him and testified."

"The Menendez brothers in Los Angeles?"

"I examined Lyle Menendez, and testified at the retrial in his case."

"Ted Kaczynski, the 'Unabomber'?"

"I worked on that case for a very long time for the FBI and later for the prosecutors from the U.S. Attorney's Office."

"You testified for the Ronald Goldman family against O.J. Simpson?"

"Yes."

"Working on the Cary Stayner case in Yosemite?" Stayner was convicted of killing Carole and Juli Sund, Silvina Pelosso, and also Joie Armstrong.

"Yes, I am."

"You've worked on some of the school shooting cases in this country; is that correct?"

"Yes. I already did exams and finished my work in the Oregon school shooting by Kip Kinkel. The Georgia school shooting by T.J. Solomon, and I have yet to do the work I've been retained to do on Mr. Charles "Andy" Williams, who did the Santee, California, school shooting.

"And a team of us this fall will be doing the psychiatric autopsies on Dylan Klebold and Eric Harris, who did the school shooting at Columbine."

Once Trice established Dr. Dietz's expertise as a forensic psychiatrist, he steered the discussion to Rex Krebs.

"Can you tell the jury the initial work of evaluation you did in this case?"

"I received a phone call from you. You sent me investigative reports about the 1987 rape and attempted rape. You sent me a psychiatric report. And you sent me transcripts of investigator Hobson's interviews and a videotape of the interviews."

"And that was all reviewed?"

"One of my employees, James Wright, a retired FBI agent, summarized the documents for me originally."

"Then the next involvement started when I called you and told you the defense had retained Dr. Fred Berlin, is that correct?"

"Yes. At that point I requested an examination of the defendant, because it appeared that the defense was going to assert a mental issue, put the defendant's mental state at issue. So I asked you to arrange for an exam. I wanted both a psychiatric interview and psychological testing."

"You actually traveled up here to Monterey in an attempt to interview the defendant, did you not?"

"Yes, I did."

"Do you remember when that was, approximately?"

"Around April fourth of this year."

"Did you perform an examination on the defendant, Rex Allan Krebs?"

"No."

"Why is that?"

"Because he refused to be examined."

"Based on your background, your training, your experience over the years, the review of the evidence in this case, do you believe that you can render an opinion as to what role the defendant's mental state may or may not have played in the commission of the crimes and criminal activity in his life?"

"Yes, I do."

"Do you believe the defendant suffers from any type of disorder?"

"Yes, I do."

"More than one?"

"Yes. Dr. Berlin diagnosed two disorders and mentioned another that he considered, and I agree with him on sexual sadism. I accept that the defendant may have alcoholism. But I come down on the other side from Dr. Berlin on the question of antisocial personality disorder."

"I think Dr. Berlin said that antisocial personality disorder was 'just a bunch of words used by doctors to describe bad behavior.'"

"It's actually a specific diagnosis, isn't it?"

Dr. Dietz began by describing the origin of the concept behind antisocial personality. He informed the jury that it had evolved from earlier medical concepts starting with the "moral imbecile," which was then replaced by "psychopath." The term "psychopath" referred to individuals who acted without conscience and exhibit poor or no moral judgment. He then described how Hollywood bastardized the term and turned it into a monster. As a result, the medical profession opted to coin a new phrase: "sociopath," to reflect individuals who behave in antisocial ways. The term was used for a number of years, and then slowly it was replaced by the phrase "antisocial personality disorder."

The doctor explained what the criteria are to determine if a person possesses an antisocial personality disorder.

"There really are four issues. First, the individual must be at least eighteen years old.

"Second, we have to make sure that the antisocial behavior is not due to schizophrenia or mania.

"We also are required to find that there is evidence of a conduct disorder that began before the individual was fifteen years old.

"And lastly, we have to find that the individual has had three or more kinds of antisocial behavior since age fifteen.

"Now, in the case of Mr. Krebs, he had been [over] eighteen years old at the time of these offenses. So the first criterion is met.

"Dr. Berlin testified that Mr. Krebs does not have any psychotic mental illness. He doesn't have schizophrenia. He does not have mania. So the second point is met as well."

Concerning conduct disorder before the age of fifteen, Dr. Dietz stated that "one of the criteria for a conduct disorder is that the individual often bullies, threatens, or intimidates others. There was testimony by the private investigator that he did intimidate other children at school.

"A second thing is whether someone has broken into someone's house, building, or car. The incident with the knife and the ski mask is an example of that.

"The third would be often lies to obtain goods or favors, or to avoid obligation. Mr. Krebs was sent to a psychologist because of his lying and stealing when he was eleven or twelve years old.

"These are examples of behaviors before he was fifteen. When we look at antisocial behavior since age fifteen, he has examples of antisocial behavior in at least four different categories.

"The first of those categories is repeatedly performing acts that are grounds for arrest. Examples that Mr. Krebs has engaged in were the burglary of the house in 1981 when he took the twenty-two-caliber revolver.

"His possession of marijuana.

"His derailing the motor car on the train track.

"His assault on Jenny Everwood in 1984.

"His burglary of a garaged car in 1984.

"His rape of Shelly Crosby in 1987.

"His attempted rape of Anishka Constantine in 1987.

"The abduction, rape, and murder of Rachel Newhouse in 1998.

"The abduction, rape, and murder of Aundria Crawford in 1999.

"Those are all acts that are grounds for arrest."

Dr. Dietz continued with his list of antisocial behaviors. "The second kind of antisocial behavior is deceitfulness, as indicated by repeated lying, use of aliases, or conning others for personal profit or pleasure.

"Examples that Mr. Krebs has shown of deceitfulness include his lying to the police about the burglary in 1981.

"His problem with lying at the North Idaho Children's Home from 1981 to '83.

"His lying to the police about the car theft in 1984.

"Dishonesty, which was described in the records of the North Idaho Correctional Institution from 1984 to 1986.

"He lied to the police about the rape and attempted rape in 1987.

"When he was first interviewed by Investigator Hobson about the present charges, he lied about killing Ms. Newhouse or Ms. Crawford.

"He lied about ever having met them, saying he never met either woman.

"He was asked if he knew where they had been taken from and he lied about that.

"He was asked about the eight ball and lied about where that had come from.

"The jump seat. He lied about that too.

"And then, even after he admitted the murders in subsequent interviews, he still lied. He lied about why he confessed. He lied about the thirty-five-millimeter camera.

"The third kind of antisocial behavior is irritability and aggressiveness as indicated by repeated physical fights or assaults. Examples of that are the assault on Jenny Everwood in 1984. The fights at the North Idaho Correctional Institution in 1984 and 1985.

"His assault on Shelly Crosby in 1987.

"His assault on Anishka Constantine in 1987.

"His assault on Rachel Newhouse in 1998.

"And his assault on Aundria Crawford in 1999.

"That is more than enough adequate evidence to indicate that Rex Krebs has shown irritability and aggressiveness through repeated fighting or assaults.

"The fourth category is reckless disregard for safety of self or others. Four examples of that are that after injuring the man in the car derailment, he was told that the man could have been killed, and his response was 'So what?'

"Mr. Krebs claims that he was driving drunk while he had Rachel Newhouse tied up and captive. He claims that he left Rachel Newhouse alone with a rope tied around her neck. He claims that he was driving drunk with Aundria Crawford. Recklessly disregarding safety.

"So taking all of that together, he's over eighteen. He doesn't have the serious mental illnesses. He has evidence of a conduct disorder before fifteen, and he has at least four of the criteria of antisocial personality disorder since age fifteen, that indicates that he meets the *DSM-IV* criteria for antisocial personality disorder."

Trice asked the doctor, "Now, Dr. Berlin expressed a

different opinion, and you disagree with him, why? Just because the criteria are met?"

"Yes. He meets the criteria; therefore, he has it."

Trice approached the subject of sexual sadism with Dr. Dietz. "There's a second disorder that you've diagnosed, is that correct?"

"Yes. That would be sexual sadism."

"Dr. Berlin spent a lot of time talking about fantasies. What are fantasies?"

"Fantasies are voluntarily invoked mental imaginations. And I agree entirely with Dr. Berlin when he says that people do not choose their sexual deviations. They do not choose to become a sexual sadist. Or to become a pedophile. They discover that they have these disorders.

"Nobody chooses which things turn them on and arouse them. But when an individual's favorite masturbation fantasy is of a sadistic act, such as tying someone up, when they have that fantasy, they are not experiencing that any differently from someone normal who has a fantasy about being with an attractive person of the opposite sex who's naked. It's equally arousing. It is equally pleasant. It's equally used for the purpose of sexual arousal.

"For the sexual sadist in particular, there's a variety of things that fit in the category of what is arousing to a sexual sadist. Bondage, which usually means tying someone up with leather restraints, or chains, or ropes, or duct tape, or any other material. We also make a distinction between motor and sensory bondage. Motor bondage is the tying up where someone can't move. Sensory bondage is impairing their senses by blindfolding, putting earmuffs on them, or putting them in a dark space such as a coffin or a cage in the dark.

"Captivity is another common theme. Having someone captive who is available for sexual use.

"Dominating someone. Many focus on humiliation. And the humiliation can be making someone do embarrassing things in public. Or by humiliating her by calling her abusive names in front of her children, or her family, or her friends. Or it can be a ritual form of humiliation like smearing food on her body while she's tied up.

"Spanking and whipping. Flagellism. Beating is a common theme with sexual sadists.

"Choking and strangulation are very common themes in sexual sadism. And cutting, burning, and torture.

"Mr. Krebs has said that he prefers bondage, and captivity, and domination, and he's denied that he prefers beating, and strangulation, and torture. His behaviors have included bondage, and captivity, and domination, but they have also included beating and strangulation."

"Can you explain this disorder, this sexual sadism?"

"Sexual sadists discover this about themselves, typically by puberty. This condition has existed for at least two hundred years, and one would think a lot longer than that.

"Throughout history there's been examples of individuals who have committed horrible crimes in the service of this particular disorder. Caligula, for example, in Ancient Rome, was a sexual sadist. But we do not really know what the causes are. We do know that people who have this disorder vary tremendously in how they cope with it. Some people confine themselves entirely to fantasy and masturbation. Some of them use a defense mechanism called sublimation, in which they will actually find a way to do pro-social things through this interest. They could become a scholar of sexual sadism, or write a biography on the Marquis de Sade.

"A second kind are those who have consenting partners. Many individuals find someone who will consent to the simulation of sadistic acts. Will consent to spanking. Will consent to tying up. And will allow the sadistic partner to enjoy those activities in a way that are not harmful to the consenting partner.

"Many use pornography. And there is a large volume of pornography devoted to this. Something like twenty percent of the imagery was sexually sadistic imagery.

"There are also bondage and domination services available.

In some of the larger cities, there are clubs specifically devoted to this. Prostitutes too include some who will act the submissive or the slave for a fee.

"Some people engage in nonviolent crimes through sexual sadism." Dr. Dietz described a case he worked on for the FBI in which a man placed threatening notes on women's cars at shopping malls. The man videotaped the women's reactions as they read the more disturbing sections in which he bound and gagged them with a knife to their throats.

"And then some sexual sadists commit violent crimes in order to fulfill their desires. That's just a tiny group of the sexual sadists that ever get to that point. That's the group that I have studied the most, and the group that, of course, causes the most harm."

"Having made this diagnosis," prodded Trice, "what evidence in this case do you think supports this diagnosis?"

"The self-reported sexual fantasies," responded Dr. Dietz, "in which Mr. Krebs talks about having from age twelve or thirteen. Rape fantasies.

"The assault on Jenny Everwood, which was a sexual assault, involved both beating and manual strangulation. And I think that is evidence of his sexual sadism.

"The Shelly Crosby rape is another example that involved bondage, the attempt to gag and blindfold, cutting the clothing, attempted anal penetration and vaginal penetration. All of that is consistent with the behavior of a sexual sadist committing a violent crime.

"The Anishka Constantine attempted rape also is consistent with a sexual sadist committing a violent crime. He brought binding materials with him. He attempted to bind her, but she grabbed his knife and got the better of him.

"And, of course, both of the homicides. Rachel Newhouse—the defendant admitted that he beat her. He abducted her. He gagged her. He kept her captive. He bound her in a variety of positions.

"In the Aundria Crawford homicide, the defendant admitted that he beat her. He abducted her. He gagged her. He blindfolded her. He kept her captive. He bound her too in a variety of positions. He cut her clothing, and he raped her both vaginally and anally. He has admitted to many varieties of behavior that are consistent with sexual sadism."

Both Dr. Dietz and Dr. Berlin agreed that Rex Krebs was a sexual sadist. Trice's job now was to draw out of Dr. Dietz the impact of sexual sadism on Krebs's criminal behavior.

"But you disagree with the nature and effects of sexual sadism, is that correct?"

"Yes, it is. First of all, I don't consider sexual sadism as a mental disease. There are many, many disorders, ranging from not serious to very serious. Only a few of all the things in the *DSM* deserve to be called mental diseases. Those are the conditions that cause a human being to have a perception of reality that is fundamentally different from what any other person can ever experience.

"There are a number of conditions that can do that. Sexual sadism isn't one of them. Someone whose only problem is sexual sadism has only one fundamental difference from normal people and that is a difference in what excites them sexually. It doesn't affect how they think. It doesn't affect their emotions. It doesn't affect their ability to control themselves. It only affects what it is that turns them on sexually.

"I believe they can control what they do with their sexual desires just like other people do."

"This concept of the 'policeman at the elbow' rule, are you familiar with that phrase?"

"I am. That's a term borrowed from a test for whether someone's not responsible for their behavior. Would the defendant have committed this crime had there been a policeman at his elbow at the moment? The answer in this case is most certainly that had there been a policeman at his elbow, he certainly would not have committed these crimes. He even looked around for witnesses when he was on the bridge with the skull mask before he abducted Rachel Newhouse. If there had been any witnesses there, he wouldn't have done it. If there had been a policeman there, he wouldn't have done it.

"He was fully aware that this was wrong behavior and capable of stopping it with those kinds of external controls."

Dr. Dietz also acknowledged to the court that he agreed with Dr. Berlin's assessment as to Rex Krebs's potential alcoholism.

Trice asked the doctor whether he believed psychotherapy could have cured Rex Krebs's antisocial personality.

"I think anyone in the mental professions," Dr. Dietz informed the court, "would say if somebody has the kind of risk factors he was addressing, that psychotherapy is a good thing to offer. It's almost a platitude to say and to offer it.

"The question becomes if somebody has developed an antisocial personality disorder, which they have by the time they're eighteen, what impact can psychotherapy have on that disorder? Unfortunately, despite a hundred years of efforts to find some psychotherapy that would help such people and make a difference in their crime rates, nothing whatsoever works. The recidivism is the same for people who have received the treatment and people who haven't.

"It's one of the great disappointments of modern psychiatry that we do not know how to change the antisocial behavior of people with antisocial personality disorder. The only thing that cuts down their rate of offenses is incarceration."

"Dr. Berlin talked about the sexual sadism and the fantasies almost becoming a compulsion," stated Trice. "Is that opinion widely held in your field?"

"No, it isn't. The difference between Krebs as someone who does such things when he's cruising, drinking, and finds a proper victim and many other sexual sadists, who don't do those things, is the difference between a person of good character, and morals, and conscience, and a person with an antisocial personality who does not have good character, and conscience, and morals, but who behaves aggressively and deceitfully."

"I'd like to ask you whether the offenses were committed

while the defendant was under the influence of extreme mental or emotional disturbance?"

"I believe that these offenses were not committed while he was under the influence of extreme mental or emotional disturbance. Antisocial personality disorder is certainly not an example of extreme mental or emotional disturbance. It's an example of a maladaptive pattern of social relationships.

"Sexual sadism is not an example of extreme mental or emotional disturbance; it's an example of a perversion, a sexual deviation which is not about the emotions or mental disturbance. It's about sexual desire."

"The other question Mr. McLennan asked Dr. Berlin was whether the defendant acted under extreme duress. Do you have an opinion on that?"

"I think Rachel Newhouse was acting under duress and Aundria Crawford was acting under duress, but not Mr. Krebs."

Trice asked Dr. Dietz whether Krebs could appreciate the criminality of his conduct at the time of the murders.

"First of all, I don't think that the conditions that anyone has described Mr. Krebs as having are a mental disease or defect. But even if he did, I think we have evidence that his volitional control was there, that is, that he did have the capacity to conform his conduct to the requirements of the law.

"His decision to drink was a decision to put other people at risk. Because he knows how he behaves when he drinks. When he decided to cruise, that's a decision to put other people at risk. His decision to carry a rape kit with him was a decision to prepare for sadistic sexual assault. Those are reflective of choices to put himself in a position where he will find himself behaving in the way he's always wanted to and where other people are at risk.

"His decision to stop resisting, to stop trying to conform his conduct, is a choice, a bad choice he made, rather than his not having the ability to control himself."

"No further questions," Trice directed toward Judge LaBarbera.

FIFTY-EIGHT

May 7, 2001
Superior Court Room 16, Monterey, California
2:00 P.M.

John Trice was ready for the closing argument of the sentencing phase for Rex Krebs. He approached the attentive jury.

"We are now at the last step in the criminal-justice system, where the people, the jury, will decide what is the appropriate punishment for this defendant for the slaughter of Rachel and Aundria.

"You have been immersed in this terrible story. You too will never forget this. You realize now you have been in the presence of one of the most cruel, calculating, and brutal individuals on the planet, Rex Allan Krebs.

"You will decide if we did what I said we would do: prove the horrific facts of these cases and his brutal and extensive criminal background substantially outweighs the pathetic blame-game defense that has been thrown at you in the past two or three weeks.

"I don't want to finish my work on this case after two years talking about the defendant and his mitigation. I want to finish my work on this case talking to you about what should be the focus here. The focus here should be Rachel. It should be Aundria. It should be their families, and it should be his monstrous mentality."

Trice's argument focused the jury's attention on the crimes perpetrated on the victims by Krebs. He did not want them to fall under the spell of "poor pitiful Rex" and the horrible treatment he received throughout his youth. He informed the jury that sympathy for the family of the defendant is not a mitigating factor for them to entertain. And he informed the jury that Allan Krebs was a bad father.

"But the story the defense wants you to believe is that because of that you should feel sorry for Rex Krebs. And that, ladies and gentlemen, is where the leap is. This thirty-five-year-old rapist who brutalized these two coeds in San Luis Obispo, he deserves nothing from you."

Trice went on to chastise the defense's expert witness, Dr. Fred Berlin. The attorney spat out in disbelief of Dr. Berlin's "ridiculous concept of sexual compulsion." Trice sarcastically stated, "He has evil thoughts, so he has to brutalize a twelve-year-old girl in Sandpoint, Idaho, in 1984? He has to brutalize a woman named Shelly, who's asleep in her bed? He has to brutalize Anishka, who's sleeping in her home with her seven-year-old daughter. He just has to kidnap two coeds in San Luis Obispo, rape, and strangle them to death.

"That's the defense. He has bad thoughts. He just can't help himself." Trice's disgust was evident to everyone in the warm courtroom.

"The defense will say, 'But he confessed.' The defense may say Rex brought closure to Montel and Phillip and Gail. But Rex Krebs only told us what he wanted us to hear after he was confronted with the blood evidence."

Trice wanted to make sure that during all of the defendant character testimony the two reasons the jury was there would not be forgotten. "Just as the defense attorneys want to humanize Rex Krebs, so it is proper for us to humanize those he killed. It's important because sometimes in our criminal-justice system there are flaws. And sometimes we forget the victims. And it shouldn't be that way.

"Someone with much more insight than I once said: 'When

one person kills another, there is immediate revulsion at the nature of the crime. But in a time so short as to seem indecent to the members of the person's family, the dead person ceases to exist as an identifiable figure.

" 'To those individuals in the community of goodwill and empathy, warmth and compassion, only one of the key actors in the drama remains with whom to commiserate, and that is always the criminal. The dead person ceases to be a part of everyday reality, ceases to exist. She is only a figure in a historical event.

" 'We inevitably turn away from the past toward the ongoing reality. And the ongoing reality is the criminal. Trapped, anxious, now helpless, isolated, often badgered and bewildered, he usurps the compassion that is justly his victim's due. He will steal his victim's moral constituency along with her life.'

"So that's why you got to know a little bit about the girls."

Trice prepared to conclude this all-important facet of the trial. He approached the jury. "Justice, ladies and gentlemen, is not served until the citizens of our community are as outraged by what Rex Krebs did as the families of the victims. Rachel and Aundria were not taken by an act of God, but by an act of that man," he firmly stated as he pointed toward Krebs, who did not look at Trice or the jury.

"It is now appropriate that justice be administered by an act of man, by our government, by our criminal-justice system, by this court, by you, the jury. The death penalty is supported by the evidence in this case. It is the only appropriate judgment for him.

"Thank you."

Trice nodded his head toward the jurors and silently turned around. He headed toward his seat. The courtroom sat completely still.

Only Judge LaBarbera's mention of lunch recess broke the reverie.

The defense, just as Trice predicted, focused not on the vic-

tims, but instead on the mitigating factors in Rex Krebs's life
that possibly drove him to kill the two girls. Both attorneys
spoke before the jury. A weary but determined James Maguire
III began the defense's closing arguments. The attorney spoke
of the various "risk factors" in Rex Krebs's life. He alluded to
the things that Trice mentioned, that Krebs chose. Now he
wanted to talk about something uniquely different.

"I'm going to talk about the things that he didn't choose.
Let me start with his parents. Rex didn't choose to be born to
Allan Krebs, a man with a reputation for brutality. He didn't
choose to be born to Connie Krebs, an alcoholic woman who
cared more about having a man in her life than she did about
her son's well-being."

Maguire moved on to the various risk factors. He mentioned poverty, constant moving around, instability within the
family structure, neglect, and verbal, emotional, and physical
abuse.

"I'm saying to you," Maguire stated firmly, addressing the
jury, "that each of these is also a factor in mitigation. They are
an explanation. They're not an excuse. They are an explanation for why Rex Krebs is in this courtroom today. They are
the forces that form the person that Rex Krebs became, and
they damaged him in a major way. By damage, I mean mental illness.

"You know," Maguire continued, "if you were to describe
to someone who hasn't been present at this trial the criminal
conduct that Rex Krebs has engaged in here—conduct that
he's admitted to—a person listening to this account would
say, 'This is sick. This is a sick person.' And, of course, he is.
He is sick. This conduct is so abnormal that we know intu-
itively that a person who does this has to be sick, has got to
be mentally ill in some form."

Maguire went on to make the point that Krebs often sought
help, but never received it. He also spoke of how every time
Krebs seemed to get better, he would end up back with his
father and eventually would get in trouble again.

Maguire also compared the expert witnesses, Dr. Fred Berlin and Dr. Park Dietz. Naturally, he was less kind to the latter. "Dr. Dietz seems to be some sort of professional witness who doesn't treat people anymore. He hasn't since the early '80s. He just goes around making lots of money testifying in cases." Maguire mentioned that both Berlin and Dietz agreed that Krebs suffered from sexual sadism, that it is an uninvited illness, and that there are treatments to prevent it from reoccurring.

Maguire also castigated Dr. Dietz about his testimony of Krebs's bad acts that proved the defendant suffered from antisocial personality disorder. Specifically, when Krebs drove Rachel home while intoxicated and endangered other people's lives.

"It didn't seem to make any sense to me," Maguire quizzically stated of Dietz's testimony. "Frankly, five hundred dollars an hour, I expected a little tighter presentation."

Maguire wound up his closing by stressing the option for treatment for Krebs. "It doesn't matter whose fault it was that Rex Krebs didn't get the treatment that he needed. It does matter that it's available to him now. There is an antidote now. This means that his dangerousness, his evil side, can be taken away.

"There is no need to kill him. So if he is sentenced to life in prison, the evil Rex Krebs can be eliminated without destroying the good Rex Krebs."

Maguire concluded with one last plea for his client's life: "It was the good in him that made him offer himself up to your judgment. So now I ask on his behalf that you allow the good in him to live, that you break the cycle of violence, that you vote for the good. Life without the possibility of parole is a sentence that will punish him, that will protect society and is the appropriate sentence in this case. Thank you."

Judge LaBarbera gave everyone a breather. There was still one more closing argument remaining.

Upon return from a twenty-minute recess, defense attorney

Patricia Ashbaugh approached the jury one last time. Her job was to remind them of the job they had to do, that they could not let their emotions cloud their judgment.

It would be a tough job. They had to decide whether to send a man to his death.

"Vengeance can sometimes be like a seductive, elicit lover. It will take you in. It will make you feel good for the moment, but then it vanishes. Vengeance is destructive. It destroys good people and it can destroy good people like you. Vengeance will not bring back Rachel Newhouse. Vengeance will not bring back Aundria Crawford. Do not embrace it."

Ashbaugh then appealed to the jurors' conscience.

"Whatever decision you do make, you will have to live with (it) for the rest of your life. You will think about it over and over and over, not just next week, not just next month, not just next year, but perhaps your entire lifetime. Because if you vote for death, there will be some executioner who will put poison into the veins of my client, Rex Krebs, because you have ordered it, and he will die."

Ashbaugh then appealed to the jurors' sensibility that a life sentence behind bars would be a just punishment.

"I suggest a conclusion that you could reach is that Rex Krebs will not hurt or be a problem for anyone if you render a verdict of life without possibility of parole. Life will not be glamorous for him. He will not get to see his son grow up, attend his graduation or his wedding. He will not see the ocean again. He will not feel the sand beneath his feet. He will not walk in the mountains. And he will not walk among us. He will have to live with himself and what he has done.

"I really don't know what else to say. But this I will say to you. Life is nothing to fear. Life is nothing to be ashamed of. Life is what I am asking from you. Thank you."

The defense rested.

Rex Krebs's life lay in the hands of twelve fellow Californians.

After four long days of deliberation, on the evening of May

11, 2001, the jurors sent word to Judge LaBarbera that they had reached an agreement on a sentence for Rex Krebs. The judge summoned both parties to the courtroom. The judge also sent for the jurors.

The time was 6:50 P.M.

"The jury is present." The judge signaled the room. "I understand you've reached a verdict?"

"Yes, we have," replied one of the jurors, who handed a sheet of paper to the bailiff, who, in turn, handed it to the judge.

Judge LaBarbera read the sentence and handed the paper to the clerk: "The defendant will please stand, and the clerk will read the verdicts."

The clerk did as instructed.

"Superior Court of California, County of San Luis Obispo. *The People of the State of California, Plaintiff,* versus *Rex Allan Krebs, Defendant,* verdict of jury, penalty.

"Count one, Penal Code Section 187, murder of Rachel Lindsay Newhouse. We, the jury, having convicted the defendant, Rex Allan Krebs, of the first-degree murder of Rachel Lindsay Newhouse and having found true the special circumstances pertaining to her murder, now fix the penalty at death."

Once again the pressure cooker released in the courtroom. Sighs, cries, and winces rose above the fray.

The clerk continued to read the sentence.

"Superior Court of California, County of San Luis Obispo. *The People of the State of California, Plaintiff,* versus *Rex Allan Krebs, Defendant,* verdict of jury, penalty.

"Count two, Penal Code Section 187, murder of Aundria Lynn Crawford. We, the jury, having convicted the defendant, Rex Allan Krebs, of the first-degree murder of Aundria Lynn Crawford and having found true the special circumstances pertaining to her murder, now fix the penalty at death."

Judge LaBarbera took control of the room. "All right. You may be seated. Ladies and gentlemen, the verdicts at this time complete your service." The judge complimented the jury for their impeccable behavior.

Judge LaBarbera then sent through an order to have the prisoner transferred to the San Luis Obispo Jail.

Rex Krebs still had one more court appearance.

FIFTY-NINE

July 20, 2001
Superior Court, San Luis Obispo, California

The same cast of characters gathered one last time for the formal sentencing of Rex Krebs. In addition to the judge, the attorneys, the defendant, the court reporters, and the bailiffs, the contingent was also joined by Rachel's sister, Ashley Newhouse, and Jody Crawford and Gail Eberhart Crawford, who had added her daughter's last name before the trial.

Judge LaBarbera assembled the group for the final time. He complimented the attorneys on both sides for their professionalism. He also complimented Rex Krebs for his exemplary behavior in the courtroom. The judge then stated that he had read the probationary report conducted on Mr. Krebs and then asked John Trice if he had anything to add.

The prosecutor stated, "I'd like to present some written statements." Cindy Marie Apsey and Karen Coffey from the victim witness division of the district attorney's office read the victim impact statements. Apsey first read a letter written by Jeanne Steffan-Skelly, Rachel Newhouse's aunt. The letter related Steffan-Skelly's fears of being a mother, a parent, of sleepless nights fretting over the dangers the world presents to children. She spoke of how she dealt with those fears, but how she could not deal with "a phone call saying that your child is missing."

Apsey continued to read Steffan-Skelly's letter which

spoke of the pain suffered by her sister, Montel Newhouse, and the entire Newhouse family. She worried about their mental health after losing Rachel. "When will their lives ever be the same again?" she wondered. "That answer is more obvious. Never."

As Aspey continued to read the letters, tears welled up in the eyes of many in the gallery. She spoke of life not being fair. That even despite creating a loving environment, terror could strike a family at any time. And that to deal with the terror, one had to get out of bed every day and face what life throws at you.

"The pebble that ripples a pond does not stop at the shore," Apsey quietly read. "It affects every moment from that second on and every living thing around it."

She spoke of how people who suffer a tragedy must find a safe place to deal with their pain and suffering.

"It is my prayer that each of us who have loved Rachel in our own way can find the strength to go to that newly created place where we can repair our lives and rediscover happiness and trust. I wish that most for my sister and her family.

"Jeanne Steffan-Skelly."

Karen Coffey then read a letter from Jody Crawford. In the letter, Aundria's grandmother spoke of unfulfilled dreams. She also spoke of the necessity of executing Rex Krebs. She was very succinct.

"The day he took Aundria's life, he gave up his own."

Finally, Apsey again rose before the court. This time, she read a letter written well over a year earlier by Gail Eberhart Crawford.

"My heart is gone. My life, my being, the person I thought I was is gone. Aundria was my only daughter, my only child. She was my future. She is my past. I now have only past memories and pictures." Apsey continued to relate the torment that Aundria's mother endured since Aundria's murder. More tears began to flow in the courtroom.

Apsey then read about Rex Krebs. "He murdered many

lives when he murdered Aundria." Apsey forged onward. "But she, of all of us, suffered more than anyone can imagine." The letter continued to lay into Krebs, striking out at his lack of mercy, his lack of compassion, his inability to explain why he did what he did.

"This person knows right from wrong; he simply has no concern for any life other than his own."

The letter conveyed Crawford's disgust at Krebs's crocodile tears. "He cries only for himself. I truly hope he is a dead man walking." She spoke of how Krebs attacked her daughter, "like a snake in the grass, like the devil himself strikes in surprise, tortures and kills without mercy.

"Aundria is an angel now, and Rex Allan Krebs should burn in hell for all eternity."

Apsey folded the sheet of paper and stepped back.

"Mr. Maguire," inquired Judge LaBarbera, "do you or Ms. Ashbaugh or Mr. McLennan want to say anything?"

"No, Your Honor. However, I did tell Mr. Krebs that he would have an opportunity to speak to the court today if he wished. He asked me to inform the court that he tried to express how very, very sorry he is for the harm and grief that he's caused. He tried most of last night to put that in words and found that the words were inadequate."

"Thank you," the judge replied. "All right. I'll begin by reading from this judgment." The judge read each count against Krebs for which he had been convicted, including the two charges of murder for which he would be executed. The judge ordered that Krebs pay $70,000 in restitution to Gail Eberhart Crawford.

"Mr. Krebs, it is now that I would ask you to stand.

"It is the judgment and sentence of the court that for the first-degree murder of Rachel Lindsay Newhouse, committed with the attendant special circumstances alleged in the information as Enhancements One, Two, and Six, defendant Rex Allan Krebs shall be put to death within the walls of the California State Prison at San Quentin in the manner pre-